# Aspects of
# South African Literature

▼▼▼▼▼▼▼▼▼▼▼▼▼▼▼▼▼▼▼▼▼▼▼▼▼▼▼▼▼▼▼

*Edited by*

CHRISTOPHER HEYWOOD

*Senior Lecturer, Department of English Literature,*
*University of Sheffield*

HEINEMANN
London . Ibadan . Nairobi . Lusaka
AFRICANA PUBLISHING COMPANY
New York

Heinemann Educational Books Ltd
48 Charles Street, London W1X 8AH
PMB 5205, Ibadan · PO Box 45314, Nairobi
PO Box 11190, Johannesburg · PO Box 3966 Lusaka

EDINBURGH MELBOURNE TORONTO AUCKLAND
SINGAPORE HONG KONG KUALA LUMPUR NEW DELHI KINGSTON

ISBN 0 435 91340 9 (cased)
0 435 91341 7 (paper)

Published
in the United States of America 1976
by Africana Publishing Company
a Division of Holmes & Meier Publishers Inc.
101 Fifth Avenue
New York NY 10003
Library of Congress Card No 76-25033
ISBN 0-8419-0292-5

Printed in Great Britain
by Cox & Wyman Ltd
London, Fakenham and Reading

# Contents

▼▼▼▼▼▼▼▼▼▼▼▼▼▼▼▼▼▼▼▼▼▼▼▼▼▼▼▼▼▼▼▼

# Acknowledgements

▼▼▼▼▼▼▼▼▼▼▼▼▼▼▼▼▼▼▼▼▼▼▼▼▼▼▼▼▼▼▼▼▼

These papers have been taken from contributions to two conferences which were held in March and April 1975, at the University of Texas at Austin, and in England at the University of York. Thanks are given to the organizers, Professors Dennis Brutus and Bernth Lindfors, of the English Department of the University of Texas at Austin, and Christopher R. Hill, Director of the Centre for Southern African Studies at the University of York, and to the other members of the Steering Committee at York, for their unstinting efforts in assembling the material and the speakers for the two conferences. Thanks are also given to the many Departments and Programs at the University of Texas who supported the inaugural meeting of the African Literature Association at Austin, and to the Nuffield Foundation for their support of the York Conference, which was the fourth in a series of conferences organized by the Centre for Southern African Studies. The contributors and members whose presence ensured the success of both conferences are thanked as well.

Thanks are due in addition to the International Writing Program at the University of Iowa, where the paper by Oswald Mtshali was first given in January 1975. Alan Paton gave his paper as an opening public lecture at the start of the conference at York, and both he and his audience are thanked for having provided a memorable occasion.

The staff of the British Library in Bloomsbury and elsewhere, and the Librarian and his staff at the University of Sheffield, are thanked for their untiring assistance in the pursuit of reference material sought in the course of preparing these papers for the press. Thanks are due to Julia Blake-Rywinia for her assistance in preparing the final typescript.

The fragmentary nature of this volume is recognized. If these essays stimulate further reading and writing about a difficult literature in a problematic social setting, they will have served their purpose.

The author and publishers would like to thank the following for permission to reproduce copyright material in this:

The Bodley Head for extracts from Roy Campbell: *Collected Poems Vol. 1*, 1949; Roy Campbell: *Broken Record*, 1934 and Roy Campbell: *Light on a Dark Horse*, 1951

Heinemann Educational Books for extracts from Arthur Nortje: *Dead Roots*, 1973

The International African Institute for extracts from Thomas Mofolo: *Chaka*, 1931

Oxford University Press for extracts from I. Schapera: *Praise Poems of Tswana Chiefs*, 1965 and Oswald Mtshali: *Sounds of a Cowhide Drum*, 1972

Victor Gollancz for extracts from Bessie Head: *Maru*, 1971

The following journals are also thanked for material which has appeared as articles: *English Language Notes* (article by Christopher Heywood); *Journal of Commonwealth Literature* (article by Rowland Smith); *Journal of Southern African Studies* (article by Nadine Gordimer) and *Umoja: A Journal of Black Experience* (article by Chidi Ikonne).

It has not been possible in all cases to trace copyright sources, and the publishers would be glad to hear from any such unacknowledged copyright holders.

For it is only the miraculous vanity of man which ever persuades him, that even for the most richly gifted mind, there ever arrives an earthly period, where it can truly say to itself, I have come to the Ultimate of Human Speculative Knowledge; hereafter, at this present point I will abide. Sudden onsets of new truth will assail him, and overturn him as the Tartars did China; for there is no China Wall that man can build in his soul, which shall permanently stay the irruptions of these barbarous hordes which Truth ever nourishes in the loins of her frozen, yet teeming North; so that the Empire of Human Knowledge can never be lasting in any one dynasty, since Truth still gives new Emperors to the earth.

HERMAN MELVILLE: *Pierre: or the Ambiguities*

While there have been few Negro visionaries to solve American problems, there have been fewer white visionaries. The only truly dedicated ones are three, three Southern ladies – Harriet Beecher Stowe, Lilian Smith and Carson McCullers. In South Africa Alan Paton fights with dedication.

TABAN LO LIYONG: *The Last Word*

There are advantages, indeed, in coming from a large flat country which no one wants to visit: advantages which both Turgenev and James enjoyed.

T. S. ELIOT: '*In Memory of Henry James*'

# Introduction: The Quest for Identity

▼▼▼▼▼▼▼▼▼▼▼▼▼▼▼▼▼▼▼▼▼▼▼▼▼▼▼▼▼▼

CHRISTOPHER HEYWOOD

IN listing over eleven hundred works in the 'Tentative Edition' of his *Biographical and Bibliographical Record of South African Literature in English* (Grahamstown, 1938), E. R. Seary laid the foundations for a modern study of a neglected branch of modern literature. Of the works listed, seven were by black writers. The subsequent expansion of black writing on the continent can hardly have been envisaged at the time: but the pressures which brought it about were by then fully formed. The works of the black and white South African writers in English both before and since form an important body of writing, but one which has been most markedly neglected by critical and historical scholarship. The first novel of African life to be written in Africa by a black African writer was Plaatje's *Mhudi* (Lovedale, 1930): recently re-issued, edited with an introduction by Tim Couzens,[1] it forms part of a succession of works by the Dhlomos and Mofolo which lead by imperceptible stages to the writing of Abrahams and Ekwensi, Mphahlele and Achebe, and thus to the modern literary consciousness of Africa. On the other side, the work of Schreiner, Campbell, Plomer, and Doris Lessing forms a part, integrated yet distinct, within the literary formation of the twentieth century.

From its beginnings, South African literature has both reflected and transformed into its own idiom the preoccupations of the parent communities, of which Regency, Victorian, and Edwardian England is one. The colonial past of Caribbean, West African, or American literature leads by delicate gradations from the remote past to the immediate present. The same process is traceable here. The traditions of John Stuart Mill and Herbert Spencer reappear in the work of Olive Schreiner; the works of Pauline Smith and the controversies begun by John William Colenso penetrated the life and times of Arnold Bennett. The Victorian devotion to the cause of social, sexual, and racial enfranchisement stirred in, and was stimulated by, the colonies, in a chain of circumstances no less minutely dovetailed than those traced by George Eliot in the society of *Middlemarch* or by Achebe in *Things Fall Apart*.

The critical problem of bringing into a single focus the issues at work in South African literature began after the war of 1939–45 in the work of Ezekiel Mphahlele. His *African Image*, in its two divergent versions of 1963 and 1974, sprang from his academic thesis for the University of South Africa; his thinking underpins the modern study of literature in Africa. He wrote:

> My subject was *The Non-European Character in South African English Fiction*. The study of Afrikaans literature which has created a stock non-white figure led me to inquire into the 'enigma' as it emerged in English fiction. I made a quick survey of English literature inside Africa and outside, where the non-white character is portrayed: Conrad, E. M. Forster, William Faulkner, Kipling, Mulk Raj Anand, Pearl Buck, William Plomer, George Orwell, Harriet Beecher Stowe, Carl van Vechten, Countee Cullen, Langston Hughes, Richard Wright, Claude McKay, Roger Mais, George Lamming, John Steinbeck and David Karp. Then I dealt with the early emergence of the non-white character in South Africa from Thomas Pringle to Rider Haggard; a body of literature where the non-white character appears either as a barbarian on the battlefield or as a noble savage . . .[2]

Subsequent studies by Martin Tucker[3] and G. D. Killam[4] have expanded Mphahlele's work, bringing its issues into sharper focus and emphasizing some of its central themes: that before alien societies the white writer is as powerless as the child with whom the settler conventionally compares the 'natives'; and that within the patterns of a westernized society, the kinship and family ties of African societies remain indestructible. The full record of the literature which has resulted from the colonial experience from the time of Shakespeare remains to be constructed, but its inner structure can only pursue the lines traced by Ezekiel Mphahlele and another scholar of penetrating sensitivity, Eldred Jones, in his *Othello's Countrymen* (London, 1964).

As Professor Albert Gérard has suggested, a full history of the literature of southern Africa could only be undertaken by 'carefully allocated and organized team-work'.[5] But collaboration dulls the clarity of focus which the pioneering studies have attained, and the freshness would be lost. South African writers have historical and environmental reasons for remaining rooted in the patchwork of their original society, and finding, as Olive Schreiner did, a unifying principle in the patchwork itself. The obsessive pursuit of identity by South African writers reflects their insecurity in a maze of contradictory loyalties. In his speech to Parliament in

Westminster on 27 July 1909, Lord Crewe urged the case for sovereignty on behalf of the settler communities and distinguished the white linguistic groups as 'races'. In the characteristic phraseology of his day, the disfranchised or partly enfranchised sections were known as 'classes':

> The inhabitants of South Africa are some of British, some of Dutch and some of French Huguenot descent. Their ancestors through many years of history suffered and fought for freedom. They underwent forfeiture and exile and imprisonment, and on the scaffold and on many battlefields they bore witness in the cause of civil and religious liberty. It would have been one of the most tragic ironies of all history if men descended from such races as these had remained permanently estranged. Now I hope we may look forward to seeing them joined in a free union under the supremacy of the British Crown, with a guaranteed freedom, for as many years in front of us as the imagination of man can venture to look.[6]

Among the many issues which changed the character of English liberalism in the twentieth century, the presence of substantial non-white minorities, and in certain suburbs majorities, in English towns, was still undreamed of by 1910. It is perhaps not stretching credibility to claim that in contrast, South African 'liberal' traditions in thought, literary sensibility, and politics contained from the outset a fusion of social, political, and racial egalitarianism more advanced and radical than was possible for its equivalent movements within the imperial society. The verdict of Anthony Trollope in his book *South Africa* (1878), after his tour of 1877, expresses indirectly, by its insouciance, the magnitude of the problem which Trollope failed to discern: 'The difficulty as to the savage has at any rate not been solved in South Africa as in other countries in which our Colonies have settled themselves.'[7] Like his literary judgements, Trollope's political opinions still bear consideration and are a mixture of perceptive sympathy and obtuseness, 'South Africa', he pronounced in a frequently noted verdict, 'is a country of black men and not of white men. It has been so; it is so; and it will be so'; and again: 'I find that the very men who are the friends of the negro hold the theory but never entertain the practice of equality with the negro. The stanchest disciple of Wilberforce and Buxton does not take the negro into partnership, or even make him a private secretary'; and 'The Kafir is not a bad fellow' (II, pp. 92–3).

Trollope's views stem from the tradition of radical journalism in the Cobbett manner which had earned Pringle banishment from the Cape; Pringle's *African Sketches* (1834), as Nadine Gordimer observes, inaugurate the traditional scope of English writing in South Africa. Pringle relates a characteristic anecdote and advances the nostrum of his age, emancipation, as the cure for all South Africa's ailments:

Mr Read married a woman of the Hottentot race, and his family are consequently Mulattoes, a circumstance which in South Africa still involves a *social* proscription (though the 50th Ordinance has swept off all legal difficulties) only inferior to that existing in the United States; but now that the dragon Slavery is destroyed, its odious brood, the prejudices of caste and colour, must ere long also expire.[8]

In *God's Stepchildren* (London, 1924), Sarah Gertrude Millin adopted a contrary thesis, but the materials of her argument are the same. The tragic consequences of ancestral mingling are explored in more penetrating dramatic depth by Peter Abrahams in the most ambitious of his early novels, *The Path of Thunder* (London, 1952); and in *Maru* (London, 1971), Bessie Head adroitly re-opens the perennial subject despite the avoidance of white characters in the *dramatis personae*. The prominence of this theme and the variety of forms which it assumes in the literature of South Africa (perhaps most tragically in the moral defeat of the central character of Plomer's *Turbott Wolfe*, published by Leonard and Virginia Woolf in 1924) springs from the reality seized upon by the writers in English since the time of Pringle and hinted at by Camara Laye in *Le regard du roi* (*The Radiance of the King*, London, 1956), that South African society includes the polarity outlined in *Othello* and is based on romantic social or sexual interests, as inevitable as those traced by E. M. Forster in *Where Angels Fear to Tread*, and similarly blind to ethnic, moral, and legal frontiers.

Against the more facile optimism of both conservative and liberal attitudes in nineteenth-century Europe, colonial and post-colonial societies, led by the writers of the New England 'renaissance' of the 1830s, interposed a picture of life which was intensely tragic but which emphasized the redemptive value of death. In *Moby Dick*, Melville portrays the fanaticism of Ahab as a counterweight to the humanitarianism of 'Ishmael'; but Ishmael is drawn into the toils of Ahab's monomania: 'The subterranean miner that works in us all, how can one tell whither leads his shaft by the ever shifting, muffled sound of his pick?' (*Moby Dick*, XL). The Janus faces of industrial society, its ruthless practices and its democratic theories and impulses, are exemplified in the clash between Ishmael and Ahab. Ahab represents the obsession with destiny of a modern world which has not shed a patriarchal conception of itself: 'The path to my fixed purpose is laid with iron rails, whereon my soul is governed to run' (XXXVI). The opposing spirit of Ishmael, brooding in the end over the aboriginal calamity which overtakes the ship and all its crew, dramatizes the other expression of an ambiguous figure, here seen as the brotherly love engendered by industrial toil: 'Come, let us squeeze hands all round; nay, let us all squeeze ourselves into each other; let us squeeze ourselves universally into the very milk and sperm of kindness' (XCIII). A vision of opposites so extreme can only end in death.

In its various guises, the haunting figure of a society torn by a tragic ambiguity has gripped the imagination of the modern writer. Works such as Camara Laye's *Le regard du roi* and Hamidou Kane's *L'Aventure ambiguë* (*Ambiguous Adventure*, London, 1972) have extended the arguments of post-colonial America and the Antilles into the major works of modern Africa. Through the intermediary force of their European admirers (as the work of scholarship has only recently begun to show), notably Dickens, Zola, Kafka and Camus, the New England writers conveyed to their successors a literary heritage of the greatest possible significance, based on a perception of reality at once minutely psychological and ambitiously intellectual. The detailed polemicism of mediaeval allegory was replaced by the obscurity of a modern allegory which was not always certain of its doctrinal content. 'Some of us, my dear Sir,' Melville wrote to his publisher, 'always have a certain something unmanageable in us, that bids us do this or that, and be done it must, hit or miss'; the whale, Melville wrote elsewhere, was at once a factual reality and a means of examining 'this great allegory – the world'. The revival of interest in two modes of tragic writing in England, the Moralities and the Jacobean melodramas, has owed much to the work of T. S. Eliot, whose academic training lay in metaphysics and Idealism and whose experiment in late mediaeval dramatic form, *Murder in the Cathedral*, was another signal of his rejection after 1928 of the traditions of liberal eclecticism. But the submission of Beckett to the will of God and his ensuing death do not constitute a return to the counter-Reformation dogmatism of *Everyman*: rather, Eliot provides the reverse of a coin bearing Ahab on its face. Beckett's submission, like Diallo's in *L'Aventure ambiguë*, is the other side of Ahab's defiance: 'That inscrutable thing is chiefly what I hate, and be the White Whale Agent, or be the White Whale principal, I will wreak that hate upon him.'

Ambiguity, recently a critic's toy but in its origins an apocalyptic, visionary force, takes its rise in modern times in the post-colonial literature of America. George Eliot's reply to Emerson, made in a Coventry garden, that her favourite books were *The Scarlet Letter* and Rousseau's *Confessions*, is a pointer to the new spirit of her age. More abrasive, less abundant but more searching and practical in her thought than George Eliot, Olive Schreiner carried the literature of modern tragedy to a new form in *The Story of an African Farm*, and captured the imagination of her generation. Her thinking reflected the intensity of the liberal, humanitarian movement as it had emerged from the more comfortable America and from the hands of her admired master, Emerson. One of the few authorities on

South African literature in English, J. P. L. Snyman, notes: 'Two features of the South African novel are the prominence of the Native and the fact that most of the outstanding writers are women.'[9] Snyman's reasoning, that in a frontier society women have more leisure to write than men, carries less weight than that of Van der Post, who argues more cogently that in the case of Olive Schreiner at least, the frontier society dramatized universal masculine failing: 'the deep rejection of woman in our man's world proceeds directly from the failure of man to honour the woman in himself'.[10]

The argument from linguistics and infantile castration fear advanced by Freud as the basis of ambiguity[11] and sustained by Empson in his study *Seven Types of Ambiguity*[12] can be advanced as an alternative to Van der Post's construction of the psychological forces at work in the problem. It is Van der Post, however, who has seen the value of the social setting in Olive Schreiner's writing. In her novel, as in many others which handle the double face of colonial society, the tragic view of life derives from despair about the efficacy of the liberal impulse. The pilgrimage made by D. H. Lawrence, the greatest of many admirers of her literary work, brought him from the Nottinghamshire coalfield to New Mexico, in search of the colonial situation which her works and those of Frobenius and others had outlined. The opposition between an untenable idea of progress through industrialization and an equally untenable reverence for a past which includes massacres, slavery, human sacrifice, and cannibalism, is pursued to its limits by Soyinka in *Madmen and Specialists*. Here, the particle 'as', deified by a characteristic Soyinkan pun, announces a state of mind resembling the schizophrenia which R. D. Laing has argued to be a potent weapon for survival in modern society.[13]

South African literature in English falls into three periods, 1830–1910, 1910–60, and 1960 to the present day. The early writers were preoccupied with the formation of a society among the settler communities; the following period saw a shift of conscience among white writers and the emergence of black writing; after 1960 the balance shifted further towards the acceptance of claims made by or on behalf of the African societies of southern Africa. These periods coincide with transitions in international colonial development and are less peculiar to southern Africa than may be supposed. The emphasis laid on such dates as 1881 or 1899 or 1948 in many pronouncements about South Africa exaggerates the importance of conflicts among the settler communities; the emphasis should rather be on the questions of land tenure and industrial development which underlie the debates. In a revealing paper, Adrian Guelke provides a timely warning against the facile assumption that all the problems of modern South Africa began in 1948: most of the legislation of the past quarter-century has its origin in the heritage of early industrial practice in the decade following Vereeniging.[14]

Besides Paton and Van der Post, Plomer and Campbell, Doris Lessing, Nadine Gordimer and Dan Jacobson, the spokesmen for the middle period include the Dhlomos, Plaatje, Abrahams, and Mphahlele, whose works demonstrated the cultural achievements of the non-white communities and typified the American accent of literature in the industrializing phase. Behind their work lay the radical thinking of such men as Edward Carpenter, E. M. Forster, and E. D. Morel, writers indebted at many points to American thought and feeling. The more radical internationalism of the Padmore circle in London of the 1930s and 1940s yielded its harvest in South Africa after 1960, giving notice of its arrival in the preceding decade in the magazine *Drum*: 'It wasn't so much a magazine as it was a symbol of the new African cut adrift from the tribal reserve – urbanized, eager, fast-talking and brash', as Lewis Nkosi noted in a much-quoted passage.[15] Campbell wrote in *The Wayzgoose*:

> Plomer, 'twas you who, though a boy in age,
> Awoke a sleepy continent to rage,
> Who dared alone to thrash a craven race
> And hold a mirror to its dirty face

but Nkosi, Kunene, Nortje, La Guma, Rive, Bessie Head, and the lately published Dikobe have shown the interest, variety, and sinuousness of the indigenous cultures. South Africans who live or buy books abroad are now able to find out about themselves, if not at first hand, then through the tranquillizing mirror of art.

The sources of life in any literature are oral; we should, as G. M. Young has said, 'go on reading until we hear the people talking'. But the application of oral tradition to printed texts varies from one culture to another. Behind the printed texts of modern writing in southern Africa lie the gestures, overlooked in much literary criticism in the twentieth century, of social tradition: but the division between the politically dominant Germanic cultures and the politically submerged African societies remain as acute as they were in the times of the literary founders. 'Today the black man, brought low by his brother Bantu, is subjected and bewildered', Sarah Gertrude Millin wrote in the last edition of her book *The People of South Africa* (London, 1951, ch. VI); in her first attempt at the subject she wrote: 'Today the black man is subjugated and bewildered. The white man is his lord, his teacher, his tyrant. He has been broken by the white man, and must be mended by him.'[16] More correctly, from the literary point of view, the white writer can learn from contact with writers whose English, like the English of Conrad, the German of Kafka, or the French of Oyono and Laye, is a subordinate or second language, painfully acquired, carefully sharpened, and applied with medical precision to the wounds that history has created. Oral traditions include satire, irony, ambiguity, and invective, as Okot p'Bitek has shown; the novels of Bessie Head and Dikobe, constructed like folk-tales in an idiom different from that of the *Drum* generation, have the consistency and mathematical balance of ballads. In Africa, where speech is often like song, poetry – Campbell argued – can find a natural home: 'Poetry has gone to the Southern Hemisphere: it is really a pastoral art.'[17]

In its outlines, sketched in these papers rather than studied, South African literature follows the movements of the world in the last two centuries. It is a literature closely integrated with the movements in the rest of the continent and with the communities facing the Atlantic on its northern shores at least. No clear-cut polarization of 'white' and 'black' aesthetics is possible in this literature, though much of its past lacks sensitivity to the interaction of the societies in conflict and assimilation. 'Larry Neal quotes Brother Knight on the "black aesthetic",' Mphahlele observes, and quotes as follows in the complex textual succession:

> To accept the white aesthetic is to accept and validate a society that will not allow him to live. The Black artist must create new forms and new values, sing new songs (or purify old ones); and along with other Black authorities, he must create a new history, new symbols, myths and legends (and purify old ones by fire). And the Black Artist, in creating his own aesthetic, must be accountable for it only to Black people.[18]

This point is more firmly made than can be sustained in practice, but remains a tenable view. The South African writer has a less fixed notion of his audience, who may be white and who are, if so, the target for the message of the work. In defining the artist's attitude to his subject, Wilson Harris has provided the most workable formula for the writer in a colonial society with a complex history which has its roots in the mercantile expansion of Europe:

> At the heart of that necessity lay the arts of a new vision grounded in the long-suffering infinity of man as well as the savaged limits of man, grounded therefore in something [as] infinitely vulnerable, infinitely marvellous as the texture of man, the inner shadow of man seeking a dimension of creativity and freedom that involved a partial and deeply painful unravelling of investitures of fate by which he was so deeply conditioned that they were printed on every organ of the premises of existence.[19]

*References*

1. Sol T. Plaatje, *Mhudi*, ed. with introduction by T. J. Couzens (Johannesburg, 1975).
2. Ezekiel Mphahlele, *Down Second Avenue* (London, 1959/71), pp. 194–5.
3. Martin Tucker, *Africa in Modern Literature* (New York, 1967).
4. G. D. Killam, *The Image of Africa in English Fiction, 1870–1950* (Ibadan, 1969).
5. Albert Gérard, 'Towards a History of South African Literature', in Hena Maes-Jelinek (ed.), *Commonwealth Literature and the Modern World* (Brussels, 1975), pp. 79–88.
6. *Selected Speeches and Documents on British Colonial Policy, 1763–1917*, 2 vols, ed. A. B. Keith (London, 1918), Vol. 2, p. 45.
7. Anthony Trollope, *South Africa*, 2 vols (London, 1878), Vol. 1, p. 20.
8. Thomas Pringle, *African Sketches* (London, 1834), p. 517.
9. J. P. L. Snyman, *The South African Novel in English* (Potchefstroom, 1952).
10. Laurens van der Post, 'Introduction' to William Plomer, *Turbott Wolfe* (London, 1965), pp. 9–55.
11. Sigmund Freud, 'The Medusa's Head', in his *Collected Papers*, ed. Ernest Jones (London, 1950), Vol. IV, pp. 105–6.
12. William Empson, *Seven Types of Ambiguity*, 3rd edn (London, 1953), p. 194.
13. I am indebted to Annemarie Heywood for her penetrating study of this question: *Apostasy, Community and Madness in the Work of Wole Soyinka* (MA dissertation, University of Sheffield, 1974).
14. Adrian Guelke, 'Apartheid and the Labour Market', in *Collected Papers I* (Centre for Southern African Studies, University of York, 1975), pp. 96–117.
15. Lewis Nkosi, 'The Fabulous Decade: the Fifties', in his *Home and Exile* (London, 1965), pp. 3–34.
16. Sarah Gertrude Millin, *South Africa* (London, 1934), p. 23.
17. Roy Campbell, *Broken Record* (London, 1934), p. 125.
18. Ezekiel Mphahlele, *Voices in the Whirlwind* (London, 1973) p. 65.
19. Wilson Harris, 'Reflection and Vision', in Hena Maes-Jelinek (ed.), *Commonwealth Literature and the Modern World* (Brussels, 1975), pp. 15–19 (p. 17).

# Yesterday

Yesterday

# Roy Campbell

▼▼▼▼▼▼▼▼▼▼▼▼▼▼▼▼▼▼▼▼▼▼▼▼▼▼▼▼▼▼

## ALAN PATON

YOU can read all about Roy Campbell's boyhood in his two autobiographies, *Broken Record* and *Light on a Dark Horse*. All I can say is that you can't have that kind of boyhood any more, certainly not in those parts. Housing schemes have swallowed up the haunts of the red duiker and the mpiti, the python and the mamba, the porcupine and the bush-pig, the giant crane and the sunbirds, the bou-bou shrike, *boboni*, with those striking calls from mate to mate, and the wood dove, with that sorrowful lament that captured my heart too when I was a boy: *my mother is dead, my father is dead, all my relations are dead, and my heart goes du du du du du.*

Nature was one of Campbell's great loves, and literature – mostly poetry – another. Campbell was not a master of prose, but he could write it, as the examples will show. The trouble was that once he got a pen in his hand to write prose, he had to boast and to shock and to goad. Everything had to be big, and if it wasn't big enough he made it bigger. His autobiographies are works of selective recollection and vivid imagination. His ideas about politics and society and the social order were often so irritating that many readers found his prose writing bad for their blood pressures and gave him up.

He tells us why he wrote these books:

> Ever since that first night out at sea and my last view of Durban, my memories have become clearer and clearer until I have at last been literally forced to write them out ... so as to repay my debt both to Almighty God and to my parents, for letting me loose in such a world, to plunder its miraculous literatures, and langagues, and wines: to savour its sights, forms, colours, perfumes, and sounds: to see so many superb cities, oceans, lakes, forests, rivers, sierras, pampas, and plains, with their beasts, birds, trees, crops, and flowers – and above all their men and women, who are by far the most fascinating of all.[1]

To this one may add that this did not apply to all men and women. It did not apply to Quakers, Jews (though Campbell would later have liked to deny it), or to the English until the bombing of London, or to the non-equestrians, the shopkeepers, and those not spiritually fitted to be killers of bulls.

His satirical verse, though without doubt witty, could so easily be made tedious by his swashbuckling and contempt. But he did not allow his politics – if they can be called that – to affect his lyrics. When they have defects, they are of quite another kind.

Out of the writings of his boyhood and young manhood he kept, so far as is known, only one poem, and that is 'The Theology of Bongwi, the Baboon':

> This is the wisdom of the Ape
>   Who yelps beneath the Moon –
> 'Tis God who made me in His shape
>   He is a Great Baboon.
> 'Tis He who tilts the moon askew
>   And fans the forest trees,
> The heavens which are broad and blue
>   Provide him his trapeze;
> He swings with tail divinely bent
>   Around those azure bars
> And munches to his Soul's content
>   The kernels of the stars;
> And when I die, His loving care
>   Will raise me from the sod
> To learn the perfect Mischief there,
>   The Nimbleness of God.[2]

This poem disposes of the criticism that Campbell had no brains. He had a good brain. That some strange and unpleasant ideas got into it cannot be denied. But he had in his verse that gift, so closely allied to wit and so essential to imagery, of seeing the concealed relation, which when revealed delights the hearer and reader with its aptness and its unexpectedness, and often, too, its beauty.

He went to school at the Durban High, under A. S. Langley, whose legend lives on. Campbell called him 'the surly tutor of my youth'. He holidayed in Rhodesia with his cousins, whence comes the poem 'The Zebras', written probably some seven or eight years later:

> From the dark woods that breathe of fallen showers,
> Harnessed with level rays in golden reins,
> The zebras draw the dawn across the plains
> Wading knee-deep among the scarlet flowers.

> The sunlight, zithering their flanks with fire,
> Flashes between the shadows as they pass
> Barred with electric tremors through the grass
> Like wind along the gold strings of a lyre.
>
> Into the flushed air snorting rosy plumes
> That smoulder round their feet in drifting fumes,
> With dove-like voices call the distant fillies,
> While round the herds the stallion wheels his flight,
> Engine of beauty volted with delight,
> To roll his snare among the trampled lilies. (*CP*, p. 40)

It is interesting to note that Campbell, after describing the zebra as an 'engine of beauty volted with delight', wrote in *Broken Record* that the zebra was an inferior animal with no stamina, and little intelligence.

Campbell's hero at the Durban High School was the master Bill Payn, a genial giant, who as far as he was able, protected Campbell against Langley's intense dislike. Campbell wrote appreciatively of Bill Payn and of Natal rugby at that time, in a magnificent piece of prose:

> That tremendous phalanx with Wally Clarkson at the centre, and Payn at the wing, has been bolshevized out of existence. Anyone who has seen that great rugby, the fury and fire of the Attack, with the ball flashing from hand to hand, and everywhere caressed by great sculptors of motion; and above all the triumphant gaiety and humanity of men like Payn; anybody who has seen that kind of rugby laughs at the modern edition.
>
> The Australians have taught us a great lesson: they nearly beat us, and by generous spectacular play. All play *should* be spectacular: it should take for granted the intelligence of the spectator. The duty of the player towards the spectator should be as great as that of a matador . . . or as his duty to win. The great player is a sort of priest or poet (as actors are), and he should always parade his excellence. Payn, an intellectual athlete, never forgot this duty. Sometimes, for sheer fun, he would catch the ball, like an egg, in one hand: in his obligingness and decency towards his public, he was as reckless and generous as possible, and what is more, he could afford it. Personally, I think that his spectacular play was superior to any serious movement that I have seen on the part of exact warriors like Benny Osler. Whenever Payn got the ball, I could feel him smiling and laughing. After he got a move of about ten yards, his impetus was something superhuman. His knees used to come up almost to his nose, and every stride he took seemed a thunderbolt. I have seen him running with three or four Britishers attached to him, and treating them almost as if they were parcels which he was bringing home to his wife.[3]

Out of these Natal days came two notable poems, though they also were written some years later. One was 'The Serf' and the other 'The Zulu Girl'.

They have been much anthologized, but that is not surprising. In my opinion they are two of the finest lyrics of the twentieth century:

### The Zulu Girl

When in the sun the hot red acres smoulder,
Down where the sweating gang its labour plies,
A girl flings down her hoe, and from her shoulder
Unslings her child tormented by the flies.

She takes him to a ring of shadow pooled
By thorn-trees: purpled with the blood of ticks,
While her sharp nails, in slow caresses ruled,
Prowl through his hair with sharp electric clicks,

His sleepy mouth plugged by the heavy nipple,
Tugs like a puppy, grunting as he feeds:
Through his frail nerves her own deep languors ripple
Like a broad river sighing through its reeds.

Yet in that drowsy stream his flesh imbibes
An old unquenched unsmotherable heat –
The curbed ferocity of beaten tribes,
The sullen dignity of their defeat.

Her body looms above him like a hill
Within whose shade a village lies at rest,
Or the first cloud so terrible and still
That bears the coming harvest in its breast. (*CP*, pp. 30–31)

Where did Campbell get the lines: 'An old unquenched unsmotherable heat/The curbed ferocity of beaten tribes/The sullen dignity of their defeat'? And again: 'Or the first cloud so terrible and still/That bears the coming harvest in its breast'? Or what made him see the Ploughman in 'The Serf' as one 'That moves the nearest to the naked earth/And ploughs down palaces, and thrones, and towers'?

*Broken Record* is in its early pages the story of a white South African boy, member of the master race, whose Zulu servants are real gentlemen and born aristocrats and dear companions, but one does not marry their sisters or invite them to dinner. One must remember that although these are the adventures of a boy in the early years of the century, the book was not published until 1934. One must suppose that Campbell had his white eyes opened at Sezela when he came home briefly from 1924 to 1926, in the days of *Voorslag* and in the company of William Plomer and Laurens van der Post, and that by 1934 he had closed them again. In fact after he returned to England he wrote to Plomer saying that they had 'overdone the black man stuff'.

Campbell left South Africa for the first time in 1919 'exiled by his own disdain'. It was a country where you relax 'to shear the fleeces or to fleece the blacks'. But one may speculate that his disdain was not for what we call the traditional way of life. And one may also speculate that the idea of settling down in South Africa and doing what his father Dr Sam Campbell might well have called 'a job of work' was repellent to him. His father, who was a patron of culture and education and all the high arts, just could not get used to being the father of a poet, who lay about writing on pieces of paper and tearing them up, and sometimes just lay about. Nor could Campbell get used to having a father so industrious, so conventional, so public-spirited.

Campbell arrived in London a teetotaller and a non-smoker, and then went on to Oxford. He met William Walton, musical genius, aged 16 and already famous. He consorted with Robert Graves, Edmund Blunden, L. A. G. Strong, Beverley Nichols, A. E. Coppard, Louis Golding, Edgell Rickword. He met T. S. Eliot and the Sitwells. He shared a flat with T. W. Earp, Russel Green, and Aldous Huxley. He wrote of Huxley, 'I felt ill at ease with this pedant who leeringly gloated over his knowledge of how crayfish copulated . . . but could never have caught or cooked one' – which tells as much about Campbell as about Huxley. He talked literature day and night. His knowledge of literature grew immense, though how deep I shall probably never know. He began to read French. He ran away from Oxford to the Camargue, and became a fisherman, a jouster, a bullfighter of the French sort, and a lover of Provence.

In 1921 he returned to England, and entered the world of Augustus John, Liam O'Flaherty, Philip Heseltine, and Wyndham Lewis. Then happened one of the three great events of his life. He met Mary Garman, a most beautiful young woman, fell in love with her, and on 11 January 1922, married her. By this time he had become a heavy drinker, and when he and Mary left for their honeymoon, Dr Garman said to his daughter, 'You have married a dipsomaniac'.

Campbell writes this of the marriage:

Though we were very happy, my wife and I had some quarrels since my ideas of marriage are old-fashioned about wifely obedience and in many ways she regarded me as a mere child because of being hardly out of my teens. But any marriage in which the woman wears the pants is an unseemly farce. To shake up her illusions I hung her out of the fourth-floor window of our room so that she should get some respect for me. This worked wonders for she gazed, head-downwards, up at the stars till the police from their H.Q. on the opposite side of Beak Street started yelling at me to pull her back. She had not uttered a single word, and when I shouted out pleasantly across the street, 'We are only practising our act, aren't we Kid?' she replied 'Yes', as calmly and happily as if we did it every ten minutes. The police then left us alone, saying: 'Well, don't practise it so high up over other people's heads, please.'

My wife was very proud of me after I had hung her out of the window and boasted of it to her girl friends.

This infuriated them, as their young men always gave in to them: and they got no excitement or 'polarity'. But it was five or six years before we broke each other in to our complete satisfaction and I wore the pants for good. We both had such fiery temperaments that all our acquaintances had predicted a speedy and ruinous finish to our romance, which up to now has lasted thirty years.[4]

Campbell never wore the pants for good. He had married a woman with a will of steel, in the same class as Florence Nightingale and the late Mrs Hofmeyr, mother of Jan Hendrik. She was powerfully to affect his life, his view of the world, his authoritarian ideas, his religion. But she left two things alone, his drinking and his writing. Over the first she was powerless. In the second she recognized the working of genius, and was content to watch it. When the urge to write came upon him, the urge to drink left him.

Being penniless they left London and went to wild Wales, to Ty Corn, an old stable which cost them 36 shillings a year. Here in poverty and happiness he wrote *The Flaming Terrapin*, and here his daughter Tess was born. He sent his poem to Augustus John, Heseltine, and Rickword. John gave the manuscript to T. E. Lawrence, who wrote to Jonathan Cape: 'Normally rhetoric so bombastic would have sickened me. But what originality, what energy, what freshness and enthusiasm, and what a riot of glorious imagery and colour! Magnificent I call it.'

What was the Flaming Terrapin? It is, Campbell says:

> This sudden strength that catches up man's souls
> And rears them up like giants in the sky,
> Giving them fins where the dark ocean rolls
> And wings of eagles when the whirlwinds fly.

It is, says Campbell:

>                     a great machine,
> Thoughtless and fearless, governing the clean
> System of active things; the winds and currents
> Are his primeval thoughts; the raging torrents
> Are moods of his, and men who do great deeds
> Are but the germs his awful fancy breeds. (*CP*, p. 60)

What does it mean? A great machine, thoughtless and fearless, governing the clean system of active things? I don't know what it means. And I don't think Campbell did either. But is it not extraordinary that a young man of twenty with that Durban background should write such lines? The 'Flaming Terrapin' is the very Principle of Life. He is power, energy, strength, mastery. He is in the bull, the eagle, the horse, the storm, the lightning. Before this elemental tempestuousness, even the Devil slinks away.

The imagery is endless and incredible. The Ark is launched, and Campbell writes this of Noah, standing to the wheel:

> Beside the keel he saw the grey sharks move,
> And the long lines of fire their fins would groove,
> Seemed each a ghost that followed in its sleep
> Those long phantasmal coffins of the deep.

and again:

> Now by each silent pool and fringed lagoon
> The faint flamingoes burn among the weeds.
> And the green Evening, tended by the Moon,
> Sprays her white egrets on the swinging reeds.

and again:

> from his track
> Slithering like quicksilver, pouring their black
> And liquid coils before his pounding feet,
> He drove the livid mambas of deceit. (*CP*, pp. 65, 91, 63)

But one must stop. The late Professor William Gardner, Professor of English at the University of Natal, considered that the great promise shown in *The Flaming Terrapin* was not fulfilled thereafter. If he meant that the promise began to fade then, I would not agree. But certainly after *Adamastor* it began to do so. It seems to me that a poetry of such striking sounds and such vivid colours, of such life, clangour, shocks, eagles, storms, of such sustained imagery, cannot itself be sustained. Campbell could not help becoming repetitive. He was like one of his own tempests that had blown itself out. In Yeats and Eliot the emotional and intellectual growth went on. In Campbell it faltered and finally stopped. When he was converted to Roman Catholicism, his poetry took on a new vigour, in part because a new world and therefore a new vocabulary and a new imagery had been opened to him.

*The Flaming Terrapin* made Campbell famous. His father was moved to pride in his strange son. Dr Sam Campbell had been very angry when Roy, at the age of 19, married an unknown young woman, just as angry as Dr Garman had been when his daughter married an unknown young man. According to Mary, when the two doctors met they wept on each other's shoulders over the ingratitude of children. But now at the age of 22 the unknown young man was famous. Dr Garman was not to know of his son-in-law's fame; he died in 1923.

In 1924 Campbell returned to South Africa. Although he was famous, his father could not get used to his apparent indolence. Campbell lectured at the technical college that his father had founded, but when Mary and Tess arrived he was glad to be able to take them to Peace Cottage, and then later to a cottage lent to them by Lewis Reynolds, the sugar baron of Sezela. It was a time of great creativity. During this visit to South Africa he wrote 'The Serf', 'The Zulu Girl', 'The Albatross', and at least the first draft of 'Tristan Da Cunha'. It seems likely that he also wrote 'Hialmar', 'Mazeppa', 'The Pioneers', 'Buffels Kop', and 'To a Pet Cobra' at this time. The last eleven poems of this collection were, probably, all written in France, though Laurens van der Post avers that 'The Palm' was written at Sezela.

Campbell writes in *Broken Record* (p. 103): 'Since I re-attached myself to my original muse of the *Terrapin*, as in the last quarter of *Adamastor*, *The Georgiad*, and in *Flowering Reeds*, I have had such formidable luck that it has become a proverb not only among my contemporaries, but publicly in the press.' Was Campbell repudiating 'The Serf' and 'The Zulu Girl'? He was surely not repudiating 'Tristan da Cunha'. Did he who made the *Terrapin* make *The Georgiad*? I confess that I find this a baffling statement.

The *Adamastor* collection, as it appears in the *Collected Poems*, is magnificent. We have already seen 'The Zulu Girl'. Here are four stanzas from 'Tristan De Cunha':

> Hurled by what aim to what tremendous range!
> A missile from the great sling of the past,
> Your passage leaves its track of death and change
> And ruin on the world: you fly beyond
> Leaping the current of the ages vast
> As lightly as a pebble skims a pond.
>
> The years are undulations in your flight
> Whose awful motion we can only guess –
> Too swift for sense, too terrible for sight,
> We only know how fast behind you darken
> Our days like lonely beacons of distress:
> We know that you stride on and will not harken.
>
> Now in the eastern sky the fairest planet
> Pierces the dying wave with dangled spear,
> And in the whirring hollows of your granite
> That vaster sea to which you are a shell
> Sighs with a ghostly rumour, like the drear
> Moan of the nightwind in a hollow cell.

> We shall not meet again; over the wave
> Our ways divide, and yours is straight and endless,
> But mine is short and crooked to the grave:
> Yet what of these dark crowds amid whose flow
> I battle like a rock, aloof and friendless,
> Are not their generations vague and endless
> The waves, the strides, the feet on which I go? (*CP*, p. 43)

And here the beautiful 'Mass at Dawn':

> I dropped my sail and dried my dripping seines
> Where the white quay is chequered by cool planes
> In whose great branches, always out of sight,
> The nightingales are singing day and night.
> Though all was grey beneath the moon's grey beam,
> My boat in her new paint shone like a bride,
> And silver in my baskets shone the bream:
> My arms were tired and I was heavy-eyed,
> But when with food and drink, at morning-light,
> The children met me at the water-side,
> Never was wine so red or bread so white. (*CP*, p. 47)

It is clear from this poem that although Campbell was not yet a Catholic, he was on the way to becoming one.

One of Lewis Reynold's reasons in lending the Campbells a cottage was so that they, assisted by Van der Post, Plomer and Roworth, could start a modern South African review. This was called *Voorslag*, which means a whiplash. Campbell was to be the editor. Now Campbell was no manager of any kind whatsoever. Nor could he abide Maurice Webb who had been appointed business manager, and he ridiculed him, his vegetarianism, the size of his bottom, and gave him the name of Polybius Jubb. He disliked Roworth and he later ridiculed Reynolds in the poem 'To a Young Man with Pink Eyes'. In *The Flaming Terrapin*, Campbell had lambasted mediocrity, and for him Webb and Reynolds were mediocrities. In addition to all this he was drinking a great deal. It was not surprising when he announced his resignation from *Voorslag* in the third issue.

While the Campbells were at Sezela, Dr Sam Campbell died. Although he was proud of his poet son, he disapproved of what seemed to him to be a careless and undisciplined life. Whether he knew of the existence or the extent of Roy's drinking I do not know. What I do know is that it was a strain for all of them to live in the same house. However when Roy resigned from *Voorslag*, which happened after his father's death, he, Mary, Tess and Anna, who had arrived on New Year's Day 1925, plus Van der Post and Plomer, moved to the family home at Musgrave Road. Here, in two or three days of uproarious hilarity, was written *The Wayzgoose*, which poured scorn on the cultural pretensions of Durban: 'My words, O Durban, round the world are blown,/Where I alone of all your sons am known.' (*CP*, pp. 251–2) The brilliance of Campbell's satire can be seen from the opening lines:

> Attend my fable if your ears be clean,
> In fair Banana Land we lay our scene –
> South Africa, renowned both far and wide
> For politics and little else beside:
> Where, having torn the land with shot and shell,
> Our sturdy pioneers as farmers dwell,
> And, 'twixt the hours of strenuous sleep, relax
> To shear the fleeces or to fleece the blacks:
> Where every year a fruitful increase bears
> Of pumpkins, cattle, sheep, and millionaires –
> A clime so prosperous both to men and kine
> That which were which a sage could scarce define;
> Where fat white sheep upon the mountains bleat
> And fatter politicians in the street;
> Where lemons hang like yellow moons ashine
> And grapes the size of apples load the vine;
> Where apples to the weight of pumpkins go
> And donkeys to the height of statesmen grow,
> Where trouts the size of salmon throng the creeks
> And worms the size of magistrates – the beaks;
> Where the precocious tadpole, from his bog,
> Becomes a journalist ere half a frog;
> Where every shrimp his proud career may carve
> And only brain and muscle have to starve.
> The 'garden colony' they call our land,
> And surely for a garden it was planned:
> What apter phrase with such a place could cope
> Where vegetation has so fine a scope,
> Where *weeds* in such variety are found
> And all the rarest *parasites* abound,
> Where pumpkins to professors are promoted
> And turnips into Parliament are voted?
> Where else do men by vegetating vie
> And run to seed so long before they die? (*CP*, 243)

There arose a myth – Campbell-inspired – that after *The Wayzgoose* he had to flee for his life. In fact he fled from what he thought was a living death. There was no possible life for him in Durban and Musgrave Road. His mother Margaret was reputed to be a saint, but his sister Ethel had had enough. She bought clothes for Van der Post and Plomer so that they would not have the excuse of destitution for staying, and off they went to Japan. Campbell was later to say that they had run away. His real complaint was that they had run away before he did.

The Campbells returned to England in 1927 and after vicissitudes were lent the gardener's cottage by the Nicolsons at Long Barn. The Nicolsons were Harold and his wife Vita Sackville-West. Here happened the second great event of Campbell's life. It could have been catastrophic, but for reasons we shall give, it stopped short of that. This near-catastrophic event is dismissed in five lines of Nigel Nicolson's book *Portrait of a Marriage*: 'Roy Campbell, the poet, and his wife Mary, were lent the gardener's cottage, and Vita fell in love with Mary, to the fury of Roy, who wrote *The Georgiad*, a highly uncomplimentary portrait of Long Barn and the Nicolsons, in revenge.'[5]

So what for Vita with her grand passions was a passing fancy, was for Campbell a traumatic experience. Laurens van der Post would go so far as to say that after it the poetry lost its fire and colour. Professor William Gardner thought that it had ended before that. And it was for Mary a traumatic experience too, for her love for Campbell was deep indeed. After she became a Catholic she went to mass every day 'to expiate past sins'. And I, taking a past sin to be really a sin of the past, asked her if she did not believe that a sin expiated was a sin done with. And she agreed, but said there had been 'a wild time in her past'. That the wild time was Vita Sackville-West I have no doubt. But the whole responsibility was not here. Campbell had been drinking heavily, and must have been a poor lover, and by that I don't mean only physical love. Therefore, after going off in anger and despair to France, he was reconciled with his wife.

His forgiveness was not to be complete, however, until there came the third great event of his life. On 17 January 1935, he and Mary were received into the Catholic Church at Altea, and were remarried according to Catholic rites. Campbell said: 'From then on I went monogamous, and never regret it.' I have no evidence that since his first marriage he had been anything else. But he had finally forgiven her. Rob Lyle, who probably knew Campbell better than anybody else, said that the wound was healed, but that the scar remained till the end of his life.

Why did he forgive her? One reason was certainly that he was lost without her. Another reason was that for all the vulgar boasting, his nature was generous. A third reason was that he was guilty also. A fourth reason was that his reception, that is *their* reception, into the Catholic Church, and their final confirmation in Toledo in 1936, was for him so overwhelming that total forgiveness could no longer be withheld.

He wrote of their confirmation: 'On that day, before dawn, began an entirely new chapter in our lives, which had hitherto been somewhat drab and dull compared with the new splendours of experience for which we were lucky enough to be preserved.'[6] Some of Campbell's statements I do

not believe at all. Some I believe partly. This one I believe wholly, though
it is, like so many of his affirmations, exaggerated.

I have jumped to Spain, but must now jump back to England. When the
Campbells were reconciled, they, to use his words, 'eloped to Provence'.
Those were what Mary called 'the halycon days'. It is permissible so to
look back, but they were also the days, indeed the years, of trying to forgive.
Sometimes the memory of her infidelity was too strong for him, and he
raged at her, and that was more likely than not to have been when he was
drinking. These scenes caused them all great pain, not least the children.

However he did not believe in brooding. He took up water jousting
again, and the French form of bullfighting. He became a fisherman. He
experienced a revulsion against writing. It was the kind of life that his
father would have hated, of sensuousness and the sun and the sea. Tess
and Anna began to speak beautiful French, just as they were later to speak
beautiful Spanish and Portuguese. I might add that they also speak
beautiful English.

Under the influence of his reading of Mistral Campbell began to write
again, and to collect already published poems for *Adamastor*. The new
poems were 'Mass at Dawn', 'Horses on the Camargue', 'The Sleeper',
'Estocade', 'Autumn', 'An Open Window', 'Sonnet', 'The Garden', 'The
Snake', and perhaps 'The Palm'.

From 'Horses on the Camargue' come these lines:

> Then in their strength and pride
> The stallions of the wilderness rejoice;
> They feel their Master's trident in their side,
> And high and shrill they answer to his voice.
> With white tails smoking free,
> Long streaming manes, and arching necks, they show
> Their kinship to the sisters of the sea –
> And forward hurl their thunderbolts of snow.
> Still out of hardship bred,
> Spirits of power and beauty and delight
> Have ever on such frugal pastures fed
> And loved to course with tempests through the night.
>
> (*CP*, p. 48)

Another poem from this period, 'The Sleeper', is one which I have read
many times; only in later years did I understand its full meaning:

> She lies so still, her only motion
> The waves of hair that round her sweep
> Revolving to their hushed explosion
> Of fragrance on the shores of sleep.
> Is it my spirit or her flesh

> That takes this breathless, silver swoon?
> Sleep has no darkness to enmesh
> That lonely rival of the moon,
> Her beauty, vigilant and white,
> That wakeful through the long blue night,
> Watches, with my own sleepless eyes,
> The darkness silver into day,
> And through their sockets burns away
> The sorrows that have made them wise. (*CP*, pp. 48–9)

This may not be Campbell the poet at his best, but it is certainly Campbell the man at his best. *Adamastor* was a great success, and was reprinted three times in 1930. Arnold Bennett said Campbell was 'outrageously a poet', not knowing that Campbell would write of him in *The Georgiad*:

> Each knight and pundit of the weekly scrawl
> From him to Bennett (weekliest of all) . . .
>
> (*CP*, pp 216–17)

Geoffrey Grigson wrote 'first among the poetry of the year', not knowing that Campbell would later empty an inkwell over his head (though of that we cannot be sure because it is Campbell's own story). J. C. Squire, not knowing that Campbell would ridicule him also in *The Georgiad*, said that he was 'the most promising writer who has ever come out of South Africa'.

In spite of this success, the pain remained, and I think was largely assuaged by the writing of *The Georgiad*. Mary used to offer it to me as an example of Campbell's hatred of homosexuality and lesbianism. Did she know that I knew that she was the prime inspiration, she and Vita Sackville-West? She said to me: 'He turned against the Sackville-Wests because they were homosexuals.' She said even more unbelievably, 'Roy's account of Vita is not true; she had in fact a sweet nature.' She said also, 'I don't want two accounts of the Sackville-West episode.' How could I say to her, 'There won't be two; there'll be only one, and it won't be yours'? Nor did I have the heart or the hardness or whatever is required, to say to her, 'Tell me about you and Vita.' What a time that must have been, during the writing of *The Georgiad*! Did she read every day's work (for that was her custom)? Did she laugh? Did she cry? Perhaps you can write Campbell's life better when you don't know.

This is what he wrote about Long Barn:

> Now Spring, sweet laxative of Georgian strains,
> Quickens the ink in literary veins,
> The Stately Homes of England ope their doors
> To piping Nancy-boys and crashing Bores,
> Where for week-ends the scavengers of letters
> Convene to chew the fat about their betters –

> Over the soup, Shakespeare is put in place,
> Wordsworth is mangled with the sole and plaice,
> And Milton's glory that once shone so clear
> Now with the gravy seems to disappear,
> Here Shelley with the orange peel is torn
> And Byron's gored by a tame cuckold's horn. (*CP*, p. 207)

What can one say about *The Georgiad*? In the first place it is extremely clever. In the second place Campbell cannot transcend his own personal hurt and anger, and satire needs more than personal hurt and anger. What were Mary's reactions as she read about Georgiana? And what were Campbell's emotions as he watched Mary reading about Georgiana? The life of *The Georgiad* will be short. It is very probable that no one reads it now but students of Campbell's writings.

In 1932 Campbell's money began to run out. Uys Krige, who was staying with the Campbells and was tutor to Tess and Anna, advised them to move to Spain, where living was cheaper. Campbell writes in *Light on a Dark Horse* that he had lost a good deal of his popularity. The suggestion is that he was in debt. He had to have money quickly and he wrote *Broken Record* in ten days and ten nights, though Uys Krige said it was six weeks. 'It enabled us to flee in time'. He wrote in *Broken Record* that he had for a time earned money by joining a gang that stole dogs that were beloved of their owners. His mother was deeply shocked by this, but he was able to assure her that he had invented it all to fill up his book.

Then to Barcelona. According to *Light on a Dark Horse*, Mary and Roy Campbell understood the issues in Spain at once. We may be sure of their views. They were strongly pro-Church and violently anti-Communist. They were for law and order, because without law and order you cannot have liberty. They were for authority, and pretty strong authority too, because without strong authority you cannot have security.

In 1933 *Flowering Reeds* was published. The lyric passion is abating, the joy, the vigour, they are abating too. The best-known poem is 'Choosing a Mast'. Here is its last stanza:

> And when to pasture in the glittering shoals
> The guardian mistral drives his thundering foals,
> And when like Tartar horsemen racing free
> We ride the snorting fillies of the sea,
> My pine shall be the archer of the gale
> While on the bending willow curves the sail
> From whose great bow the long keep shooting home
> Shall fly, the feathered arrow of the foam. (*CP*, p. 105)

After their re-marriage in Altea they moved to the beautiful city of Toledo where Campbell became a horse trader. It is sometimes said that

South Africa was the love of Campbell's life. I find it impossible to believe. Spain was the love of his life, the Spanish peasants, the Spanish language, the Spanish wine, the Catholic Church, and finally Franco. His coming out for Franco was inevitable. For him the issues were clear – the Church against the Devil, the law against anarchy, authority against equalitarianism, the spirit against matter.

Toledo was what Campbell called a 'red' city and Mary was warned not to go to daily mass with a mantilla and carrying a missal. She was told she would be killed and she ignored the warnings. I have no doubt that she would have chosen to die rather than submit, just as Florence Nightingale and Mrs Hofmeyr would have done.

Out of these Spanish and Catholic years came *Mithraic Emblems* in 1936. Mithras was a god who mediated between God and man. Campbell claims that Mithras was the genuine precursor of Christ, his cowboy in fact. He says in his forthright fashion that Christ is his king, but Mithras is his boss. One can understand that, for Christ the King entertained some very un-Campbellian views about life and conduct, while Mithras the Boss was more accommodating. There is a deep religious feeling in these poems, expressed in that dazzling and unconventional imagery that is Campbell at his best: for example, in 'To the Sun':

> Oh let your shining orb grow dim,
> Of Christ the mirror and the shield,
> That I may gaze through you to Him,
> See half the miracle revealed,
> And in your seven hues behold
> The Blue Man walking on the Sea;
> The Green, beneath the summer tree,
> Who called the children; then the Gold,
> With palms; the Orange, flaring bold
> With scourges; Purple in the garden
> (As Greco saw): then the Red
> Torero (Him who took the toss
> And rode the black horns of the cross –
> But rose snow-silver from the dead!) (*CP*, p. 127)

Campbell fell from a horse in 1936, and limped ever after. This was the famous wound that he received fighting for Franco, a legend that he did not actively deny. His lameness was increased when a fragment of metal from a hand-grenade pierced his hipbone, in Kenya in 1943, during a demonstration of the missile.

Campbell decided to give up drinking until Franco had won the war, and he went to make his vow at the shrine of Our Lady of Fatima. In view of the fact that he was going to undergo the great hardship of total abstinence, he brought a skin of wine which he intended to drink before making the vow. When he held it up over his open mouth, out came water. He went back to the wine-shop but the shopkeeper declared it had been full of wine. Thereupon Campbell proclaimed the miracle of the wine that turned into water. I cannot tell you if he bought a second skin, but I can tell you that he kept the vow. This seems to show that one cannot dogmatize about alcoholism and dipsomania. One would never call Campbell either a drunk or a drunkard. After Franco's victory he returned to drinking, and his record thereafter is one of ups and levels and some very, very deep downs.

His championship of Franco cost him the regard of most of the English-speaking literary world. His championship of Hitler revolted many Jews, though not all as we shall see. He saw true modernity working in Fascism and Hitlerism, ornamentally and efficiently. As he saw it, it effected two complete revolutions without bloodshed, untidiness, and dirt, and compared with workers' revolutions and their bloodshot frenzy, these two bourgeois revolutions indicated the infinite superiority of bourgeois over workmen, from the point of view of humanity.

Was Campbell a Fascist? I would say he was not. I don't think for a moment that he understood the true nature of Nazism and Fascism. To put it bluntly, he was deceived by these two ranting bullies. Their swagger blinded him to their wickedness. Why was this so? Was the secret back there in his boyhood, in his father's home, in A. S. Langley's school? I don't think I shall be able to answer such a question. It is a question for Freud. Freud said that only psychoanalysts should be allowed to write biographies, but the truth is that only writers should be allowed to write them. I do not think a biographer must be able to answer fully the question, *what* made his subject tick. But I think he must be able to describe fully *how* his subject ticks.

During the Spanish War Campbell wrote *Flowering Rifle*, which he described as a poem from the battlefield of Spain. I tried to read it for this paper, but failed to finish the course. It is unrelieved polemic; the imagery has almost gone. He intensified the enmity already felt for him by such lines:

> A tyranny far worse than blamed on Hitler
> Whose chief oppression is of the belittler,
> The intellectual invert, and the Jew,
> Whose tyranny's the harder of the two.[7]

Yet one must not think Campbell liked this isolation. When the Second World War broke out he decided that he must fight for decadent Britain. But he did not arrive in England till July 1941. Professor Gardner wrote he had 'allowed the tide of war to pass over his head'. But unbelievable as it may be – and it certainly was to me at first – he worked for British Intelligence in 1940 and the first part of 1941. In London he became an air raid warden, and was overwhelmed by the courage of the Londoners. He was accepted by the Army at the end of 1941, and wrote to Mary expressing his pleasure at finding himself so popular with the younger men, a popularity to which he had become unaccustomed. He was popular in Kenya too, a poet-sergeant much sought after by the young officers, many of whom were Jews. But his health broke down and he returned to Britain via Durban.

On 1 January 1946, he joined the BBC as a talks producer. In that year he published *Talking Bronco*. That was virtually his last poetry. The poem which gives its title to the book is another wearying polemic, and for some reason I have yet to discover was omitted from the *Collected Poems* (1955). But Campbell's translation of the poem of St John of the Cross entitled 'En una Noche Oscura' did much to polish up his tarnished image, and brought him a last round of applause. Campbell's admiration for St John of the Cross is shared by André Brink, and one of the reasons is that St John, though a holy man, was not afraid of the flesh. And though the poem is a song of the love of the soul for her Lord, the imagery is sexual through-out. It is my belief that Campbell, in these declining years of his Muse, would have given a great deal to have been able to write a religious poem like that. But his Christ is not so much the lover as the Red Torero, Him who took the toss, or the Man with outspread arms, the Man they made an Albatross. The dead Torero

> . . . died the sudden violence of Kings
> And from the bullring to the Virgin goes
> Floating his cape. He has no need for wings. (*CP*, p. 143)

In 1949 Campbell left the BBC after an undistinguished period of service. Rob Lyle started *The Catacomb* magazine to give Campbell a job. It is heavy stuff, anti-liberal, anti-Communist, pro-Catholic, pro-Franco, pro-Salazar. England is clearly going to the dogs again. Campbell claims to have boxed the ears of both Grigson and Spender. He contributed poems regularly, but in the style of *The Georgiad*.

In 1951 Campbell published *Light on a Dark Horse*. If he had been easing back into favour, this work brought the process to an end. T. E. Lawrence found *The Flaming Terrapin* bombastic and magnificent. *Light on a Dark Horse* was bombastic and not magnificent. This is a puzzle difficult to solve, that a man to whom popularity was so important, could so wantonly, so foolishly, destroy it. One is forced to conclude that this poet, with the great sensitivity revealed in 'Buffel's Kop', 'The Zulu Girl', 'The Sleeper', in his response to the beauty of nature, was to a large degree insensitive to men and women, and had no conception of the deep offence he gave to them by his unbridled utterances. Mischief is the word, in its uglier meaning; it was by no means innocent, but it was to a large degree uncomprehending. Patric Dickinson on the BBC called him 'this poet, so nearly great, so hopelessly flawed and incompetent to deal with his life and times'. With these words I fully agree.

In May 1952 Campbell went to live in Portugal. Except for an undistinguished book for children called *The Mamba's Precipice*, published in 1953, and another book, *Portugal*, published in 1957, his writing was now confined to translations of Spanish and Portuguese writers. Much of this translation was done for the BBC. Mrs Helena Wood found his translation from Calderon, 'Life's a Dream', most exciting. The Third Programme 'are positively interested in more of Roy Campbell's translations'. Campbell wrote a postcard to R. D. Smith, congratulating him on his production of 'Life's a Dream', but called it, with no conscious intention I am sure, 'Life's a Drink'. Mr Henry Treece, who had earlier translated the same play, wrote to Campbell objecting to the line 'tread on my neck and trample on my crown', which he said was his own. Campbell wrote to R. D. Smith saying that in fact he had translated *La Vida Es Sueño* before Treece was born, as a school exercise. Mr Treece commented thus: '. . . Mr. Campbell's reply has the tang of the sea about it. All I would ask him is, When and Where. The answers to these questions would be most interesting.' Campbell wrote to Mrs Bray of the BBC that his original translation was done at the Natal University College when he was about 17 or 18. There was not one word of truth in this. Not to this day – that is, July 1974 – does the University of Natal offer a course in Spanish. According to Professor Will Gardner, it was not until 1925 that Campbell decided he must learn Portuguese, Spanish, and French. That was partly because he had just read an English translation of Camoës.

Campbell's letters to the BBC are humble. He was very hard up, and was always asking for his money. He was pleased with another translation from Calderon, 'Love After Death', and thought it the best he had ever done. But Mrs Helena Wood found it most disappointing, the verse mediocre, and the typewritten ms. full of errors. The translation was rejected, and the BBC decided they did not want any more for the time being. Campbell wrote asking to be given Portuguese translations. He wrote: 'I would promise to do it in my best copybook handwriting, so there could be no typing errors. (I have had my lesson.)' I find this a sad letter: the swashbuckler has become a supplicant.

There was one bright spot in these sad years. In 1954 he paid his last visit to Natal, to receive the honorary degree of D.Litt from the University of Natal in Pietermaritzburg. The *Natal Witness* said you could hear the crash of dropping bricks. Campbell defended Spain with vigour. There hardship and poverty bred courage and initiative. He said: 'My own beloved country, besides Spain, is the only country that does not win the certified approval of the United Lunatic Asylum of Disunited Nations, which is as dangerous a war factory as Geneva was before it.' He also defended his beloved country: 'Since many of our critics, especially in various other Dominions, systematically exterminated their aborigines by hand, it does not fit in well with their criticism of our more humane regime.' And again: 'The 200,000,000 Natives of Europe – victims of Yalta – were sold there for a bottle of vodka by people whom one would never have thought capable of such utter gullibility.'

I do not wish to generalize about academic audiences, but this kind of stuff does not go down well with them. It was too like *Broken Record*, of which I said in 1957 in a Campbell Memorial Lecture:

These squibs and crackers go off on nearly every page of this extra-ordinary book, and are not unlike the squibs and crackers that a small boy at a party throws at the feet of the adult guests. Some of them must have made his aunts and uncles jump, not to mention his brothers and sisters.

Campbell's graduation address aroused a variety of emotions, distaste, disapproval, disbelief, and I suppose also approval. I do not wish to generalize about Old Soldiers and Old Boys, but this kind of thing went down better with them. Campbell was surrounded by admirers and hand-shakers and comrades, and they and the flowing cup induced in him a kind of euphoria stupendosa. He wrote to Mary that he felt that he could be a leader of his people, and that she and she only had the power to draw him away. By his people, I suppose he meant us, the English-speaking people of South Africa, and as many of you know, we don't need a Campbell, we need nothing less than an Archangel.

Back to Portugal. There Mary painted his portrait, the portrait of a grave and ageing man. I said to her, it's a sad picture. She said, do you think so? Two years later I went back again to see her, and she said within a minute or two, you said it was a sad picture, well I want you to know he was not a sad man. A few days later we discovered two notebooks. They are the notebooks of a man who wants to write and cannot. The old Campbellian idiom is manifest, but the Muse, frequently after one or two lines, comes to a halt. Then Campbell moves to another page, and tries again. The prevailing themes are stones, statues, his statue, pigeons on his stone hand, the stones of Broken Hill. He writes of the purgatorial woe:

> That after so much torment such decay
> And boredom far more terrible than they
> We're tested by the purgatorial woe.

But he finishes nothing. He then turns to the Dragon Stone – 'The Dragon Stone, that shaped my course and doom'. This is clearly the Drakensberg; then in come the Tugela and the Umzimkulu, mambas, Zulus. I read these to Mary. She weeps. She says humbly, that's when I painted the portrait. Stones, Stones, and More Stones. 'The Stones that formed my childhood.' 'Coffin' comes now frequently – 'my overcoat of firewood'. From the poplar we hew our cradles, coffins, and guitars. 'Stone of the Berg.' 'Stone of the Dragon, the maternal womb.'

> I'll spend my old age in the public gardens
> While into stone my own sclerosis hardens.

He is in much pain with his hip, which has developed a sclerosis. He has a diabetic condition. He drinks much wine. A South African visits him and describes him as 'a ruin of a man'.

Then there is the second notebook. Stones again. 'By lonely outcrops in the Spanish highland.' Or the same page 'An outcrop in the Matabele highland'. Though these stones take him back to the maternal womb, they have an immediate relevance. They are building their new house, Casa de Serra, near Sintra. They have had to dig out great boulders to lay the foundations, and they lie around the house that is to be. Campbell goes there nearly every day, to see the building of the home in which he will never live.

Again the gardens, the sclerosis, the boredom, 'the fear of going crackers'. 'When one is petrified by one's own fame.' The repetition is endless but finds no end. I give the one completed stanza:

> A billion times to keep from going crackers
> I'll read my name and birth date to reclaim
> Dead selves the stones, I slept on as I came
> With my dark horse, the bugbear of the backers,
> Who put the public favourites to shame –
> The Pegasus I rescued from the knackers
> To share the petrifaction of my fame.

In April 1957 Mary and Roy went to attend Holy Week in Seville. It was a great event in Spain, and Campbell was very much at peace. On Easter Monday, 23 April 1957, they started back. Mary was driving; Campbell never drove. Campbell was far away and talked little. The roads were bad and they had a puncture, putting on a spare which was very old, and was kept for the sake of economy. At about two o'clock in the afternoon Campbell said they would soon be at Setubal and would be home for tea. As is common in Portugal, trees were very close to the road. The old tyre burst, and they went into a tree. They were found unconscious but Campbell was dying. His neck was broken. They were taken to the Misericordia in Setubal. When Mary recovered consciousness they did not tell her that Campbell was dead. When they finally told her, she was at peace, because she knew that he did not want to go on living.

So he went as he had written that he would,

> Instead of ending with a whimper
> My life will finish with a bang.

## References

1. Roy Campbell, *Light on a Dark Horse*, London, 1951, p. 9.
2. Roy Campbell, *Collected Poems*, Vol. 1, London, 1949, p. 17. References in the text to this volume will be to *CP*.
3. Roy Campbell, *Broken Record*, London, 1934, pp. 52–3.
4. *Light on a Dark Horse*, p. 248.
5. Nigel Nicolson, *Portrait of a Marriage*, London, 1973.
6. *Light on a Dark Horse*, p. 347.
7. Roy Campbell, *Collected Poems*, Vol. 2, London, 1957, p. 213.

# South African Oral Traditions

MAZISI KUNENE

ALTHOUGH my topic is South African oral traditions, I shall not deal with all South African oral traditions. For one thing they are far too many: that is, if we mean by this topic the variety of oral literatures and literary stylistics of each of the South African indigenous people. This would be a life-time's study. South African oral traditions include the sum total of Sotho, Zulu, Xhosa, Swazi, Venda, and Shangane literatures, to mention only the major ones. These can be further subdivided in a variety of regional units. For instance Sotho oral literature comprises such sections of the Sotho people as the Pedis, Khatlas, Ngwatos, Mshoeshoe-Sothos, Ngwaketse, and many others. Similarly among the Xhosas the literature is identified with various nationalities that constitute the subgroups. These include: the Gcalekas, the Dlambes, a large section of the Hlubis, and the Mpondos. All this literary variation is further complicated by the close connection in African literature one finds between history and literature; geography and literature; politics and literature. Often a particular literature, e.g. Sotho, may have numerous varieties according to where it originates and when it originated. Language in this sense does not determine the evolution of the content, so that in some cases both in style and content, a particular subgroup literature may be closer to the dominant literature of a neighbouring group, e.g. Swazi-Pedi. It is therefore clear that language does not standardize literature in this case, it acts only as a vehicle. Further research must ask various questions, for instance: what is Sotho literature? These factors and questions arise out of the fact that we are dealing with a literature which is not frozen into some book-form to act as a standard or point of reference for all those writing in that language. This is a crucial factor in examining all oral literature or rather the latter-day attempts to make translations, definitions, recordings of oral literature.

In order to make this study manageable it is necessary to focus on the literature of one national group. I have chosen the Zulus, not because their poetry is the only one that merits study and attention, but because it is the one I personally know best. Secondly because the Zulus as a nation, thanks to Shaka the Great, are the most publicized, and their literature and history has been most extensively studied. Thirdly, because of all the African national groups in South Africa their literature is perhaps most centralized and standardized. This is no claim for it to be the most meritorious; it is only easier to put under one central theme as Zulu oral literature. A little-known fact is that the Zulus, once a small nation group when the Mthethwas, the Gasas, the Shangana, the Ambos, were powerful nations, produced at that period less than impressive literature. Unfortunately the literatures of these once-powerful nations have been lost. We cannot therefore justifiably talk of Zulu oral literature as if it was always grand, epic, and excellent. Rather we have to think of it as going through the same stages of evolution and development as the history of the Zulu nation itself.

Many writers – spies, missionaries, adventurers, traders – have sought the motivations of Zulu society. This has enabled us to look into a great variety of documents reporting on the various aspects of the Zulu nation and history. In the field of oral literature we count such people as R. C. Samuelson, A. T. Bryant, Henry Fynn, Nathaniel Isaacs, Andrew Smith, and many others. These recorded numerous forms of literature which were alive in their times. This has been both an advantage and a disadvantage. Whilst preserving a tradition that would have otherwise been lost, it has given the impression that only a particular text is the one valid one, whereas the living quality in oral literature lies precisely in the varieties of contributions by different authors. It lies in keeping the particular composition closely related to a particular occasion. In this way oral literature is living literature whose excellence lies in performance. There is therefore a great stylistic difference between written or recorded literature (that was once oral) and oral literature as it is expressed and acted today.

Before we go on to analyse the content and style of African oral literature it is essential to understand the workings of the society from which it originates. Having pointed out the existence of a variety of literary types according to various nation-groups it must be pointed out that fundamentally, the South African oral literatures bear some significant common characteristics. Sometimes literary works are merely translated from one language group to another. This is particularly true of nursery rhymes, stories, and story-poems, satires, and occasionally, the literary structure of a particular heroic or epic poem, for example, the echoes from the poem on Emperor Shaka of the Zulus in the epic poem on King Sobhuza I of the Swazis. In such cases it can be assumed that the heroic literature of one nation has had a strong influence on the other. This assumption can be easily made if there are strong bonds of friendship as in this case, where there were diplomatic visits, and diplomatic marriages resulting in exchanges of poetic or cultural material and stylistic innovations.

It is, however, the similarity in social organization which has brought about a literature which can rightly be called South African oral literature. Oral literature is a direct product of two major factors, (a) the communal form of social organization, (b) the non-literate nature of the society. Without going deep into the structural forms of African society it would be enlightening to mention a few aspects that relate to the content and form of oral African literature. The central unit of the African society is the family. The family is not as in the western countries merely a biological unit which sheers itself off as soon as possible to form other biological units. It is rather a social group, a large family group which in some ways can operate as a self-sufficient unit. Some families are so large that they constitute sizeable clans, as for instance, the Dlaminis, the Phiris, the Mtaungs, and the Ngeobos. At the centre of each family is a family head who may be male or female. He/she is a replica of the king, or prince or chief. Whilst not exercising the same political power as the king he/she possesses tremendous authority within the family unit. His/her power derives from a collaborative ideology which defines survival in terms of communal action. It is these heads of families who are symbolic of the family ethos who inherit the mantle of ancestral power. Of course their power is by no means absolute, originating as it does from a pact of mutual interdependence.

If this vertical authority is important it balances up with an equally important form of horizontal authority. The latter type of authority is based on age grouping. Age here does not refer to a statistical definition but rather to a cyclical period more akin to the idea of generations in biblical terminology or an Afro-Asian time conception. Each age group is given by society certain duties and responsibilities so that society is not divided rigidly into male and female but above all into age groups.

The relations that exist within a family grouping extend naturally into the whole society. Some of the more explicitly stated forms of authority may gradually become symbolic and/or honorary, as when, for instance, a young king is addressed as 'Wena omdala' (you who are old). Some of the tales told in our literature illustrate clearly that authority based on age is totally inadequate and unsatisfactory. Thus Chakizana (the wily one) out-wits and outplays the elders as soon as he is born. His superior intellect is accepted by them and they eagerly want to know from him many of the hidden mysteries around them.

What, one may well ask, is the use of all this discussion on society when we need to know about oral literature? To those who understand, no explanation is necessary. To those who don't, it is necessary to state explicitly and emphatically that no full knowledge of African literature is possible without a grasp of the workings of African society. Perhaps few literatures in the world possess such close links with the societies from which they originate. Knowledge of the language is certainly no guarantee of an understanding of African oral literature. This is perhaps one of the crucial points about African traditional literature. It is about concrete events, concrete situations, and is therefore firmly rooted in historically traceable social events. As in Chinese literature, the abstract is incidental. This being the case, the literature changes drastically with the change in society. Thus in a particularly outstanding historical period, the literature itself improves in quality and in scope. This is by no means an inexplicable phenomenon, for herein lies one of the outstanding qualities of oral poetry – a flexible expressionism which follows closely the socially significant events. It is as if the poets and composers, having perfected their instruments, wait only for events that fit the grandeur of their artistry. This, of course, is stating the extreme in order to make a point. It can, however, be shown how the artistry evolves as the content of the literature becomes mature and more socially significant. This is clearly illustrated in the evolution of classical Zulu poetry from the sixteenth century to the late nineteenth century.

It is easy to understand why a society whose social bonds are not automatic (biological) needs a strong social ideology to maintain them. The large family group must discourage excessive individualism if it is to survive as a unit. The unit, in order not to be incidental, i.e. created by needs for food, collaborative actions against outsiders, etc., must elevate its group relations into an ideal of religious dimensions. This can only be done through a literature that is constantly allocating rewards for acts that promote strong communal relations. Equally, the literature has to punish the witches (i.e. anti-social individuals) and hold up to ridicule any transgressor against the communal ethic. This may seem a narrowing of literature into a functional instrument of religion. This however is not true of African oral literature for the simple reason that the religion itself is of a 'secular' character. You do not sin against a superior being (unless you attempt to annihilate life, in which case your fellow men act as divine instruments for your destruction or removal) but against your fellow men.

Such acts then as are considered socially significant and warranting a literary treatment constitute in time a compendium of ethics for each generation. This does not mean, by the way, as is claimed by some anthropologists, that the society is lumbered with immutable past doctrines. It is precisely the function of literature to produce in each period a relevant critique which takes into account not only past contributions but also present circumstances. In this sense the man or woman of literature is at once a philosopher, an historian, and in some cases an oracle. It is not surprising therefore that these individuals possess special privileges. They are free to make scathing criticisms against any member of society. They are also given enough by society to be free of any material obligations and stress. Literature in this sense serves more than a form of entertainment, but is at once a serious system of ethics which it enforces, a preserve of historical events, a body of philosophical speculation, a nexus that produces a logic, not only between past and present generations, but also in the whole cosmic phenomenon. All these functions it can achieve only because oral literature is not specialized in the sense that literature is for western intellectuals. Every man, woman, or child is expected to be steeped in the literature of the country. Thus each man and woman has conferred on him or her the accolades of poetry or satire according to what he or she does. Through all these devices literature achieves its universality. One can say that South African oral literature is more socially based and more universally lived than the literature of 'literate' societies. Indeed most societies in this sense are not literate but only understand very superficial elements of literature. In other words, literature in so-called literate societies gets frozen, only to be defrosted by those with a special technique, which they acquire through many years of specialized training. Those who come from societies steeped in oral literature will know that the training for literary appreciation starts at a very early age, i.e. non-verbal rhythmic stage. With each age group there is a relevant type of literature that culminates in the highest literary expression, i.e. heroic or epic poetry. Since the literature is lived in everyday activities there is a constant awareness and reference to its elements. So important is the literature to the community that it has sometimes been used as reference to settle family disputes, boundary disputes, and succession issues.

Oral literature differs in many ways from written literature. The social organization itself ensures this differentiation in form and in function. As I have stated, the specialization of literature for a certain class or group is alien to oral literature. Looking into such a literature, it is often forgotten that what we see on paper is bare bones. It is as if the books of Shakespeare were to be found by someone who has never heard of England, never read about the war histories of the English, never heard of their many kings and queens, never experienced the desiccating individualism of Shakespeare's heroes and heroines. There is in fact more to be known about African oral literature in the religions and philosophies of the African. For this study I have chosen only the most elementary assumptions of African religion and philosophy.

There are very strong reasons for linking up oral literature to religious observances. For one, it makes many a work of literature as sacred as the Old Testament was to the Hebrews or the Book of the Dead to our Egyptian ancestors. This way the highest literary expressions are not only preserved, but accorded a relevance with each occasion of religious observance. Thus the events and the literature become a perspective from which the contemporary generation maps its future thought developments.

Central to African religion is the concept that the dead exercise an influence on the living. Similarly, the living exercise an influence on the unborn. African socio-religious philosophy, being very practical, leaves the possibilities of material and immaterial dimensions to the judgement of the individual. This balance requires that the individual by his action must improve his/her material reality through exercising the physical equipment relevant to the material world. On the other hand, the same actions can be interpreted as the act of the gods (the Ancestors, the Forefathers), they who have interceded on the community's behalf with the Supreme Being. They had also by their actions whilst on earth made it possible for the following generation to live a better life. Following these examples (as contained in the heroic-epic literature), the current generation is partially guaranteed a better life i.e. until it makes its own contribution. In this sense knowledge is the celebrated and cumulative experience of the community. Because of the dual nature of life none can be punished for holding one belief against the other (material versus immaterial). The punishment lies ultimately in the sanction and isolation which society imposes on those who apparently refuse (by holding too strongly to one or the other doctrine) to participate in society. What is implied in both doctrines is communal participation which both religion and literature set out to reinforce and sanction. Each generation is relevant to itself, its history-making role, above all, the circumstances that dictate its life. Oral literature, combining these semi-religious social tenets, views life as composed of cycles of generations. These are extensions of the age-group divisions which are the microcosm of what obtains in the universe, from the minute to the peak point and final disintegration. Hence the failure to observe one's obligations and social responsibilities is followed by punishment not only from within the society, but also from profound forces that are at certain times within humanity's control. Such forces can be invoked either by a biological parent or a social parent in extreme cases of social transgression: 'The curse of the parent brings madness and death.' However wronged the parent, he/she may withhold the use of this ultimate power. Does it work? It certainly does, not only because of the psychological disposition of the victim, but because such an individual threatens by his/her act the integrity of the community and challenges the very order of the universe. The literature which projects at once a fantastical universe (myths of creation and legends) and a very strong element of realism originates from this very admixture of material and immaterial aspects.

It is obvious that since any national occasion is of necessity solemn and 'religious', society demands on such an occasion an affirmation of its ethics through the highest form of literature. It is for this reason that the African community calls on the best artistry in the country to enshrine the occasion and further set it up as a practical example providing the community with guidelines. On the first day of the First Fruit Festival (Incwala) the ceremonies are preceded by constant epic narrations of the deeds of past ancestors of the royal clan and successions of heroes who proved themselves worthy guardians of the community. The 'rebirth' or re-emergence of the king from a period of isolation symbolizes the new challenges for the contemporary generation. Through such epics and heroic poems there is a dramatic re-enactment of battle scenes.

Too often it is assumed that oral literature refers only to poetry. This is because in recent years a great deal of research has been made in this aspect. There is at present a proliferation of studies based on the African heroic epic and mythological material. Yet it is clear from all observations that whilst the heroic epic is regarded by Africans as the highest literary expression it is not half as widespread and ubiquitous as some of the less complex forms. These constitute the fertile soil on which the heroic epic grows. They train the young on the subtleties of language. They also challenge the old to unravel the inner mysteries of meaning from the simplest of phenomena. Thus their forms are to the old, hauntingly simple, and to the young, entertaining.

> Mother! Talkative one,
> Feast to which all nations go!
> I came here where the place is rich with honey
> Where you eat and leave plentifulness
> Mother of the myriad nations of ants
> Giver of plenty, generous one
> Comforter of orphans, of the desolate earth.

Unfortunately in the translation the poem loses its flexible literary response which makes it an adult poem as well as a children's poem.

Perhaps the only sensible division of oral literature is according to purpose as defined by the African society itself. Since the events determine the type of literature associated with them, it is logical that literature should coincide with these social categories. Indeed the absence of the fragmented segments of knowledge means that oral literature serves the function of synthesizing a great variety of socially relevant information or knowledge. This oral quality in African literature goes further than being only a preserver and disseminator of knowledge. Clearly, both written and oral literatures begin from different points of assumption. Written literature is explicit and detailed, often comprising long descriptions of situations and events. By its elaborate descriptions it aims at giving a pictographic image of the events. Oral literature on the other hand is not concerned with a replay of events but with their social significance. Thus oral literature begins with the assumption that the events it seeks to comment on are universally known. If some of the members of the audience are not informed or need reminding it feels it is enough to provide only summaries. These 'summaries' of necessity require a technique that fits into the structure of the whole ethical thesis. Thus oral poetry uses symbolisms which aim at operating as a common language or a short cut route to information of a generalized character. This can be illustrated in the following extract from a praise poem:

> The swift runner is very fast.
> The horses once outran the escaper,
> they once outran Tharodi Kwena,
> they outran the wind of Segotshane,
> of Modietsho and Telekelo,
> of Senthufi, Kgakge, and Kgomodimafshwi.
> Leforakwena lied to us there, excusing his greed;
> he said, 'There are no animals'.
> But the giraffes grazing in Sefoka hollow,
> can't they be attacked by the vanguard?
> Men went to keep watch at Chukuduchochwa;
> coming back they whitewashed their knees
> and twisted grass stalks round their legs.
>     I argue about him with RaKgabo,
> as the army returns with joyful song;
> I say, 'A calf is known by its breeders,
> Senese is the one who should know him.'
> I see him dragging along the king of beasts
> and bearing the mane of a swift-running lion.
>     Food-giver, brother of Kgosidintsi,
> he never gives stringy meat,

he gives only meat that is fat,
we people eat it and smear our knees.
     As he comes he kills, Sechele's son,
he comes killing, but he also spares,
he spared Kgomo's son and set him free.
We say, a chief rules through foreign children.[1]

In this extract the poet is not really concerned with detailing events so much as with the moral responsibility that must uplift society. Indeed we are told very little about the characters and the nature of the occasion. What is clearly impressed on us however is that:

(a) 'The swift runner is very fast'     (The hero outwits all by his wisdom and speed.)

(b) 'Leforakwena lied to us . . .'     (We, as part of the hero's party, punish the greedy.)

(c) 'Food-giver brother of Kgosiditsi'  (Our heroes are not only the brave ones but are also generous, they 'never give stringy meat'.)

(d) 'He spared Kgomo's son and set him free'
                                        (We can trust them because they are also kind and forgiving. It is correct that they should remain protected by better people even if such people be strangers.)

Oral literature constantly projects the examples of socially desirable actions, making heroes of those who uphold the highest communal values and villains of those who violate them. Its strategy is therefore to be effective immediately and to be of immediate application. This does not mean that it is purely propagandistic or 'pop'. On the contrary, since it starts off on the premise of what is fundamentally significant and universally desirable, it operates on a timeless basis.

To maintain its interest, oral literature of necessity links itself with various social, political, and religious events. Any gathering becomes a fit place for its expression be it a work party, a circumcision school, a diviners' get-together, a family reunion, a dance, a feast, a festival, an evening gathering by the fireside, or a shepherds' gathering. The participation of the community is an essential part for a literature that is not only 'live' but also communal in its intent. This communal quality secularizes the literature and makes accessible what would otherwise be a highly moralistic or didactic literature. The fact that it is based on concrete social and historical events brings it closer to every-day morality and action. It deals with the ethical challenges of things that can be achieved and therefore becomes more than a litany of superhuman ideals. Thus the ethical message is interwoven into a whole fabric of social drama. The 'contemporariness' of most of African oral literature derives from precisely this fact. A work of literature runs the danger of being didactic only if the author assumes a superior attitude. Literature of such a type assumes a pulpit posture. That African oral literature is without this didacticism is an achievement deriving both from a subtle literary technique and from the social context of its composition. Oral literature holds up to ridicule things that are socially inacceptable. This way it enhances the position of the author/narrator (who assumes the representative role of the whole of society) and diminishes the role of the wrong-doer. Note for instance the following stanzas:

> He is like Makopye, a spoiler of the country
> He used to make life hard for us,
> He inspanned us and used us as oxen
> He made us pull the shafts of refuse-carts
> He made us play scratch like children
> Red-faced people with pointed noses
> Stooges of the whiteman Makopye.

The author/narrator is indignant, he mobilizes those who have been humiliated by conquest. He is not cowed despite the fact that the hideous oppressors 'inspanned us and used us like oxen'. In fact, he is contemptuous of the very oppressors, who like their stooge 'Makopye a spoiler of the country' and others, were put to flight by heroes like Sekikibane.

The technique of ridiculing what is socially undesirable runs through a great deal of oral literature. It assumes its highest expression in the heroic and epic poetry where greater things are at stake. It manifests itself in various degrees in other types of literature.

It should be clear at this stage that oral literature not only affirms the positive social actions and ideas but also creates them. It is at its best the generative force that embodies all the experimental material of society. By its unconventionality it seeks to break the established norms should they prove inadequate to meet the new situation. It establishes a nexus between the various stages of change. Thus an author is not only a person who can make beautiful verses and beautiful stories, but is also a sage, a philosopher, and an historian. Naturally various artists excel in one field or another, but the basic assumption about them is that they are persons who because of their profound experience are steeped in the workings of society. In some cases the heroic poem acts as a connecting link between the different eras. The practice in most African societies of re-enacting the heroic acts of past heroes aims at reaffirming the continuity of society and social values relating to acts of self-sacrifice. It is for this reason that on very important national occasions the national poets declaim the national epics. The intention is always to remind the members of society of their duties and responsibilities, entertainment being only of peripheral significance.

The view of the society of itself, of its relations with other societies, of its relations with the cosmos, is inevitably deeply influenced by its needs and by the manner in which it has solved the problem. The African society is a society that is land based. It has evolved in a continent of vast proportions and comparatively friendly climate. Nor is the internal area of the continent cursed with impossible mountains or rivers. The result is a society whose experience and philosophy is based on keen observation of natural phenomena. The concreteness of its language, ideas, metaphor, derives from this fact. The cyclic concept of life as opposed to the fragmentary, a life defined by fragmentary time-units, comes of a society not determined by the urgency of land hunger. Hence the very strong communal ideology arising, not from a need to eke out existence as has often been suggested, but from a very real necessity to undertake collaborative action to exploit a seemingly endless land mass. The emphasis on movement as the fundamental phenomenon that dominates all life-growth, seasons, rebirth, shapes of living things, etc., is by no means isolated from the circumstances that make up African belief and philosophy. The cyclic thrusts of movement are nowhere better illustrated than in the myth of creation. According to this myth God decided at first that human beings on earth would be given eternal life. To convey this message he sent a chameleon. The chameleon was slow; it took its time going around, spending a great deal of time hunting for flies and berries. Meantime God changed his mind and sent the fleet-footed salamander. It arrived first with the terrible message that there would be death on earth. Initially the foolish humans welcomed this idea, until they learned by experience how horrible death is. The chameleon arrived eventually, but it was too late. Ever since, humankind has detested the chameleon. The symbolism is clear to those acquainted with the beliefs and philosophy of African society. The chameleon is life, for like life it is slow and takes, according to the dictates of its seed (message), a circuitous route, following an outer circle. Humanity on the other hand is confined to a smaller orbit; acceleration in this orbit presages destruction. In this contrast we see the chameleon representing life, whilst the salamander represents death (speed). But life according to tenets of African belief does not follow such simplistic categories. The chameleon that represents life gorges itself with death (flies). As if to carry this point further it also feeds on berries (summer, life, rebirth). Ultimately its message is, for those who occupy the inner circle, death. The salamander on the other hand is obedient, speedy, and devoid of alternate initiatives. It does not swerve from the direction given to it. Because of its speed it represents and carries the message of death. It is, however, rewarded for its power to make its pace coincide with the expectations of humanity (it meets the demands of humanity for instant answers). Hence it is incorporated into human society. It is welcomed by them even when its message is found to be unpleasant; it is the chameleon that is blamed. The salamander is in this sense the projection of humanity's fantasies about physical immortality, but these fantasies only emphasize the frustrating distance between its own immediate orbit and life's long-term orbit. As humanity cannot blame itself for what, after all, is the outcome of its physical possibilities (life and death) it puts the blame squarely on life's failure to satisfy its appetite for immortality.

I have dwelt on this myth not only because it illustrates the importance of understanding the life-relationship in relation to its pace but also because it demonstrates the economy of thought in oral literature. It assumes general acceptance of the importance of movement. Through this myth the society sanctifies the idea of movement, giving it a religious quality. The myth itself is structurally cast on two levels: (a) a level that appeals to children through the fantastical use of animal-life drama, (b) a level suitable for adults. This is the level requiring a deeper and more profound understanding of the symbolism and philosophy pertaining to the life of society as a whole. These levels recur in oral literature, demanding of the listener, and latterly of the reader, an intellectual alertness for ideas that have evaded many a well-intentioned anthropologist or aspiring literary critic.

In all recorded oral literature we are ultimately faced with a literature that has, by being written down, been cast on to an unsuitable framework. As a result, what is translated sounds either obscure or simplistic. Oral literature has sometimes been classified as follows:

A. *Heroic-epic*
  (i) occasional odes, divining poetry, (ii) initiation poetry, (iii) story-poetry, (iv) funeral poetry, (v) war poetry closely akin to work-party poetry and hunting poetry, (vi) nursery rhymes.

B. *Mythological literature and legends*

C. *Stories*
  These fall into various subsections, the most popular of which (among the anthropologists) has been animal stories. In fact, there are stories

comprising numerous different themes, dealing variously with themes
relating to ogres and monsters, battles and general history, etc. All these
stories are divided into two strict categories: (i) Izindaba, true stories and
(ii) Izinganekwane, tales or stories of fantasy. Ruth Finnegan in her
book *Oral Literature in Africa*[2] has, in dealing with prose-classification,
included proverbs and riddles, which I think is stretching a point a bit
too far. Neither of these categories is treated by Africans as anything
more than occasional literature, if that. Indeed, the riddles are treated
as 'children's games'. On the other hand it is rare that a Zulu speaker,
for instance, would bring up a litany of proverbs. In fact, people who
continuously quote proverbs in their speech are regarded as outright
bores. This is true also of English. I have seldom heard any good English
speaker spouting all those proverbs that we learnt at school. As literature
these two categories are of very little significance except of course to
seekers after 'exotic wisdom'.

### D. *Drama*

Drama in African society is an integral part of the dance, the per-
formed or acted song and the masquerades of the festival occasions.

Unlike European drama, African drama is not dominantly conversa-
tional but rather depends on symbolic movements and demonstrations.
The actor, the performer or re-enactor of events uses his/her body movements, voice modulation, artifacts (masks), eye movements, etc. to convey the content of a dramatic event. Since African drama is often
dependent on the demonstrative actions of a single individual or a collection of individuals, the overall impact of concerted action is often
missing. The whole drama depends on the assumption of a lot of background information. There is never an extensive attempt to inform
through action, through character development, and through the creation
of a complex plot. Drama in this sense hints at things and takes the
whole setting, including the 'spectators', as part of the drama. Hence in
the heroic epic performances the audience actively participates, responding to the skilled and subtle messages of the performer. African drama
is, therefore, essentially communal. It is an open air performance, enact-
ing interesting event or events communicated through a symbolic
language of words and /or movement. The story-teller or the historical
narrator often depends entirely on his/her skill as a one man/woman
performer to illustrate dramatic events. Among the Mende peoples in
West Africa there are dramas approximating the European type. On the
whole African drama is, like the bulk of Asian drama, non-conversational,
symbolic and integrated to social events.

The dancer, the epic poet, the story-teller portrays character only in
so far as it helps the movement of the drama. He/she is not concerned
with the psychology of the characters, this not being a society that puts
too much emphasis on individualist roles. African drama represents,
there, not persons, or even details of events, but ideas. Each actor's task
is to represent a collective and to project a composite of ideas. This can
be seen clearly in the multi-characterization of a skilled storyteller, who
may in the same story portray the ogres, the beautiful victims, usually
young girls, mimic various animals, and project the stern character who

represents the father figure in the community. The actor in *Sizwe Banzi is Dead*, a play put together by various members of a drama club community in Johannesburg and produced by Athol Fugard, gives exactly this kind of performance. He is the story-teller who often attracts audiences by his stories at dinner-break in many South African factories. Indeed what this actor says many of those from South Africa know already, having heard the story and seen its impromptu dramatization many times.

I shall now consider the Shakan period for in-depth analysis, since it is the one I have studied more thoroughly than others. It should not be assumed however that other southern African nationalities (particularly the Ngwatos, the Xhosa people (the Southern Sothos), have made lesser achievements in literature in their classic periods. These assumptions originate from definitions of history and culture that are made by foreigners who often define social phenomena according to their own experience. Unfortunately the conqueror often defines what is most clearly seen among the conquered. Be it as it may, our selection of the Shakan period can be paralleled by an equally merited classic period of the other nationalities of southern Africa.

There is a systematic development of literature noticeable in the pre-Shakan period. As literature is so integral a part of history and social drama in African society, this evolution reflects the organizational changes in the society. A time had to come in which the predominantly land-based, pastural–agricultural society would find itself at the end of the great African land mass. When this happened in the past there was a series of backwheeling movements either of an imperial kind or of friendly settlements. Obviously in the past it was easy to move from one region to another, the centres of trade and mining attracting only a small section of enterprising luxury-seekers. However as the pressures from the northern part of the African continent increased and the region in the Sahara and Kalahari became more and more unproductive, it became less and less possible to move from one area to another without encountering either natural obstacles (poor pastures) or opposition from those already settled. All this made it inevitable that there should be a sedimentation of population at the tip of the African continent. Of course, population saturation depends to a great extent on the type of economy and production; for an agricultural–pastural community population 'saturation' comes sooner. Such were the circumstances of the pre-Shakan society. Pre-Shakan society was a society that was restless and infested with many minor wars. There were numerous nation-groups speaking various languages. The method of warfare was simple, involving sometimes the confrontation between two goliaths of the opposing armies. Winning a war was sometimes a matter of how one group out-dealt and out-danced the other. Kings like Zwide of the Ndwandwes were hated and despised for their viciousness in battle. The impact all this had on literature was equally to tone down its heroic quality. This is particularly true of heroic-epic literature, which depends on the dramatic social events involving a story-teller epic poet. However the literature of fantasy – the nursery rhymes, satirical lyrics, mythic and legendary stories – reached its maximum expression. Many of the stories and legends of this period emphasize the element of physical danger which always is made to succumb to physically weaker but intellectually superior forces. Many of the monster-stories belong to this category. If some of them were not invented in this period they were at least elaborated in it. A deeper study of their unequal episodes illustrates this fact. The following examples are a few illustrations of the pre-Shakan literature:

> The mysterious pole of Nomgabi
> Where owls used to sit and doze
> It is there where Phungashe of the Buthelezis used to sit
> It is there also where Macingwane of Ngonyabalni used to sit
> Dladlama of Majola clan used to sit there.

> Child of my mother get on my back let us go
> Let us flee this Nguni land
> Where people die like flies on the pathways.

These extracts are from King Senzangakhona's 'heroic' poem.[3] They are typical of the poetry of the period in their emphasis that 'it is wiser to sit quietly or at most, to flee' than to die in the hands of 'gangsters' like Macingwane. There is, in this literature, a predominantly nomadic quality, most of the poetry emphasizes the physical beauty of the individuals. In some cases poets are shown to be engrossed in nature-images as is the case particularly with the Mkhize poets. Another common quality of pre-Shakan poetry is understandably the ability to outwit and outmanoeuvre your enemy. Many pre-Shakan individuals are known as:

> Thou deep pool that abounds in smooth stones
> Each time someone tries to take a bath
> He slips into the depths of water.

The peaceful and languid life of the pre-Shakan period was not changed by Shaka, as is generally believed, but by the anti-social and vicious war tactics of Zwide and Macingwane. Indeed a thorough and unprejudiced examination of the period shows how Shaka, by his military genius and statesmanship, brought together various warring elements. Shaka was a firm believer in unified and stable states. This, he reasoned, was the only way to guard against the endless small wars and numerous acts of gangsterism and banditry that were prevalent at the time. It was for this reason that he set out to create a state in which all who belonged to it, whatever their national origins, shared a common and an equal citizenship. (It was for this he was killed by his brothers, who in fact demanded aristocratic privilege). In a very short space of time he had welded together many dissident elements into a powerful nation. Shaka's belief in rooting out the rampant banditry of the time is illustrated clearly in his attack against the warlike Prince Matiwane of the Ngwanes. His policy of establishing strong diplomatic and close relations with established states is demonstrated in his relations with King Sobhuza I of the Swazis on the one hand and King Moshoeshoe I of the Basothos on the other. With both these stable states Shaka had strong relations. At one time he sent the able commander-in-chief General Mdlaka to attack Matiwane for having threatened his friend King Moshoeshoe after the latter had reported to him the confiscation of the exchange gifts meant for Shaka. From various historical studies it is clear that the Zulu state, far from being a destructive force, was a stabilizing factor in the whole southern African region. The conflicts between various peoples in the region (Xhosa versus Prince Matiwane; Moshoeshoe versus Mzilikazi; Ngwato versus Mzilikazi; Shona versus Mzilikazi; etc.) were not caused by the expansionism of the Zulu state, nor were they between the Zulu state and other established states, but mainly between lawless elements who were marauders and established settlements. It is obvious to any unprejudiced historian that Emperor Shaka, far from being a blood-thirsty savage, was an astute statesman and a far-sighted nation builder. His military tactics were more effective than those of others but no less inhuman than those of Alexander the Great, Ashoka the Great, and Napoleon. All Shaka's conquests had indeed a purpose and a scheme which was far more visionary than the raids of the Ndwandwes, the Ntulis, and the various bandit groups that inhabited the mountains and forests.

The creation of a Zulu state had profound effects not only on the politics of southern Africa but also on the literature. The literature of the new nation assumed dimensions never dreamt of before. The heroic poem finds its full flowering and ultimate logical form in the epic. There is a revolutionary change in style, content, and form of literature. No longer are poets and other authors of stories content with the brittle literature of fantasy. They give body to their literature centring themselves firmly on realities deriving from social and historical drama. This alone means that the literature assumes a seriousness it has hitherto lacked. The accolades of heroism and self-sacrifice are no longer conferred on reluctant heroes, nor are they any longer offered as possibilities, but as realities.

*Pre-Shakan*
Inyathi ehamba isingama amazibuko
(The buffalo that wanders examining the depths of pools)

*Shakan*
Inyathi ejame ngomkhonto phesheya koMzimubu
Ningayihlabi nani bo Gambushe
Niyothi ningayihlaba Niyobe nihlabe uPhunga
Nahlaba uMageba.
(The buffalo that awaits its enemies with a spear
Across the Mzimubu river
Dare not stab it you of Taku and you of Gambushe
Should you dare you shall have provoked
The ancestral spirits of Phonga and Mageba.)

In the Shakan stanza we see how thought is completed: the poet intro-
duces the theme, treats it and concludes with the consequences of such an
activity. This contrasts radically with the earlier loose stanza of the pre-
Shakan period. In the Shakan stanza the events are of concrete historical
significance whereas in the pre-Shakan stanza the intention is to give a
rather eulogistic treatment of the subject or hero. The infusion of content
to the literature of this period pervades all types of literary forms, so that
even the nursery rhyme ceases to be a meaningless collection of 'nice-
sounding words'. It is transformed into a satirical poem which serves as
entertainment for children whilst subtly and indirectly instructing them on
socially acceptable morality. Note for instance the following nursery rhyme.
(It is not always easy to establish the exact period of a particular nursery
rhyme but this can be inferred from the style of the poetry of the period
and by contrasting the styles).

| | | | |
|---|---|---|---|
| 1st | We mfazi ongapesheya Uthi bhu inina? | 1st | You woman across the river What is it you boast about? |
| Chorus: | Ngithi bhubhisidwala | Chorus: | I boast about my new leather skirt |
| 1st | Isidwaba yinina | 1st | What after all is a leather skirt? |
| Chorus: | Yindwangulafece | Chorus: | It is a nice soft garment |
| 1st | Afece nanina | 1st | Of what use is a soft garment? |
| Chorus: | Afece nanongwe | Chorus: | With it you can move like a snail |
| 1st | Ayi ukukhala komdoni | 1st | Alas the fall of the boastful mdoni plant |
| Chorus: | Uthi kle! wemah kle! we mah | Chorus: | You hear it cry: Oh mother I break, oh mother |

Whilst this nursery rhyme satisfies by its pleasant rhythms, it contains a salutary message against boastful and narcissistic preoccupations with dress. This is particularly serious in a society in which individualism and excess are violently discouraged.

It is impossible to discuss in full the great literary achievements of the Shakan period, the contribution to form, the invention of varied styles suitable for each type of poem and the infusion of socially significant content to the literature. One finds, for instance, great improvement to heroic poems on personalities of the stature of King Ndaba, King Jama, King Khondlo, and others. Some of the pre-Shakan poems are rhythmically more akin to hunting songs. This may well be because for man, at least, this was the commonest arena of excitement and war-simulating conflict. This is borne out by similarity with some of the early forms of the heroic poems of the Tswanas.

The great poets of the Zulu Golden Age, Magolwane and Nomnxanxa, produced oral literature which lost none of the powerful quality of the earlier poetry and became even more varied and sometimes better conceived stylistically, as evidenced by the epic poem of Cetshwayo, where Zulu oral literature becomes a true vehicle of thought and history. For the future, more research and study has to be done on the rich heritage of oral literature in southern Africa. Research carried out by the patronizing half-speakers of the Zulu language and other African languages demonstrates further that the true interpreters of African oral literature can only be Africans themselves. This literature cannot adequately be understood without the full knowledge of the language, customs and thought systems that are part of the ancient history of southern Africa, indeed of Africa as a whole.

## References

1. I. Schapera, *Praise Poems of Tswana Chiefs* (Oxford, 1965), pp. 142–3.
2. Ruth Finnegan, *Oral Literature in Africa* (Oxford, 1970).
3. Traditional.

# Olive Schreiner's influence on George Moore and D. H. Lawrence

▼▼▼▼▼▼▼▼▼▼▼▼▼▼▼▼▼▼▼▼▼▼▼▼▼▼▼▼▼▼▼▼▼▼

## CHRISTOPHER HEYWOOD

OLIVE Schreiner's position as one of the founders of the English-speaking literary tradition in South Africa cannot be questioned. Her further importance as a leader of thought in England in the field of women's freedom is attested by various writers.[1] But the importance of Olive Schreiner for the novel in English in late Victorian and Edwardian times might be said to be unexplored. T. S. Eliot said: 'No poet, no artist of any sort, has his complete meaning alone. His significance, his appreciation, is the appreciation of his relation to the dead poets and artists'.[2]

The three writers who form the subject of this paper were all living in each other's lifetimes and were discussed as pioneers of thought and art by their contemporaries, yet the links between their works are rarely shown. Among writers in the intensive intellectual and artistic activity which took place in England at the turn of the century, Olive Schreiner and George Moore were important for the development of Lawrence's literary thinking. In turn, the striking features of their art – social allegory, naturalism, symbolism, and a penetrating psychological and social sympathy – have played a part in the emergence of many works of modern African literature. This paper is an attempt to place Olive Schreiner in the context of the literary thought of two later writers, Moore and Lawrence, who owed much to her example.

The importance of Olive Schreiner was argued by Henry Norman in his essay of 1883, 'Theories and Practice of Modern Fiction'.[3] Norman attacked the generality of English novels in a spirit which had become commonplace since the 1850s, as 'a host of self-styled novelists who, with frightful facility, produce their weekly crop of volumes'. Like two other critics at work with a similar purpose in the same year, Arthur Tilley and Hugh Egerton, whose essays traced the emergence of Flaubert and Henry

James as models in late Victorian literature,[4] Norman indicated his respect both for the French masters, notably Zola, and for the newly discovered talents of Henry James and William Dean Howells: 'It is to America, beyond all doubt, that we owe today the best novels in English.'[5] Unlike his contemporaries, however, Norman also looked nearer home for important developments. Of the newly published novel by Olive Schreiner, *The Story of an African Farm*, he said:

> The modest title gives no clue to the contents. It is the story of the growth of a human mind cut off from all but the most commonplace influences, facing its own doubts, crushing its own and others' deceits, and at last beating out a music which is not very melodious, but which is thoroughly honest.[6]

Another novelist singled out was George Moore, the writer of novels 'which are something beyond mere stories', exercising the mind of the reader 'on some question beyond the mere fortunes of the people whom it describes' and generally adding to the relief of the critic on reading works which took him away 'from the domains of the ordinary novelist – from Homburg and the Highlands, from yachts, clubs, hansoms, and Piccadilly'. After some not especially illuminating remarks on Moore's first novel, *A Modern Lover*, Norman added: 'It will be interesting to watch how far Mr Moore thus employs in the future the talents which he undoubtedly possesses'.[7]

Henry Norman did not follow up his review with further studies of the late Victorian novel. The link established in his review nevertheless had far-reaching consequences. Moore wrote later about his reading at this period, which included Olive Schreiner's novel. His *Confessions of a Young Man*, first published five years later, presented the image of a modern De Musset, intellectually exacting but lacking in human sympathy. His reading of Olive Schreiner is consistent with this general purpose:

> I read with disapprobation the 'Story of an African Farm': descriptions of sandhills and ostriches sandwiched with doubts concerning a future state, and convictions regarding the moral and physical superiority of women in plenty, but of art nothing: that is to say, art as I understand it – rhythmical sequence of events described with rhythmical sequence of phrase.[8]

Against this picture of himself in a mainly literary setting there should be set Moore's other picture of himself as an artist and young man in Ireland at the time of the land agitations, in the work published the year before the *Confessions, Parnell and His Island*. A less 'mannered' impression emerges. From Moore's self-portrait in this setting, against the evictions and suffering which undoubtedly contributed to his clemency as a landlord, Moore portrays 'the mournful grey of those western skies, the morose sterility of those desert hills' (p. 71). Visiting the house of a neighbouring landlord, Moore sees 'the storm and gloom of crime and poverty that enfolds this land' (p. 182), and noting the signs of fortification in and around his neighbour's house prophesies: 'Even here the shadow of murder and outrage falls across our way.' In the midst of the turmoil he presents himself as the poet of moral simplicity, remote from metropolitan dandyism and in sympathy with rural society, the Turgenev or indeed the Olive Schreiner of Ireland:

> Those who love life welcome new impulses, and desire the emotion of unexpected impressions. I am such a one; and the simple pleasure of sitting at a farm window, watching the villagers strolling in bands and couples and single figures across the darkening green, listening to the chattering voices of loitering women, to the howl of a distant dog, to all the vague sounds and shadows that mark the sinking to rest of the world, have never failed to thrill my heart with happiness.[9]

Studies of Moore have frequently divided his complex personality into opposing parts. In his polemical journalism on the land question in Ireland he exhibits the type of sympathy which had marked the novel by Olive Schreiner. He had by this time read *The Story of an African Farm*. In response to a review in Holland he included a copy of this work when he posted a parcel of important new works to Frans Netscher, the author of the review in *De Gids*. In the following decade Moore's sympathies during the South African war echoed those of Olive Schreiner, whom Netscher described in a pamphlet as a writer 'vol van medelijden voor de zwakkeren tegenover de sterkeren en rijkeren'; Netscher further noted that Olive Schreiner had shown herself in *Peter Halket* to be 'de besliste en gevaarlijkste tegenstander van Rhodes'.[10] It was this side of George Moore's temperament, responding in 1883 to aspects of Olive Schreiner's work, which emerged in his next novel, *A Mummer's Wife* (1885) and which decisively impressed D. H. Lawrence two decades later. On reading this novel, Olive Schreiner wrote to Havelock Ellis: 'I have read *A Mummer's Wife*. I like it very much, better than *Nana*, and I think it shows a great deal of genius, and I'm going to stick up for it.'[11] Olive Schreiner meant by this that she would support Moore's quarrel with the circulating libraries; her sympathy for the work of Moore is in contrast with her distaste for the man, whom she had met on coming to England.

At a time when the English novel underwent rapid changes of form and substance, the Irish and South African writers had significant contributions to make. Many critics of the English novel in the nineteenth century have resisted the idea of strong influences from abroad, but studies of the type of Leavis's *The Great Tradition* and Raymond Williams's *The English Novel from Dickens to Lawrence* have rarely explored fully the implications of the reading interests and literary formation of writers from Thackeray, the Brontës, and Dickens to D. H. Lawrence. Echoes of Henry Norman's emphasis on the importance of Moore and Olive Schreiner for the novel in the 1880s re-appear in the early literary opinions of D. H. Lawrence, whose reading in Eastwood at the turn of the century informed the whole of his work as a novelist. The catalogue of the library in Eastwood where, according to Jessie Chambers, he 'seemed to be acquainted with nearly every book',[12] lists as item 1375 out of nearly three thousand entries Olive Schreiner's *The Story of an African Farm*.[13] Lawrence's reading was, as Jessie Chambers notes, more than mere perusal: it was 'the entering into possession of a new world, a widening and enlarging of life'.[14] The catalogue does not record works by George Moore, and it is possible that Lawrence read both authors after leaving Eastwood. Jessie Chambers reports further on Lawrence's reading at Croydon: 'He admired George Moore and sent me *Evelyn Innes* and *Esther Waters*. When he read Olive Schreiner's *The Story of an African Farm* he wrote to me: "It will wring your woman's heart some day."'[15]

George Moore's function in Lawrence's literary formation is not confined to the parallels of theme and construction emerging in Lawrence's critical handling of borrowed material, which I have traced elsewhere in the case of *The Lost Girl* and *A Mummer's Wife*.[16] In his exploration of new subject matter and in its sensuous, musical presentation, Moore prefigured D. H. Lawrence. Speaking in a broadcast of the originality of D. H. Lawrence, David Daiches said that he was:

> developing a radically new kind of novel, in which he explores kinds of human relationship with a combination of uncanny psychological precision and intense poetic feeling. They have an acute surface realism, a sharp sense of time and place, and brilliant topographical detail, and at the same time their high poetic symbolism, both of the total pattern of action and of incidents and objects within it, establishes a rhythm of meaning that is missed by those who read the novels with the conventional characters of 'plot' and 'character' in mind.[17]

These remarks were made about *The Rainbow* and *Women in Love*. Behind these novels lay the dominant impulse towards realism which characterized the later Victorian novel, and which emerged most strongly in the work of Olive Schreiner. Her novel probably added a sense of urgency to Moore's compassionate view of the land question in Ireland, and pointed towards the mature art of D. H. Lawrence. Moore's contribution to the development of the English novel is outlined by Kenneth Graham in his study of critical responses to the fiction of the period:

> One of the most interesting writers on the question of structure in the novel is George Moore, despite his eccentricities in other respects. His pronouncements on the technique of fiction are centred on the notion of organic unity, and sum up much of the fragmentary theorizing of others. Most often, his ideal is expressed in terms of music.[18]

Lawrence's similar stress upon the functions of emotional exploration and musical structure in the novel, and on the need for a language at once sensuous and sympathetic, takes its rise from the bold but limited ventures of George Moore, especially in the novels written after Moore had taken heed of the breadth of vision of Olive Schreiner. The fusion of these artistic interests into an intense vision of his childhood world produced the novels which are generally recognized as the most typical work of Lawrence's genius.

These literary relationships reflect the expansion of a literary sensibility in England in the later nineteenth century. An intensified perception of place, of individual psychological experience, and of social relationships, and the paradox that the masters of literature were in general remote from the metropolitan centres of culture, formed the basis of these developments. An early instance of this movement in the novel was Hawthorne, whose importance for Henry James was discerned by T. S. Eliot, and construed as an assertion of the centrality of the ex-colonial New England literary tradition:

> The point is that Henry James is positively a continuator of the New England genius, which has discovered itself only in a very small number of people in the middle of the nineteenth century . . . I mean whatever we associate with certain purlieus of Boston, with Concord, Salem, and Cambridge, Massachusetts; notably: Emerson, Thoreau, Hawthorne and Lowell. None of these men, with the exception of Hawthorne, is individually very important; they all can, and perhaps ought to be made to look very foolish; but there is a 'something' there, a dignity, above the taint of commonness about some English contemporary, as, for instance, the more intelligent, better-educated, more alert Matthew Arnold.[19]

Behind Hawthorne's humour and philosophical gravity there lurked a chilling sense of the harsh realities of life. This aspect was noted by the reviewers of his time, including George Eliot, whose masters, George Sand and Emerson, were Olive Schreiner's as well. An early review of *The Blithedale Romance*, edited by George Eliot for *The Westminster Review*, remarked as a failing in Hawthorne: 'He would give you the poetry of the hospital, or the poetry of the dissecting-room.'[20] In *The Story of an African*

*Farm,* Olive Schreiner ventured further than any novelist writing in English since Hawthorne into the forbidden subjects of her age: childbirth, seduction, the intellectual freedom of women, the cruelty of the settlers' conduct: and like Hawthorne she won and retained the admiration of a generation of readers. The qualification frequently made, her provinciality, can be shown in the light of experience to have been a double-edged weapon, since 'marginality' has been the basis of the artist's claim to authenticity since Napoleonic times. In their essays on Hawthorne, Leslie Stephen and Henry James define the predicament in terms similar to those with which readers of Olive Schreiner criticism are sufficiently familiar:

> His very simplicity has been in his favour; it has helped him to appear complete and homogeneous. To talk of his being national would be to force the note and make a mistake of proportion; but he is, in spite of the absence of the realistic quality, intensely and vividly local. Out of the soil of New England he sprang – in a crevice of that immitigable granite he sprouted and bloomed.[21]

Before James, Leslie Stephen had written:

> But how was the task to be performed? How was the imaginative glow to be shed over the American scenery, so provokingly raw and deficient in harmony? A similar problem was successfully solved by a writer whose development, in proportion to her means of cultivation, is about the most remarkable of recent literary phenomena. Miss Brontë's bleak Yorkshire moors, with their uncompromising stone walls, and the valleys invaded by factories, are at first sight as little suited to romance as New England itself, to which, indeed, both the inhabitants and the country have a decided family resemblance. Now that she has discovered for us the fountains of poetic interest, we can all see that the region is not a mere stony wilderness.[22]

In writing his second novel, George Moore turned for the first germs of his plot to *Thérèse Raquin,*[23] the novel with which Zola had inaugurated the venture into Naturalism. A neglected aspect of Zola's reading at this stage of his career can be traced in the series of novels by English and New England writers which moved across his desk in the course of his work as publicity agent for his employer, the publisher Hachette. The turbid symbolism, romantic sensibility, and criminal motivation of his early novel owed much to his reading in Hawthorne, Dickens, Poe, and Wilkie Collins, the principal material for the sequence of translations into French with which Hachette had sought to influence the taste of his age. Hints of Zola's debt to Dickens have been traced in the presentation of a horrific mother-figure in her wheelchair, probably taken from *Little Dorrit,* and it is probable that Hawthorne's treatment of oppressive, fatal guilt in *The Scarlet Letter* contributed to the suffocating sense of moral oppression traced in

*Thérèse Raquin*.[24] In his use of similar, related source material, George Moore remained both selective and sensitive. In a later phase of his story he departed from Zola's example, inclining towards the handling of child-birth and platonic affection in a pattern of relationships more closely resembling Olive Schreiner's in *The Story of an African Farm*. Moore's first novel, *A Modern Lover*, was a brilliant but over-ambitious study of courtship and marriage in Victorian society, set against a public debate about the nature of painting and writing. Nevertheless, *A Modern Lover* is marred by shallowness in the portrayal of the sensual egotist, Lewis Seymour, and the three women in his life. In *A Mummer's Wife*, Moore differed sharply from Zola: in the second phase of his heroine's develop-ment, the problem is not the haunting effects of a crime, but the fluctuating loyalty of the man she loves and whom, after an intervention by his friend, she has married. In her first phase, Kate Ede is constrained by her environ-ment and by her marriage to the asthmatic Ralph Ede, whose mother exercises a suffocating effect on the household.

So far, Moore's theme conforms to the repertoire of the stifled provincial life of women which derived from the English and French lineages of *Madame Bovary*, through *Thérèse Raquin* and other sources. Moore's departure from his French literary models sprang from the humanity which his experience of Irish society had helped to develop; it may be surmised that his immediate literary model in this departure was *The Story of an African Farm*. In *A Mummer's Wife*, a succession of triangular relationships, of the type developed by Zola in *L'Assommoir*, provide the framework for the nervous guilt, recrimination, and eventual death of his heroine. Kate Ede's ability to register a diversity of mental experiences, 'sensations of gratitude', 'examinations of conscience', 'analysis', 'reflec-tion', 'thinking out in her inner consciousness' (ch. XII), and many other instances, take Moore's handling of psychological experiences far beyond the range of Zola. Moore's psychological depth justifies the admiration which Moore gained from Virginia Woolf: 'Not one of his novels is a masterpiece; they are silken tents which have no poles; but he has brought a new mind into the world; he has given us a new way of feeling and seeing.[25]

Moore's second plot is concerned with the tenderness of platonic affection between Kate and the musician, Montgomery, and the attempts, against a background of increasing financial ruin, towards loyalty on the part of Dick Lennox, the father of her child and her husband after her divorce from Ralph Ede. It is here that Olive Schreiner most clearly pre-figures Moore. Despite his hostile literary criticism, in his selection of themes he echoed her treatment of the relationships between Lyndall, her 'stranger' who is the father of her child, and Gregory Rose, her admirer and the companion of her struggle towards death. These themes re-appear in Moore's later novels, *Esther Waters* and *Evelyn Innes*, and in both these works the rival claims of female independence and the heroism of a mother's struggle for the survival of her child reflect the kind of interests which had made their most poignant appearance in English in *The Story of an African Farm*.

In her single contribution to the English novel in the nineteenth century, Olive Schreiner played an important part in the development of the form. Her influence emerges again in the work of D. H. Lawrence, whose re-working of earlier novelists' work forms a little-explored aspect of his literary art.[26] The influence of Olive Schreiner can be traced in the formation of the 'Eastwood' cycle of novels, *Sons and Lovers*, *The Rainbow*, *Women in Love*, and in *The Lost Girl*; here, too, the example of Moore was powerful. *The Lost Girl* was begun as a 'pot-boiler' during the writing of 'The Sisters', which Lawrence later divided into *The Rainbow* and *Women in Love*. Lawrence gave to Alvina Houghton, the heroine of *The Lost Girl*, a quality of spirited independence which is lacking in Moore's heroine, Kate Ede. Her ability to see through the romantic shams of her society resembles Lyndall's, and her independence of the world and its principle of marriage is no security against her romantic susceptibility, which leads her to Italy to her marriage into a suffocating masculine community. Unlike Lyndall, she is able to escape. Lawrence's debt to Olive Schreiner in other novels set in Eastwood emerges in his treatment of the independence and pregnancy of Ursula Brangwen in *The Rainbow*. Ursula's reading with her friend Maggie Schofield includes a book about 'Woman and labour' (ch. XIII) – a reference to Olive Schreiner's *Woman and Labour* (1911), which Lawrence knew by the time he wrote *The Rainbow*. The story of Ursula's relationship with the fickle Skrebensky is comparable to other novels of the period, for example Grant Allen's *The Woman Who Did* (1895) and Hardy's *Jude the Obscure* (1895), but these works, too, were written in the shadow of *The Story of an African Farm*, and probably owed something of their sense of social urgency to Olive Schreiner's example.

Another instance of Lawrence's drawing towards a theme from *The Story of an African Farm* occurs at the end of *Sons and Lovers*. Lawrence's pre-occupation with the distinction between sexual and 'platonic' passion is taken to an extreme in the contrast on the one hand between Paul's love for his mother, and on the other, for the two women, Clara and Miriam, with whom he has sexual experiences. Besides the pattern of Lawrence's

personal history and relationships at Eastwood, literary parallels inform
and strengthen the picture of Paul's love for his mother. Lawrence knew
the portrayal in *Madame Bovary* and in *The Return of the Native* of a weak
son's dependence on his mother. In its intensely spiritual quality, the
relationship between Paul and Gertrude draws upon another literary
example, that of the love of Waldo for Lyndall in *The Story of an African
Farm*. Waldo does not marry, and his ambiguously presented death at the
end of the novel anticipates the nebulous 'drift towards death' claimed by
Lawrence for his hero. Paul's intuition of his mother's presence among the
stars echoes Waldo's appeal to the stars for the dead Lyndall. Thus
Lawrence:

> On every side the immense dark silence seemed pressing him, so tiny a
> spark, into extinction, and yet, almost nothing, he could not be extinct . . .
> So much, and himself infinitesimal, at the core a nothingness, and yet
> not nothing.
> 'Mother!' he whispered – 'mother!'
> She was the only thing that held him up, himself, amid all this. And
> she was gone, intermingled herself. He wanted her to touch him, have
> him alongside with her. (Ch. XV)

And Olive Schreiner:

> The dream was with him still; the woman who was his friend was not
> separated from him by years – only that very night he had seen her. He
> looked up into the night sky that all his life long had mingled itself with
> his existence. There were a thousand faces that he loved looking down
> at him, a thousand stars . . . yet he looked up at them and shuddered; at
> last he turned away from them with horror. Such countless multitudes,
> stretching far out into space, and yet not in one of the all was she!
> Though he searched through them all . . . nowhere should he ever say,
> 'she is here!' (II, xiii)

Resemblances between the works and opinions of Lawrence and Olive
Schreiner underline the quality of the enthusiasm which Lawrence felt for
her novel, and reveal the originality of her work in the context of later
Victorian and Edwardian literary thought. In *The Rainbow* and *Women in
Love*, Lawrence portrayed a contrasted pair of heroines, one submissive
and the other aggressively independent, confronting an alien civilization
and its incursion into an agrarian community, ambiguously presented as at
once doomed but precious. Like Waldo Farber, Will Brangwen carves in
wood, and in another echo from Olive Schreiner's treatment of the generations, Gerald Crich dies when his ideals have failed, following, like Olive
Schreiner's Waldo, where his father has led. Both novelists built their
action in the form of debates set against celebrations surrounding a wedding, or the movement from light to dark. The subjects of these debates –

the nature of the artistic impulse, the powers of women in society, the conflicting claims of marriage and spiritual love, and many others – are further parallels of substance and manner. In the work of his greatest literary period, Lawrence appears to have felt the dominant creative impulse which came to him, as it had come to George Moore, from the most potent and original of the South African novelists.

The importance of Africa for the modern novel in English is generally traced through the works by Mayne Reid, Rider Haggard, and John Buchan which formed the prelude to Joyce Cary's attempt at the portrayal of an African in *Mister Johnson*. Within this structure, Achebe emerges as the culmination of a process leading through familiarization to sympathy and at last to self-expression. In this rendering of literary history, the complex working of the colonial experience in English literature is overlooked. The 'dark places' hinted by Conrad's narrator in *Heart of Darkness* to be the capital cities of Europe, no less than the scenes of colonial plunder in Africa, included Moore's Ireland and Lawrence's Nottinghamshire. The fusion of social satire and special pleading for the social and imaginative experience of women, which emerged as the central strength in the work of both these writers, had its most persuasive early flowering in Olive Schreiner's novel.

The presence of African themes in modern literature can be traced back to *Othello*, *The Tempest*, and *Robinson Crusoe*, as well as to the literature of travel and settlement by white men in Africa. In the more hectic phase of modern literary experience which began in the nineteenth century, the colonial experience is persistently reflected, and is inseparable from the writers' attitudes to Africa. In Zola's *Thérèse Raquin*, the heroine is the daughter of a French soldier and an African woman: "'On m'a dit que ma mère était fille d'un chef de tribu, en Afrique'" (ch. VII). Zola's modern literary descendants include Cyprian Ekwensi and Peter Abrahams as well as George Moore. Writers work in concert across the racial barriers and never in isolation. Moore's lack of experience of Africa did not prevent him from following the lead of Zola and other writers of his age, in making use of Africa as an image for the nervous tension of his heroine in *A Mummer's Wife*: Kate Ede's nervous storms reverberate as though she epitomized 'the roaring solitude of an African forest'. Speaking for a later generation, Lawrence exploited the image in invoking a sculpture as the emblem of Birkin's impending involvement with Ursula in *The Rainbow*:

> There came back to him one, a statuette about two feet high, a tall, slim elegant figure from West Africa, in dark wood, glossy and suave. It was

a woman, with hair dressed high, like a melon-shaped dome. He remembered her vividly: she was one of his soul's intimates. Her body was long and elegant, her face was crushed tiny like a beetle's, she had rows of round heavy collars, like a column of quoits, on her neck. He remembered her: her astonishing cultured elegance, her diminished, beetle face, the astounding long elegant body, on short, ugly legs, with such protuberant buttocks, so weighty and unexpected below her slim long loins. She knew what he himself did not know. She had thousands of years of purely sensual, purely unspiritual knowledge behind her. It must have been thousands of years since her race had died, mystically: that is, since the relations between the senses and the outspoken mind had broken, leaving the experience all in one sort, mystically sensual. Thousands of years ago, that which was imminent in himself must have taken place in these Africans: the goodness, the holiness, the desire for creation and productive happiness must have lapsed, leaving the single impulse for knowledge in one sort, mindless progressive life through the senses, knowledge arrested and ending in the senses ... (*Women in Love*, XI)

Lawrence's vision of an integrated personality, a fusion of the ideals of the Pre-Raphaelites with a rendering of the new vision which Frobenius had found at Ife, reflect the change in his thinking which had been brought about by his experiences during the war of 1914–18. This later phase is marked off from the earlier thinking, in which he had approximated more closely to the 'positivist' tradition which Olive Schreiner had inherited from writers such as George Sand and John Stuart Mill. Nevertheless, Olive Schreiner's picture of society in a colonial setting had been among the most important of later Victorian contributions to thought in this context. In a frequently quoted passage she defined her view of South African social experience:

All South Africans are one. It is not merely that all men born in South Africa, from the Zambesi to the Cape, are bound by the associations of their early years to the same vast, untamed nature ... *This bond is our mixture of races itself*. It is this which divides South Africans from all other people in the world, and makes us one.[27]

What then seemed applicable only to South African society has in the last few decades become appreciably more true of societies elsewhere. The cultures to which Africa has been exposed through slavery, colonization, and settlement, no less than the Irish or Ibo societies in which 'things fall apart', have themselves changed irrevocably in the course of the exposure. Olive Schreiner's work is built around a concept of society and moral conduct which could only have been found in South Africa. The dynamism of her novel was felt not only in the literature of southern Africa, but in the literature of the English language as a whole after 1880.

*References*

1. See, for example, Vera Brittain, *Testament of Youth* (London, 1933), pp. 41, 84–5, etc.
2. T. S. Eliot, 'Tradition and the Individual Talent', in his *Selected Essays* (London, 1951), p. 15.
3. Henry Norman, 'Theories and Practice of Modern Fiction', *Fortnightly Review*, XXXIV (1883), pp. 870–86.
4. Arthur Tilley, 'The New School of Fiction', *National Review*, NS I (1883), pp. 257–68; Hugh Egerton, 'The Scientific Novel and Gustave Flaubert', *National Review*, NS II (1883), pp. 894–907.
5. Henry Norman, loc. cit.
6. ibid.
7. ibid.
8. George Moore, *Confessions of a Young Man* (London, 1888; Penguin, 1939), ch. XII, p. 161.
9. George Moore, *Parnell and his Island* (London, 1887), pp. 180–2.
10. Frans Netscher, *Olive Schreiner en Peter Halket van Mashonaland*, (Amsterdam, 1897), pp. 6–7.
11. *Letters of Olive Schreiner*, ed. S. C Cronwright-Schreiner (London 1924), p. 67.
12. Jessie Chambers, *D. H. Lawrence. A Personal Record by 'E.T.'* (London, 1935), p. 93.
13. *Catalogue of Books Belonging to the Library of the Eastwood and Greasley Artizans and Mechanics' Institute* (Eastwood, 1895). Kindly lent by the Librarian of the Nottinghamshire County Library.
14. Jessie Chambers, op. cit. p. 96.
15. ibid., p. 121.
16. See my article: 'D. H. Lawrence's *The Lost Girl* and its Antecedents by Bennett and Moore', *English Studies*, XVIII (1965), pp. 131–4.
17. David Daiches, *D. H. Lawrence*, privately printed (1963), p. 16. (Nottingham University Library.)
18. Kenneth Graham, *English Criticism of the Novel, 1865–1900* (Oxford, 1965), p. 118.
19. T. S. Eliot, 'The Hawthorne Aspect', in F. W. Dupee, ed., *The Question of Henry James* (London, 1947), pp. 127–33; first published in *The Little Review*, 1918.
20. 'Contemporary Literature of America', *Westminster Review*, II (1852), p. 593.
21. Henry James, *Hawthorne* (London, 1879), p. 3.
22. Leslie Stephen, 'Hawthorne', in his *Hours in a Library*, 1st series (London, 1874), p. 183.
23. Milton Chaikin, 'George Moore's *A Mummer's Wife* and Zola', *Revue de littérature comparée*, XXXI (1957), pp. 85–8.
24. Stuart Atkins, 'A Possible Dickens Influence on Zola', *MLQ*, 8, 1947, pp. 302–8; Robert J. Niess, 'Hawthorne and Zola – an Influence?', *Revue de litt. comparée*, XXVII (1953), pp. 440–52.
25. Virginia Woolf, 'George Moore', in her *The Death of the Moth* (London, 1942), pp. 100–4.
26. See my article, 'D. H. Lawrence and Olive Schreiner's *The Story of an African Farm*', *English Language Notes*, XIV (September 1976).
27. Olive Schreiner, *Thoughts on South Africa* (London, 1923), pp. 60–1.

# Purpose versus Plot: The Double Vision of Thomas Mofolo's Narrator

▼▼▼▼▼▼▼▼▼▼▼▼▼▼▼▼▼▼▼▼▼▼▼▼▼▼▼▼▼▼▼▼▼

CHIDI IKONNE

THOMAS Mofolo's narrator does not tell us why he tells his story. He only alludes to the 'purpose',[1] and confesses how it influences his attitude towards the material available to him:

> Chaka's whole life was filled with important happenings, with marvels and mysteries that the ordinary person cannot understand. We have chosen out one side of his life only which suited best our purpose, for it has not been our intention to tell everything. (p. 182)[2]

Certainly, he does not 'tell everything' known about the man, Chaka, the son of Nandi and Senzangakona – the Chaka who actually lived between 1787 and 24 September 1828. It is not the intention of this paper, therefore, to read Thomas Mofolo's *Chaka* as a history of the founder of the Zulu nation – definitely not as 'an impartial biography'.[3]

This, however, is not to suggest that the book does not contain any historical truths. For instance, even though the woman, Nandi, was not murdered by her son, Chaka, there is no doubt that Chaka's action in sending his lover, Mbuzikazi, and their son to Tembeland 'contributed to Nandi's sudden decline and death, which occurred not long thereafter'.[4] *Chaka* bears testimony to its author's powerful imagination and virtuosity. We will, therefore, approach it as we would approach a fiction *per se*. After all, there are very few works of art which do not contain some verifiable truths.

Yet the problem is not completely solved. There are two principal ways of looking at *Chaka* even as a fiction. One is to accept the characters and their actions at their face value. The other is to recognize some of the characters as visible symbols of invisible aspects of Chaka's own nature. The narrator seems to encourage the adoption of any of these approaches. He certainly encourages the first one when he prefaces his main story with a 'value' statement:

> Our story is concerned with eastern tribes, the Kafirs, and before we begin it we must describe the state of these tribes in the early days so that the reader may be able to follow the narrative in the succeeding chapters ... The people of this tribe [Kafirland] surpassed all the other tribes in South Africa in their traditional medicines, for they belonged to the bush country where medicines abound. Medicines for bewitchment, for enchantment, for murder, for fascination, for scattering one's enemies, for making oneself to be loved by people – in using these they were without rivals ... They were also famous for being able to converse with those who had died long before, and to receive advice from their spirits ... Water snakes are held in great reverence in Kafirland ... The reader must understand that we are speaking of the positions of the tribes long ago, when the land was first inhabited. (pp. 1–3)

Nevertheless, most of the material he chooses to include cannot be understood by 'the ordinary person' unless it is approached mainly in the second way. This is what the present paper intends to do. Without rejecting the existence of witch-doctors[5] and spirits 'long ago, when the land was first inhabited', it will assume that Isanusi, Malunga, and Ndlebe, the characters 'from nowhere' (xiii), are inhabitants of Chaka's own mind, or what Ayi Kwei Armah calls 'facets of Chaka's genius'.[6] And the decision is not as arbitrary as it sounds. It is difficult to imagine a human being like Ndlebe.[7] Physically, Malunga looks like a real man; but the facility with which he appears and disappears beats an 'ordinary person's' imagination. As a matter of fact, it is significant that as long as Chaka lived with the 'prudent' Dingiswayo, who was always jealous of his chieftainship, he, Malunga, 'prudently' hid himself. His recall to normal open life when Chaka (who had regained his father's chieftainship) lived far from his overlord and benefactor, looks like an attempt on the part of Chaka to give the reins to the warrior in himself – the invisible and insatiable conqueror whose visible symbol Malunga is:

> Malunga, this is my day. I will be crossed in naught. When I was with Dingiswayo I was forced to do as he wished. What I did not wish that I was forced to do, if he wished it. But this is my day, on which I work my will, and therefore I say to thee, stay thou with me as has been determined, and hide not thyself any more, for he from whom thou didst hide hath no power here. (p. 94)

As for Isanusi, his arrival could have taken place nowhere except in Chaka's mind. For instance, in the first encounter, the hungry and exhausted Chaka sees him only when he, Chaka, is half-awake. His story of Chaka's past is mainly a response to perceptible stimuli – cues which could have brought forth the same response in Chaka's consciousness: his tired eyes tell him that he has not slept for some days; his swollen feet tell him that he has walked a long distance; the hair of hyena on his blanket tells him that he has killed a hyena, etc. (p. 45). Then, after listening to the story, Chaka 'leapt in the air for joy, and was like a man who dreams' (p. 46). Above all, only Chaka sees him. He does not even inform his mother, Nandi, of this or any other encounter with Isanusi and his servants, Malunga and Ndlebe, despite the fact that he 'was accustomed to tell his mother everything concerning the medicines given him by the witch-doctor' (p. 65).

Incidentally, 'the witch-doctor' in question here seems to be the 'woman witch-doctor at Bungeni', a real human being whom Nandi knows. Thus Thomas Mofolo's narrator actually draws a line between this woman and the characters 'from nowhere'. Some critics' attempt to locate the woman witch-doctor in Chaka's mind is, therefore, misleading.[8]

All this – this externalization of a man's motives to the extent of making them live and move and have their being in reality – is, of course, an index of the virtuosity of Thomas Mofolo's narrator. So also is the manipulation of his double vision.

Subjectively approached, the story of Chaka, for some readers, is the story of a man who, without asking, is raised high and, against his will, crushed. It suggests a tragic 'plot',[9] and Chaka himself does not lack some of the basic qualities of a tragic hero. None the less, his personal life and death do not for the most part 'move us to either pity or fear', because, according to Aristotle, 'pity is occasioned by undeserved misfortune, and fear by that of one like ourselves'.[10]

Perhaps to say that Thomas Mofolo's narrator purposely decides to make Chaka's fate untragic will be an overstatement. A careful reading, however, reveals that Chaka's stature as a tragic hero is greatly stunted by the narrator's manipulation of his two visions or focuses – one on the plot of the story; the other on the unrevealed 'purpose' of the story. The first exposes; the second modifies. The result is the creation of a man who is not really a man.

Chaka is not the type of man for whose safety one can reasonably be concerned. A born superman,[11] he is not 'one like ourselves'. Thanks to a subtle timbre in the narrative tone, almost everything about him looks like a miracle. Immediately after his birth, he is recognized as 'an ox to feed the vultures' (p. 7),[12] and the narrator assures the reader that he will see this prophecy come true later. The old Jobe, hearing about his birth (without as much as seeing him), like the three wise men, or the old Simeon after the birth of the Christ, 'showed by his words that he knew what the child would become in the world' (p. 7). Chaka himself 'as a baby . . . never cried even when he fell down. Even when he was beaten he did not often cry' (p. 8). He was so hardy, and so unlike a human infant, that people 'who saw him used to say "It is a lion's whelp; it is a wild beast cub brought up by hand"' (p. 8). He was above the fate of ordinary infants; for when his roommates arranged to have him carried away by a hyena, 'the hyena would only smell at him and then move on into the centre of the hut and take someone from there' (p. 32). He was 'the favoured' of the gods (p. 29).

Thus, as a little boy, he stood his ground, and killed a lion when older men ran away. Alone, and when it was still dark, he bathed in a river where no one would dare bathe:

> It was so awesome a place even in the daytime that no man would bathe there alone: it was a place fit only for the 'tikoloshi' (water-devil). Chaka used to bathe there alone, but that was because he was Chaka. (p. 25)

The supermanhood which the child Chaka has unconsciously acquired the man Chaka confirms. When he changed the tribe-name people

> praised him. His beautiful countenance, his tall figure, his fearless heart, and his leadership in war bore witness that Chaka had been sent by the Gods to men. It was said that a heart like Chaka's and a spirit like his were not merely human; they were the heart and spirit of Nkulunkulu himself. (p. 126)

With regard to his defeat of Zwide, 'the young men and women were all saying: "This is the real Chaka. It were better that those who fight against him should join battle first with the Gods and overcome them, and then they could come against Chaka"' (p. 126). People said that he and his fiancée, Noliwe,

> were both messengers of Nkulunkulu. When Ndlebe and Malunga [symbols of aspects of his ambition] heard these sayings they confirmed them and said that Chaka had been sent by Nkulunkulu to teach his children war. Their words were easily believed and found credence because they agreed with what was already in the people's minds. (p. 126)

In fact, Chaka encouraged them in their belief: 'People knelt and prayed to Chaka and Noliwe.[13] This pleased Chaka, but Noliwe was sad because she knew that she was still a woman like other women (p. 126). He actually asks his subjects to hail him "Bayete" which means "He that is between God and men," that is to say, "The Little God through whom the Great God rules all the chiefs and tribes upon earth"' (p. 139).

The narrator has many other details which show that Chaka is not an ordinary man on whose account we can feel that type of fear aroused only by tragedy. We can hardly identify with him. What is more, the idea of making him present himself as 'The Little God through whom the Great God rules' tends to negate his very *hubris*, a quality which is almost indispensable to a tragic hero. He certainly challenges his fate; but this fate, unlike that of most great tragic heroes, looks like the *bona fide* work of men as distinct from the plot of men who are only agents of capricious gods, whose darling he is anyway. Consequently, his very fight against the fate looks like a conspiracy with the gods against men 'like ourselves'. Our reaction, therefore, is hate instead of pity. Our sympathy is with the victims of his 'crimes'.

This is the frame of the picture we see through one of the narrative lenses. It is within this frame that Chaka is furnished with freedom of choice. We shall return to it later. Meanwhile let us peep through the other lens.

The Chaka in this frame is not guilty of his 'crimes' since he is not responsible for the circumstances and training which have led to their perpetration. For instance, in chapter five, the narrator shows how the necessity to kill his companions has been imposed on him by the cowardly jealousy of his ungrateful half-brothers and the action of his father when he orders his men to kill Chaka: 'And now we see, if we have not seen it before, that Chaka was indeed the hare whose ears are struck, an orphan, a buffalo standing alone; for all who saw him attacked him without any reason at all' (p. 39). His father's action is unjust:

> Alas. Our chief is without truth,
> He is without truth, a chameleon . . .
> Alas. Senzangakona fears where he should love.
> He loves where he should despise.

The narrator makes it clear that Chaka cannot be held responsible for what has happened:

> In this chapter we have seen that the fruit of sin is wonderous bitter, for we know that Chaka had not been to blame for what had happened, but none the less, his father had ordered him to be killed. The great crime which started everything was the sin of Nandi and Senzangakona; and Senzangakona fearing that what he had done might become known, had determined to kill his son. (p. 40)

He has earlier shown how the cruelty of the herdboys had toughened the quiet, inoffensive Chaka into a pugnacious aggressor (p. 17). This present (adolescent) experience, the narrator reveals, is even more crucial. It brings Chaka almost to the peak of his self-awareness. For example, he tells us that as Chaka hides in the bush and perceives the confusion into which the whole village has been thrown as a result of his involuntary killing of his friends: 'he thought to himself, "All this has happened because of me, and I am only small and weak. What will it be when I am a man and have

the power of a chief? I will have my revenge when my day dawns"'
(pp. 41–2). Above all, he shows how, now a hunted outlaw with no communication with any human being, Chaka lets his mind go and dwell upon
his childhood:

> he found that it was evil, terrifying, fearsome. He thought of the time
> when he was herding the cattle and discovered that there was a plot
> against him, of how the boys attacked him in the field, of his killing of
> the lion and the hyena, and he saw that on earth man lives by might and
> not by right. He saw that on earth the wise man, the strong man, the
> man who is admired and respected is the man who knows how to wield
> his spear, who, when people try to hinder him, settles the matter with
> his club. (p. 42)

He has learnt the rules that govern relationships in his society: 'He
resolved that from that time on he would do as he liked; whether a man
was guilty or not he would kill him, for that was the law of men' (p. 42).
Extracted from this framework, this resolution, as we shall see later, will
be welded into the pivot of Chaka's freedom of choice. None the less, the
Chaka we see through this narrative lens is human enough to inspire us
with pity. The only difficulty is that this particular vision is not as sustained
as the other. While the lens that offers us the other vision spans the whole
stretch of the hero's life, the present one focuses mainly on his childhood.
Even then the vision it offers is not as bright as the other one. It is only a
star at the dawn of Chaka's supermanhood. It actually begins to grow dim
in chapter four, when the awareness we have been discussing begins to
take a recognizable form. The visit of the snake is the case in point.

There is no doubt about the reality of the snake itself, since Nandi also
sees it: 'Nandi, too, by this time had covered her face, for she was afraid to
look upon her child being swallowed by the monster of the water' (p. 27).
But the voices from the reeds are clearly the 'voice' of Chaka's
consciousness:

> Chaka only heard the words . . . Nandi did not hear the voices, she only
> saw the snake and the turbulent water and the whirlwind in the reeds.
> But as for the voices, she did not hear them, although she was not very
> far away: which clearly shows that they were intended for the ears of
> Chaka only.

He has experienced triumphs. He is safely bathing in 'the turbulent water'
of hate. He must have been born (the 'voice' in his consciousness tells him)
for something great:

> Abe, ahe. The world is thine, child of my own people,
> Thou shalt rule the nations and their governors,
> Thou shalt rule all the nations of men,

> Thou shalt rule the winds and the storms of the sea
> And the deep pools of the mighty rivers,
> And all things shall obey thy word.
> They shall kneel down beneath thy feet.
> E, oi, oi. But beware thou takest the right path. (p. 29)

It is, however, the warning of the last sentence that alerts us to the gradual dimming of the focus on Chaka's human face. It is less bright by the time we come to see Chaka at the peak of his self-awareness; that is, when he recognizes and accepts the ideals of Isanusi – the symbol of all the aspects of his vaulting ambition combined. The reader's eyes, henceforth, are more steadily focused on Chaka's freedom of choice and, therefore, responsibility for whatever he chooses. The result is the steady fade-out of the reader's awareness of the fact that this ability to judge and choose has been moulded in Chaka's unsolicited childhood: the injustice of his companions, half-brothers, father's wives, and his father himself; in other words, that owing to an unsolicited training, Chaka has come to accept injustice as a valid societal value, 'for this is the law upon earth' (p. 57).

Invited to see this pessimistic conclusion (with the resolution based on it) subtly welded into, and used in, a frame where it does not really belong, the reader forgets how Chaka has arrived at it. He forgets that Isanusi's face first appeared to Chaka as an embodiment of 'malice, wickedness, and treachery' (p. 43), and only gradually became an epitome of 'perfect kindness, a sympathetic heart, and the truest love' (p. 44).

Without any intention of suggesting that the narrator ought to have told a different story from the one he has told, it must be pointed out that if Chaka's 'resolution' had been left where it really belongs, if his freedom of choice had been solidly established within the framework that reveals his human face, the hero would have been more sympathetic. More innocent, and slightly deprived of the heat of his early supermanhood, his fight could have looked like a struggle for life – a struggle against the conspiracy of gods and men to destroy him. But the vision which could have established this image is progressively dimmed by the intensification of the spotlight on a Chaka that is not really a man.

We have already witnessed this trend in the first appearance of Isanusi. It continues on pages 95–6. Here, Chaka, who is presented as reviewing his vaulting ambition, makes what amounts to a deliberate choice of life-styles:

> Isanusi, I Chaka, when I have resolved a thing cannot turn back until the end is reached. I still hunger, I still seek. Let the sow continue to give milk, lord. I pray thee use all thy power and all thy wisdom that I may reach the goal whither thou art bringing me, and which thou in thy boundless wisdom alone dost know. As for the spear of which thou dost speak, it shall be red with blood on both blade and shaft. (p. 96)

It is, however, in Chaka's move to sacrifice Noliwe that the trend is most unmistakable and effective. The reader sees a Chaka who has acquired his father's domain and Dingswayo's chieftainship, and still aims at 'a greater chieftainship three times as much again' (p. 121). When it comes into his consciousness that this will cost him the life of the person he loves, the narrator slows down the flow of the story to enable the reader to feel the deliberateness and consciousness of Chaka's choice:

> Chaka made as though to answer, but Isanusi restrained him with his hand and said that he must first take thought without haste. Then he left him and after a long while returned. 'Hast thou taken careful thought?' 'Yea,' said Chaka. 'Dost thou understand well what thou art doing?' Chaka affirmed that he did. And then Isanusi said: 'Tell me, that I may learn thy decision.'
>
> 'I, Chaka, had no need of deep thought. I have decided upon the chieftainship of which thou hast spoken. But I have no children and I do not know if the blood of my mother or my brothers would be sufficient. But if it is, I will give it you that ye may compound your medicines of it.' (pp. 122–3)

His readiness to sacrifice his mother and brothers is very significant as it cannot easily be labelled 'revenge', and classified as a corollary to his earlier relationship with these people. They are, at least, the persons he believes he loves. Besides, Dingana and Mhlagana did not challenge his right to their father's chieftainship, hence even his evil genius, Ndlebe, begged him to spare their lives after Mfokazana's death (p. 93). As for his mother, Nandi, he hardly has any excuse for wishing to kill her unless his decision can be established as manifestation of a protracted Oedipus complex.

In any case, there is someone he loves more than he does any of these people who have come into his consciousness: Noliwe. He must therefore make a choice: the chieftainship he already has with Noliwe, or a greater chieftainship without Noliwe. He initially has a whole day to make up his mind. Then the decision is postponed; he has nine months to decide what to choose. But the nine-month period passes without any decision being confirmed because 'Isanusi had allowed it to pass on purpose so that Chaka might be fixed in his resolve' (p. 143). Meanwhile, the narrator takes time to show the reader not only that Noliwe's death cannot, justifiably, be regarded as revenge, but also that everything that has been done for Chaka up to this point can be undone, and Chaka knows it (p. 144).

He further brightens the vision when the moment of choice finally arrives. Three more times, Chaka is represented as being free to change his mind and repudiate his old ways:

Think well, Chaka. What has been done by my servants can be undone, but that which I will do through the blood of Noliwe, thy wife, even I cannot undo. What will be done will be done for ever. Therefore a man must understand what he doth while there is yet time, lest afterwards he repent and it is of no avail ... I will ask thee yet again and do thou answer speaking the truth that is in thy heart and fear nothing, fear not even that I shall weary thee again to no purpose. Which dost thou choose – Noliwe, or the chieftainship? (p. 145)

Three more times, Chaka is represented as choosing the chieftainship.

There is nothing wrong in making a tragic hero a conscious chooser even if he is not responsible for what he chooses. Oedipus chooses consciously although he is not completely responsible for his choice. William Faulkner's Joe Christmas is a conscious chooser although he is in no way responsible for his doom and the choice it results in. To come nearer home, Chinua Achebe's Okonkwo chooses consciously although he is hardly responsible for what he chooses. The 'tragedy' of Chaka is that the hero's unsolicited doom is progressively shifted out of focus, and with it the mould of his misjudgement – error in judgement, but judgement well founded on observable societal values. Consequently, he emerges as a die-hard criminal – a criminal who knows fully well that his actions are criminal:

> although he was bartering her [Noliwe] away in this fashion and was planning to kill her, yet his conscience troubled him, and gave him no rest, telling him always that he had descended from the level of a man. But because of the chieftainship he smothered his conscience and pressed on, bearing death on his shoulders ... he swallowed his fears and hardened his heart. (p. 143)

He knows that it is wrong to keep concubines; he therefore calls them '"his sisters," that is to say [the narrator takes time to explain] people with whom he could not unite. But it was into the huts of these same girls that he went to visit them, and despoiled the maidenhood of these unhappy girls, and plucked the flower of their youth, so that when the time came' (p. 132), 'when their breasts had fallen and it was said that their bloom had gone he passed them on to his councillors' (p. 177). Besides, he often kills 'these unhappy girls' and his own offspring to hide his 'crime'.

Of course, the reader has almost (if not completely) forgotten why Chaka does not want to marry and have children: the experience of Jobe and his sons in whose family 'a multitude of children diminish the might of the chieftainship that passes to the heir' (pp. 119–20); the situation in his own father's house where 'marriage is a hinderance to a chief, and breeds dissension in his house ... Children contend against one another without love; blood is spilt and lives are lost' (p. 119).

This manipulation of the reader's human sentiments contributes to Chaka's loss of the reader's admiration – the admiration which, following the trend of its internal counterpart (that of characters around Chaka) changes into fear (not for, but of Chaka) and then into hate. We admire and sympathize with him briefly when he is persecuted 'without any reason at all' (p. 39). We fear him when he kills innocent people. We hate him when, among other things, he causes famine and 'because of the famine people first began to eat men, as the flesh of a slaughtered animal is eaten. They hunted each other like wild animals and ate what they killed' (p. 162). In other words, he is the opposite of Noliwe and her brother, the 'good' Dingiswayo.

As a matter of fact (and the narrator seems to encourage our suspicion), Chaka, to some extent, is responsible for Dingiswayo's death since his effort to save the 'good' chief's life is sabotaged by 'facets' of his own 'genius', Malunga and Ndlebe. They confess:

> We hindered thy messengers from going and it was we who spread the report that Dingiswayo had been killed although he was still living ... Thou must not forget that we are here because of thee. We came to win for thee the chieftainship, and our desire is that thou mayest find it soon that we may receive our cattle, our reward ... If thy messengers had gone to Zwide perchance Dingiswayo would not have been killed, and then thou wouldst not yet have been a chief. Now thou art a chief and there is none greater, thou art greater than all; but thou hast not yet won the full chieftainship that we hear by Isanusi thou dost seek. But today we can have confidence that all will be made smooth; all will come to pass as thou dost wish. (pp. 118–19)

That Chaka is capable of resorting to this type of subterfuge in order to save his face is well demonstrated by his mother's death. After killing Nandi with his own hands, he turns round, accuses innocent people of having 'bewitched his mother', and orders his army to kill them.

The narrator's 'purpose' is not stated. That his attitude towards the material available to him results in the reader's hating his hero does not necessarily mean that his 'purpose' is to make Chaka detestable. None the less, most of his undramatized utterances (and there are many of them) seem to confirm the contrary. Ayi Kwei Armah points out that 'in writing *Chaka*, Mofolo seems to have anticipated publication difficulties. Hence the occasional insertion of preachments against Chaka for being a pagan.'[14] He is perfectly right since the Chaka we have in the novel is the materialization of these 'preachments' and the narrator's basic attitude towards his material. He is a contemptible little pagan god. No one is responsible for his action; he alone is responsible for everybody else's action.

This is the compelling projection of the narrator's well-controlled double vision; it is also the bane of Chaka's stature as a tragic hero. With very little attention to *why* Chaka acts in the way he does, it concentrates our focus on *how* he acts. Consequently, our conception of the hero as a man derives not from our perception of his entire personality, but from our emotional involvement in his adult relationships – relationships which sit in judgement on him because their unconscious bases are too weak to justify and carry the weight of their horrors. The projection, nevertheless, is effective. If it is indeed the objectification of the narrator's unrevealed (but conscious) 'purpose', Thomas Mofolo's *Chaka* is a huge success.

## Notes and References

1. Ayi Kwei Armah sees the story as an 'attempt to understand and explain Chaka'. Ayi Kwei Armah, 'Chaka', *Black World* (February 1975), p. 251.
2. All page references are to Thomas Mofolo, *Chaka: An Historical Romance* (London, 1931).
3. Ben Nnamdi Azikiwe, review of *Chaka* in *Opportunity*, x, 5 (May 1932), p. 155.
4. E. A. Ritter, *Shaka Zulu: The Rise of the Zulu Empire* (New York, 1957), p. 310.
5. In fact the 'woman witch-doctor at Bungani' cannot be regarded as a symbol of a faculty or instinct of Chaka's own nature since Chaka was only a baby when his mother invited the witch-doctor to come and see him (pp. 8–9).
6. Ayi Kwei Armah, 'Chaka', *Black World* (February 1975), p. 87.
7. Armah's comment on Ndlebe and Malunga is not entirely correct (ibid., pp. 86–7). Confusing the two strange persons, he attributes Ndlebe's traits to Malunga, and those of Malunga to Ndlebe.
8. ibid., p. 85. On the other hand, Ayi Kwei Armah rightly identifies Malunga and Ndlebe as the externalization of Chaka's 'extreme intelligence, efficiency and precision in execution, on the one hand; and extreme guile, secretiveness and deceptiveness in planning, on the other' (ibid., p. 86).
9. Henry Newbolt actually sees the action of the novel as a tragedy in five acts. He does not, however, belong to the above-mentioned class or readers, since he grants Chaka very little or no innocence. Henry Newbolt, 'Introduction', *Chaka*, pp. xii–xiv.
10. *Introduction to Aristotle*, ed. Richard McKeon (New York, 1947), p. 639. Aristotle defines the arousal of fear and pity as 'the distinctive function' of tragedy.
11. Some readers tend to confuse Thomas Mofolo's Chaka with the Chaka of history books and traditions. Consequently they see Mofolo's Chaka as a superman only when he is 'corrupted' by power.
12. Although this phrase is generally applied to male children, the narrator makes it significant by assuring the reader that it will come true.
13. There are indications that the narrator wants Noliwe to be accepted as Chaka's conscience. For instance, when Chaka thinks of waging war against peaceful tribes to bring them under his sway, the narrator more or less equates Noliwe with Chaka's conscience: 'Then it was that he sacrificed his conscience for his chieftainship, so that he forgot Noliwe' (p. 129). And we know that Chaka does not actually become 'terrible' until after the death of Noliwe (his conscience?): 'In the first place all remnants of humanity still left to him disappeared and vanished in the terrible blackness of his heart. His capacity to distinguish

between war and murder or mere killing was gone – absolutely' (p. 151). The only difficulty is that Noliwe is too human, and too unlike Isanusi and his servants, to be translated from the real world of the fiction to Chaka's mind.

14. Armah, 'Chaka', *Black World* (February 1975), p. 89. Henry Newbolt would not endorse this opinion since he believes 'that the Bible narratives have filled a large place in the author's education, and have helped to form his thought'. In other words, he could see no conscious effort on the part of Thomas Mofolo to 'appease' his missionary publishers ('Introduction' to *Chaka*, p. x).

# The Social Ethos of Black Writing in South Africa 1920–50

▼▼▼▼▼▼▼▼▼▼▼▼▼▼▼▼▼▼▼▼▼▼▼▼▼▼▼▼▼▼

TIM COUZENS

> I translated Shakespeare when what was known as the Zulu programme
> was steadily growing and I tried to mimic the white broadcast as much
> as possible, and I tried to solidify my position as much as possible. I
> didn't like my masters to say, 'Uh, well, you can go away now. This
> thing you have started here is not worth it,' so I tried as much as pos-
> sible to make it as good as theirs.
>
> King Edward Masinga[1]

WRITTEN in the 'sixties, *The Marabi Dance*,[2] by Modikwe
Dikobe, is an historical novel. The novel ostensibly begins in
1938, since the heroine, Martha, is 16 years old and was born
in the year of the 1922 General Strike. The novel ends in the period just
after the Second World War. The earlier date, however, may be only
impressionistic as the marabi dance was really at its height in the early
'thirties. The author, born in 1913, is clearly recalling the period of his
early manhood. The world of the book is absolutely authentic; its tone
captures the tone of the period perfectly.

The two major themes of the novel seem to be the tensions between
town and country life on the one hand and between the aspirant middle
class and the working class on the other. And all of this is seen against the
background of racial discrimination. The novel is thus a reasonably objective, *post facto* analysis in novel form of life in Johannesburg, the 'centre'
of South Africa, in the 'thirties and 'forties. The novel is, in a sense, a
product of that time; and this paper attempts to show, with *The Marabi
Dance* as a kind of commentary, something of the society which produced
the novel's literary predecessors (the works of such writers as Vilakazi, the
Dhlomo brothers, Solomon Sidzumo, Walter Whlapo, R. V. Selope Thema,
A. C. Jordan, Peter Abrahams, and many others who succeeded Mofolo,
Plaatje, and Dube), what options were open to them, and where they might
derive their inspiration.

In the *Marabi Dance* Martha has the choice of marriage with Sephai, the 'country' man, or George, the 'town' man. She also has the opportunity of becoming a singer in a middle class, 'European' fashion but is tempted by the shebeen-culture of George. Like Martha, most of the black writers of the 'thirties and 'forties (who were almost invariably journalists as well) were aspirant middle class. There was much intermarriage and close relationship amongst writers and politicians. Plaatje married into the Mbelle family, his daughter into the Molema family. There was an Mbelle–Msimang marriage link. The Dhlomos were related by marriage to the Dubes and the Vilakazis. The Twalas were related to the Msimangs. The bitterness (present in undertone even then, palpable after the late 'forties) was perhaps due to the frustration of these aspirations, the blocking of black capitalism, trade unionism, etc. In 1925 H. Selby-Msimang was able to express this tension:

> Bantu intellectuals now find themselves thrust in a whirlpool created by two opposing extremes with a powerful cross current which tends to overwhelm them in their struggle to maintain an appreciable equilibrium at an era in their life when they are dodging the visissitudes of a transitory stage. As far back as from the time they first came into close contact with Western civilization to this day, the State, speaking generally, has never been solicitous, nor sufficiently generous, in its attitude towards the regeneration of the Bantu. Missionaries, for the most part, found themselves isolated in the effort to transform Bantu life by a process of education and Christianity that it may embrace a higher culture.[3]

On the one hand, then, there is the acceptance, at first missionary-inspired, of much of 'European civilization' and the values of urban life. In 1934, in an essay competition in the newspaper *Umteteli wa Bantu*[4] entitled 'What I Expect of Africa', Junietta Maqalika expected 'improvement in agriculture . . . race peace from Africa . . . more schools to be built . . . Christianity to be encouraged among the Africans'. Furthermore she expected 'the Bantus not to be discouraged, by seeing the Europeans at a high stage. They should remember that it took Europeans centuries and centuries to attain their present standards.' In a similar competition in 1924 on the danger of town life, Douglas C. Zulu, in the winning essay, warned a hypothetical cousin, coming to Johannesburg for the first time, to stay in the Hostel of The Helping Hand Club:

> An Auntie of mine (a Mrs Molemo) stays at the Club and she will put you in the way of things . . . join healthy outdoor games . . . Basket Ball . . . or Tennis . . . Good music, educative lectures and pictures, social and religious gatherings are all good and uplifting, but in attending these use your common sense and pick your companions carefully because on this particular point of company might lie your undoing.[5]

R. R. R. Dhlomo's *An African Tragedy* derives from this kind of writing –
it is by no means an isolated event.

On the other hand, even the middle-class blacks were subjected to strong
pressures from the state and prevailing economic and social conditions. In
1923 a newspaper competition on 'Native Grievances' listed the complaints
and their frequency of occurrence in the submitted essays as follows:

| | |
|---|---|
| Land | 33 |
| Education | 24 |
| Colour Bar | 22 |
| Franchise | 21 |
| Pass Law | 20 |
| Taxation | 19 |
| Wages | 11 |
| Segregation | 11 |
| Injustice | 11, etc.[6] |

In his novel *Mhudi*, published in 1930,[7] Plaatje implicitly but strongly
attacked land distribution. The land squeeze is strongly implicit in *The
Marabi Dance*. Also, in the later novel Mabongo approaches a policeman
and asks where he can get a 'special pass'. 'What special?' is the reply.
'There is a special for travelling, a special for a visit, a special to go out at
night and a special to seek work' (p. 50). In an article in *Sjambok* in 1930,
H. D. Tyamzashe (who held a high post in Kadalie's ICU) identified
twelve kinds of passes needed at various times. 'The pass law system', he
wrote, 'teems with irregularities and anomalies . . . The whole thing is
unjust.'[8] In the same year R. V. Selope Thema (who became the first
editor of *Bantu World* at its founding eighteen months later) wrote that
the main objections to the pass laws are:

(1) that they restrict the free movements of the Natives;
(2) they make it difficult for them to bargain with their labour to their
advantage;
(3) they exclude them from the benefits of the Industrial Conciliation
Act and the Wage Act;
(4) they are to a large extent responsible for the degradation of Native
character and for Native crime.[9]

Though most of the writers would have had genuine exemption passes like
the one the Reverend Ndlovu manages to get by fraud in Dikobe's novel
(p. 13) – what Tyamzashe in *Umteteli wa Bantu* called the 'Big Boss' of all
passes – the benefits were nevertheless of dubious value. In the same article,
Tyamzashe wrote:

This in effect means little. Exempted Natives, for example, cannot pro-
cure liquor, cannot vote, and cannot board trams. An exempted Native
can be stopped at any time by a constable and asked for his tax receipt.
Further, the exemption does not render him immune from going or

coming as he pleases. If he visits a strange Native location he must produce a location permit-pass. At the railway station or the post office, when cashing money, he will be asked for his pass, and will produce his exemption slip like the ordinary Native. So here there is no difference whatsoever and the whole system is camouflage.[10]

The frustration of this privileged-class-which-is-not-a-privileged-class of blacks is reflected in H. I. E. Dhlomo's unpublished play *The Pass* (probably based on an incident which actually happened to the author) where the hero's exemption certificate is not accepted by the police and he lands in jail – it is a play where the corruption of the pass system is also exposed. Possibly the Ndlovus of the time had already made the police over-suspicious of 'exempted natives'.

Liquor flows through the pages of *The Marabi Dance*. The issue is by no means a simple one. Clearly, many people had a vested interest in the illicit liquor trade. An unofficial commission of the South African Temperance Alliance and the South African Institute of Race Relations found, in 1935, that Syrians were the chief suppliers of European liquor to blacks. Although most whites could perhaps have rationalized this away as being the actions of people 'one would expect that sort of thing of', they must have found the revelations of *Sjambok* (and the commission) about the supply of yeast for illicit brewing less palatable. As *Sjambok* (the magazine run by Stephen Black) wrote, 'At present six times as much yeast is being made as we need for bread. Roughly speaking, the rest goes into Skokiaan!' It went on to say that its 'object was to lay bare the iniquities that are permitted by law, the colossal output of yeast and the exploitation of the native by way of his natural, human craving for alcohol . . . It is our unpleasant duty to show that some of the men most honoured in South African trade and industry are making large fortunes out of the sale of yeast used for the fabrication of skokiaan', and accuses the family of the then Chairman of the Public Health Committee of Johannesburg of being directors and shareholders in one of the most notorious slum properties of Newtown, 'a property frequently raided by police in search of "the honey dew of Nigger Heaven".'[11] No doubt the 'black spot' of Doornfontein in *The Marabi Dance* covered up similar vested interests. Of course the illegal nature of liquor may have been of some ironic advantage to the blacks since, as a 'home industry', it may have allowed for the accumulation of some capital whereas the municipal beerhalls and the later legalizing of liquor in the 'sixties could have only let in the dominating influence of the big liquor companies, which had few black shareholders.

Finally, overshadowing the life of Johannesburg, were the mines. The black newspaper *Umteteli wa Bantu*, owned by the Chamber of Mines, seldom made a point of criticizing the mines and for many years mine propaganda of an enticing nature appeared in the black newspapers. A fairly typical one describes 'compound conditions':

> You no doubt have often wondered what a Compound is like. You know that your menfolk live in Compounds, and therefore it will be of interest to you to hear of what such a place is really like.
>
> Some people when they think of a Compound imagine it to be a grimy unattractive barrack – but this is far from true. Your menfolk within the Compound live in rooms each capable of accommodating twenty persons. They each have their own bunk, and the bunks are placed around the room. In the centre there is a brazier, on which they can cook their food if necessary; for instance, raw meat which they get two or three times a week. This brazier also keeps them warm in the cold weather, and the coal used is provided free by the mine baases.
>
> When outside of this room, instead of a bleak barrack square you will find lawns and gardens and trees under which your menfolk can recline in off-duty hours.
>
> Then there are change-houses dotted about the Compound, where hot and cold water is provided. There are special places set apart where clothes can be washed, and in the centre there is the communal kitchen and beer hall where your menfolk go to draw their rations.
>
> You will see from this brief outline that a Compound is really synonymous with communal living on modern, up-to-date lines – and not a Victorian barrack room square.[12]

In *The Marabi Dance* Martha sees a group of foreign miners on a railway station, returning home. 'Martha thought of Tiny's father who had returned from the mines to die. "Are these men also returning to their homes to die?"' (p. 105). Perhaps Tiny's father had never read the kind of descriptions of which the above is one! The tensions created by the labour system raised such issues as appeared in the 1928 campaign to have 'the Blantyres' expelled from South Africa because of their competition in the labour market. H. Selby-Msimang wrote, 'The South African Native is fast gaining race consciousness . . . After all is said and done, the Blantyre Natives are more of a nuisance than an asset to the Union. Their chief occupation is domestic service – work which is the true sphere of women.'[13] It is possibly this prejudice which leads R. R. R. Dhlomo to choose 'a Blantyre' as the murderer over the card game in *An African Tragedy*, published in the same year, 1928.[14] In *The Marabi Dance*, the Reverend Ndlovu 'sent his wife and children to Rhodesia during the mass raids against the "foreign natives"' (p. 13).

Perhaps the most pathetically eloquent plea against all the foregoing injustice is contained in a letter to *Bantu World* in 1937 where Phil Mathole suggests that an SPCA could be created for Africans:

Africans, it is time that we demand for a prevention society like animals. Surely we will find ourselves more free, because today at any time and anywhere an African is shot, is assaulted, is run over by a car, and the offender escapes.

What about a dog when run over by a car? What about an African who hit a cat on the nose and has to pay £5? It is ridiculous; may the law be repealed! We are thirsty for justice and satisfied with injustice; we are deprived of everything – so give us freedom and keep everything.[15]

Perhaps the address he gives of 'General Hospital, Pretoria', adds point to his suggestion.

In the face of these conditions the intellectual *élite* – the writers, journalists and politicians – perceived their role as being both educators of their people to a new life-style and values-system and as voices of protest against injustice. Opposed to tribal rule which, like 'Enquirer' (Horatio Mbelle), they found 'reactionary and opposed to general progress',[16] they were nevertheless forced by racial discrimination into nationalistic reassessing of 'black history' and into political opposition. And this nationalist-minded aspirant middle class determined to create a national literature. In an article entitled 'Towards Our Own Literature' printed in *Ilanga Lase Natal* in 1923, for instance, 'A Special Correspondent', after discussing art and music, writes:

We must have our own literature here in S. Africa sooner or later, and the sooner the better. We do not want to force too much the growth of literary feeling, nor have we a desire to foster any narrow national or racial spirit. But we want to intensify, through literature, our individual experience. We want, as it were, to pool our emotions; to identify our common aspirations; we want mental communication in mediums that we can understand. We want to establish a brotherhood of the heart.[17]

In 1933 the great Zulu poet, B. W. Vilakazi, is already assuming the desirability of a 'national literature' based on 'Euro Bantu civilization'.[18] Repeatedly, too, these men would turn certain events, such as Mendi Day or Dingaan's Day, into triggers for nationalist (though conservative) statements. The war in Abyssinia, for instance, produced poetry like the following of Stanley Silwana in 1936:

> I sing of Afric' my Native land.
> Let England hear if she hath ears.
> Ethiopia yet shall stretch her hand
> To vanquish all who caused her tears.[19]

The questions next arise as to where African artists obtained their inspiration, recreation, audience, and outlet. Undoubtedly one of the crucial institutional attractions for black artists was the Bantu Men's Social

Centre at the southern end of Eloff Street in Johannesburg (and, later, its sister-organization the Bantu Social Centre in Beatrice Street, Durban). The foundation stone was laid on 20 January 1924; and the centre was, to a large extent, the idea of the Reverend F. B. Bridgman, an American Board missionary. It was run jointly by blacks and whites – many well-known white 'liberals' were connected with it, such as the Reverend Ray Phillips, Rev. J. Dexter Taylor, Howard Pim, Walter Webber, and Professor R. Hoernlé. As the 1931 *Annual Report* noted:

> The Bantu Men's Social Centre, was founded in 1924 by public spirited men, who saw the necessity of helping young Native men to devote their leisure time to the best advantage in healthful recreation and good citizenship, the development of worthy character, and the promotion of real sympathy between Europeans and non-Europeans . . .

In the 'thirties the membership ranged between 350 and 450 and it was virtually the only institutionalized social meeting-ground for blacks. Its activities were varied: there was a room for the Gamma Sigma Club (a debating society begun by Ray Phillips); there were concerts and balls; there was the Glee Club, a choir which gave numerous concerts; there were night classes; innumerable clubs and societies met there – ranging from the Mine Clerks Association to the Pathfinders and Wayfarers (scouts and girl guides); there were lectures, draughts, and ping-pong; there were also cricket, tennis, and football teams. As the 1928 *Annual Report* noted, 'A considerable number of Native men practically make the building their home during their leisure hours.' It was clearly the home of the 'progressive'[20] blacks. In *The Marabi Dance*, one of Martha's objections to marrying the country boy is that, 'He won't allow me to go to the Social Centre or bioscope', to which her mother replies, 'My child, marriage is very hard. But Soshal Senta and baiskopo will give you a baby and no father' (p. 67). The BMSC plays a prominent part in *The Marabi Dance*: 'The Bantu Men's Social Centre was the only entertainment place built exclusively for African men to join' (p. 71). Its somewhat snobbish values – since it was the home of the black *élite* – are what Martha aspires towards. All the respectable black writers and public figures would be present at important functions, not of least of which, for instance, was the ball held at the BMSC in honour of Prince George on 13 March 1934. Amongst the several hundred guests on that occasion were R. V. Selope-Thema, H. Selby-Msimang, Griffiths Motsieloa (the musical entrepreneur), Dr A. B. Xuma (President of the ANC in the 'forties), J. R. Rathebe, A. S. Vil-Nkomo, H. I. E. Dhlomo and D. R. Twala, who was to organize much black sport for many years to come.[21] For a fair idea of the composition of the black *élite* and white liberals at this stage there can be few better lists than the names of some of the 2,000 mourners who attended the funeral of Mrs Amanda Xuma on 2 May 1934.[22] The array of black dignitaries was imposing. H. I. E. Dhlomo sent Dr Xuma a copy of Donne's 'Death Be Not Proud' as condolence.[23]

There were other facilities that intellectuals were in dire need of: libraries, for instance. Jacob Nhlapo (later to become well known as principal of the Wilberforce Institute) wrote in 1933 that 'the time has come for our people to awaken to the great value of libraries and to strain every nerve to have them established in all our locations and townships'.[24] In 1937 the poet and playwright H. I. E. Dhlomo became the first black Librarian-Organizer of the Carnegie Non-European Library, based in Germiston, and he helped organize numerous library branches in the Transvaal until his resignation in 1940. One of these branches was in the BMSC and it played a crucial part in the development of at least one writer. Peter Abrahams described his first visit to the BMSC in his book *Tell Freedom*:

> I moved over to the bookshelves. I wanted to touch the books but held back. Perhaps it was not permitted. Typed slips showed what each shelf held; novels, history, sociology, travel, Africana, political science, American Negro literature ... I stopped there. American Negro literature ...
>
> In the months that followed I spent nearly all my spare time in the library of the Bantu Men's Social Centre. I read every one of the books on the shelf marked: American Negro literature. I became a nationalist, a colour nationalist through the writings of men and women who lived a world away from me.[25]

These American Negro books would almost certainly have been chosen by either H. I. E. Dhlomo, the Librarian, or Dr Ray Phillips, the American Board missionary who often used to write about Negro writers in his regular column in *Umteteli wa Bantu* in the 'twenties. It is this Phillips who is undoubtedly 'Mr Phillip, the organizer' in *The Marabi Dance* who 'on a certain Friday night' showed Charlie Chaplin in *City Lights* (p. 72). Phillips was very pleased with his films which he showed regularly at the BMSC. The rather ambiguous role of the liberals of the time is also evident in his film-shows on the mines. He was extremely proud of an incident which he describes in his first book *The Bantu Are Coming* where he managed to defuse a riot:

> We got word that the natives in the compound were furious, that they were forging weapons, and intended to retaliate that night! ... Then the movies moved in the direction of peace ... We could hear the noise long before we reached the compound ... Finally the gate was opened a foot and we squeezed through with our apparatus. We shivered as we made

our way to the projection stand and prepared our equipment. The compound had been turned into a munitions plant. A few, comparatively,
gathered around us, and they were silent. Not the usual happy crowd.

The lights went out and the picture flashed on. Sure enough, there was
Si Dakwa! For a moment only the silence continued, then uproar!
Listeners far outside the compound trembled. Were the natives coming
out? It was an attack, but an attack by the film comedian on the outraged feelings of the New Primrose workers. Soon all the 4000 were
shouting themselves sick with laughter as they watched Charlie, Larry
Semon, Buster Keaton, and others do their funny stuff. Never was there
such a treat; so many laughs. At the end of two hours the compound
was limp and weak from shouting, the vengeful spirit had long since
vanished and the great crowd bade us good night in the usual jovial
way – many still laughing. There was no murder that night at the New
Primrose.[26]

Films were thus accessible to writers at the BMSC as well as at black
theatres, though certain films were passed for exhibition to 'Europeans
Only'. In 1936 the names of some of these films banned to black audiences
are intriguing: 'Escape from Devil's Island', 'Jewel Robbery', 'Crime
without Passion', 'Too Much Harmony', etc.[27] But Phillips was not the
only pioneer in the movie field for blacks. He was emulated by at least one
well-known black: Sol T. Plaatje.

In 1924, after his return from America, Plaatje brought his 'bioscope' to
Johannesburg 'as he wished the people – and the Native press – to come
and see for themselves the wonderful progress attained by our American
kinsmen at Washington College and other places. Space forbids one to
paint a vivid word picture of the films depicting scenes in and around that
wonderful College founded by the late Dr Booker Washington.'[28] Because
of bad publicity, however, less than 100 people attended, in contrast to the
'Bloemfontein Natives' who 'fairly stampeded to see this show'. This did not
deter him, for 'the Plaatje bioscope' made a very successful tour of the
Barkly West district in 1925.[29]

I have discussed elsewhere the role that newspapers had to play as the
only regular outlet for creative writers – for radio was not available to
blacks as a medium of expression. The first Zulu broadcaster on the SABC,
King Edward Masinga, was appointed on 21 December 1941; and, at first,
he had only five minutes broadcasting-time a day. Furthermore, as implied
in the headnote, he had to imitate the whites in order to prove he was
worthy of more time:

I translated Shakespeare; I dramatized Shakespeare; I called the people,
the artists, I trained them and Shakespeare was heard for the first time
over the air by the Zulus. They were surprised when they heard something like *The Comedy of Errors*; they were dumbfounded when they

heard *Romeo and Juliet.* Really that was something new to their fairy tales . . . just something new.

My time for broadcasting was extended to say 30 minutes. I was very grateful, well, I had to prove to them again that 30 minutes was still very little, was still very little; I mimicked them again some more (chuckle). What they did, I looked at it and then I came to the Zulu programme and did it too; everything they did I came over and did it. After which I went to the Manager and said 'My time is very short . . .'[30]

Masinga went on to translate and produce for radio nine Shakespeare plays, some of which may still be preserved on glass records, but the pragmatic necessity of imitating 'European' models, together with the lack of informed criticism, clearly plagued radio productions as it did literary productions of the 'thirties and 'forties.[31]

Furthermore, the intellectuals of the time could find some outlet for their creative expression in sport – a field not to be neglected in any social history of black South African literature. 'The Bantu Sports Ground' which appears in *The Marabi Dance* (p. 114) was that of the Bantu Sports Club located on ground donated by Messrs Pim and Hardy. H. I. E. Dhlomo played left-half for Pure Vuur ('Pure Fire'), one of the BMSC football teams, and in Dikobe's novel Mr Samson teaches boxing at the Social Centre (presumably it was also encouraged there as opposition to the Amalaita gangs). In view of recent efforts, begun in 1974, to introduce multi-racial sport into South Africa, it is interesting to note that the Bantu Sports Club was officially opened in April 1931 by the Mayor of Johannesburg – which opening was followed by a cricket match, attended by 10,000 spectators, between a 'Bantu' and a 'European' side.[32] For the record, the black team scored 155 runs for 7 wickets declared, the white scored 118 for 9 wickets, and the match was hence drawn.

The only question that remains to this paper is to attempt to assess the artistic response, to try to determine how the artists used what facilities there were and how they overcame the problem of lack of opportunities. In all arts there was a constant plea for institutions, clubs, etc. For instance, in 1937, G. F. Khumalo expressed the thoughts of many when he pleaded for literary clubs:

Many people do not see why they should read any papers at all – they see no value in reading – they say it is useless. Many also think it is only a waste of money on abstracts. Some read only to pass time – some to show off that they are learned. Few read with concentration and interest, thus they can hardly understand and so get no benefit from their reading. The few intelligent readers quickly lose what they have got – because they can seldom apply it quickly. Life's worries cause mind wanderings and soon they forget what they have read, before they use it . . . I am appealing to all our papers to come together in one effort of national value – the establishment of an association of Bantu Literary Clubs under the Bantu Cultural Society, so that we can be all active in the furtherance of our national progress.[33]

Various attempts of varying success were made to form such clubs. On 12 May 1934, for instance, there was a meeting of African journalists and writers with J. G. Coka as the main driving force. They began a Journalists' and Writers' Union.[34] Unfortunately, it does not seem to have lasted very long, nor to have really achieved its aims for, in 1944, we find, Sgt Henry W. Nxumalo writing: 'Deep down memory lane, I recall hard-boiled Jameson G. Coka broaching up an idea of this sort. Employed journalists, however, did not give it the support it deserves. That was way back.'[35] It is interesting to note that Nxumao in the same article, written in the offices of *Bantu World*, feels a sense of continuity with earlier writers:

> In this very office were, once, versatile guys like Jameson G. Coka, author; Guybon Sinxo, novelist; H. I. E. Dhlomo, playwright and poet; P. D. Segale, a shrewd political writer, now late – other contributors being Mweli Skota, auto-biographer; Obed S. Mooki, poet, now in the Clergy; Peter Abrahams, poet, now in London; S. S. Rhune Mqhayi, the Xhosa poet and National 'Mbongi'; and H. D. Tyamzashe, the doyen of Bantu freelance journalists. Godfrey Kuzwayo ('Gossip Pen') of 'Umteteli's' social page fame was then gossiping like blazes.

This paragraph contains a greater sense of continuity than appears immediately on the surface, since the man who is here acknowledging this feeling of continuity was, in the 'fifties, to become Mr Drum.

In the field of art the paintings of Pemba and Bhengu are fairly well known and make an extremely interesting comparison with their contemporary writers. Gerald Sekoto was later to achieve even greater fame. Less known, however, is 'the famous African landscape painter',[36] John Koenakeefe Mohl. Mohl founded an African School of Art which, in 1944, functioned 'in a little studio behind his home at Sophiatown'. I have, as yet, not been able to determine the fate of this school.

Much literary activity of the period was associated with the BMSC. For instance, in the early 'thirties, there was founded the Bantu Dramatic Society whose first production (to a mixed audience) was Goldsmith's *She Stoops to Conquer*, in 1933. A repeat performance was put on one Friday night, followed on the Saturday night by a kind of pageant of Xhosa traditional life.[37] One of the most interesting of the performances occurred on 3 June 1934. *Umteteli wa Bantu* announced the forthcoming event as follows:

> In aid of the Bridgman Memorial Hospital preparations are being made for a fine concert at the Bantu Men's Social Centre on Sunday, June 3,

and the opportunity is being taken to link up this concert with the Emancipation Centenary celebrations which are reminding readers of great men like William Wilberforce, Abraham Lincoln, and David Livingstone ...

The choir numbering 65 voices will render several items. We are able in this issue to give a picture of the choir members. The promoter of the concert is Mr H. I. E. Dhlomo, and other officials are: Elocutionist: Griffiths Motsieloa; Playwright: R. R. R. Dhlomo; Speakers: R. V. Selope Thema and Dr Xuma; Accompanists: E. Motsieloa and M. S. Radebe; Reciters: S. Teyise, R. Mabuellong, and M. Jones; Violinist: O. Kumalo.[38]

The programme is a beautiful example of the conflicting cross-currents of the period:

1. Speech: Slavery: Mr R. V. S. Thema.
2. Music and Recitations: (a) Negro's Complaint (Cowper) Motsieloa Group; (b) Sixoshiwe (Caluza) The Choir; (c) The Witnesses (Longfellow) Motsieloa Group; (d) Mendi (Mphahlela) The Choir.
3. Scene I: Slave Auction Place.
4. Incidental Music and Recitations: (a) Violin Duet (Pleyel) Kumalo – Dhlomo; (b) Give a Plea to Africa (Bokwe) The Choir; (c) Ode to Ethiopia (Dunbar) Motsieloa Group; (d) O Rest in the Lord (Mendelssohn) Mrs Radebe; (e) The Slaves Dream (Longfellow) Motsieloa Group; (f) Violin: Madrigale (Simonetti) Mr O. Kumalo.
5. Scene II: A Cotton Field.
6. Incidental Music: (a) Ave Maria – Violin – (Gounod) Mr H. Dhlomo; (b) What Are These (Stainer) The Choir.

### Part II

1. Music and Recitations: (a) Gettysburg Oration (Lincoln) Motsieloa Group; (b) I Waited for the Lord (Mendelssohn) The Choir; (c) Brotherhood Song of Liberty (Lowell) Motsieloa Group; (d) The Trumpet Shall Sound (Handel) Phillip Molopi.
2. Scene III: The Coming of Freedom. Incidental Music: (a) Spiritual Music (Thompson) Rose Khumbane; (b) God so Loved (Stainer) The Choir; (c) O Taste and See (Goss) The Choir; (d) And the Glory of the Lord (Handel) The Choir; (e) Hallelujah Chorus (Handel) The Choir.
3. Closing Music and Recitations: (a) Selections from Tagore: Motsieloa Group; (b) Land of Hope and Glory (Elgar) The Choir; (c) I, too (Hughes) Motsieloa Group; (d) Self-Determination (Hill) Motsieloa Group; (e) To America (Johnson) Motsieloa Group; (f) Thanks Be to God (Mendelssohn) The Choir; Speech: Slavery: Dr Xuma.
NATIONAL ANTHEM.

The keynote of Selope Thema's speech was expressed in the following statement, 'Tonight I want to ask you how we, Africans, can live together peacefully with the White population of this land of our birth'. There was a 'record attendance', despite short notice.[39]

Writers were not wholly isolated either: there were, for instance, two writers' conferences held in the 'thirties. The first of these took place on Thursday 15 October 1936, in Florida, Transvaal. Among the writers present were D. D. T. Jabavu, R. T. Caluza, R. V. Selope Thema, H. I. E. Dhlomo. J. J. R. Jolobe, S. E. K. Mqhayi, T. Mofolo and R. R. R. Dhlomo tendered their apologies. Several whites attended. Amongst issues discussed were the difficulties of getting published, the establishment of a 'Bantu Academy', the lack of magazines, the problems of orthography and language media, and the lack of training in literary appreciation and criticism amongst the writers themselves.[40]

But *The Marabi Dance* has, as its main background image, music, and it seems appropriate to end this paper with a discussion of the variety of music at the time and how the contrasts throw light on social phenomena. The first kind was tribal music and dancing and needs little explanation. Then there was the music of R. T. Caluza who tried to keep an African flavour in his music. B. W. Vilakazi described his work:

> There is no name in music libraries for purely Caluza music but for lack of apt word we call it jazz. Jazz music is somewhat inferior to the sort of music found in Caluza's compositions. In Caluza's own words found in the Southern Workman published by the Hampton Institute: 'A Zulu singer hums a tune or sings meaningless exclamatory syllables, such as "oha! oham! oji!" As he sings he makes bodily movements which thoroughly agree with the tune. He stamps and the women join with clapping of hands and queer ejaculations of derision.' Caluza's music which is now heard widely in Zonophone records, has transformed these exclamatory and primitive 'oha, ojis' in refined music that tells a story of a Zulu tribe in the days of western civilization. There is no loss of that wonderful drive which puts one's feet into action and clapping of hands and bodily movements. This is a peculiarity of African music, to combine physical movement with music.[41]

The 'thirties saw the formation of a number of well-known black bands: there were the Rhythm Kings, the Jazz Maniacs, the African Hellenics, the Harlem Swingsters, etc. but the most famous of the bands was The Merry Blackbirds. Founded by Griffiths Motsieloa and his wife, it was led by Peter Razant and, with a number of changes, survived into the early 'sixties. Elegantly tuxedoed, it was the leading South African band, playing to both black and white (it was, for instance, engaged by the Schlesingers and by the Barlows). It concentrated on western-style music. Peter Razant's explanation of the origin of the band is interesting: 'The idea why the band was really formed was this – that the upper-class, the non-white, didn't want to associate itself with the type of music that this band was playing that was in existence (a marabi band). They thought that it was music of no significance.'[42] Associated with this relatively élitist style were the expectations raised by the Transvaal African annual Eisteddford, begun in 1931.[43] The music of the shebeens was anathema to the aspirant middle class. In 1933 'Musicus' could triumphantly claim: 'King Jazz is dying! His syncopating, brothel-born, war-fattened, noise-drunk, is now in a stage of hectic decline.'[44] But the marabi dance was at its height in 1933. In a further article later in the year, 'Musicus' contrasted the *élite* with the shebeen music:

> The problem of African music must eventually be solved by Africans. The 'Marabi' dances and concerts, and the terrible 'jazz' music banged and wailed out of the doors of foul-smelling so called halls are far from representing real African taste. They create wrong impressions. The Transvaal Bantu is to be complimented in the circumstances on the annual Eisteddford, which, to a great extent, will help to abolish the 'Marabi' menace.[45]

On the one hand, one has the music of the BMSC and Inchcape Hall (scene of much ballroom dancing); on the other hand, one has the marabi, the music of Prospect Township, of the shebeens and 'low' halls. The marabi was responsible for the creation of its own language – the word 'sponono' (girl), for example, was a marabi creation.[46] But, according to Peter Razant, this 'indigenous' music died with the destruction of Prospect Township and with the removal of its inhabitants.[47] By 1941 marabi had been replaced by Tsaba-Tsaba[48] (which in turn has given way to Phatha-Phatha, the Hula Hoop, Twist, Mayfair Jive and Hippie Jive). At its height marabi was played by Sidney Strydom (a trombone player) and his band The Japanese Express, and George in *The Marabi Dance* is perhaps modelled on a pianist by name of Thebajane.[49] The fact that the writers were mainly aspirant middle class meant that there was little propagation of music like the marabi in contemporary writings – its acceptance in literature had to wait thirty years for the necessary detachment. Peter Razant gives an analogy: 'Just like you would . . . if you go into Cape Town particularly now it's very much abroad now the Carnival of the Coons; now there the upper-class Coloured thinks that it's degrading to have this. I think that in time they will come to accept it as their own . . .'[50]

At the end of the novel, a lone marabi dancer is asked to leave the church where Martha and George are being married (p. 118); it is only in the 'seventies that *The Marabi Dance* is allowed in from the cold.

## Notes and References

1. Interview, Umlazi, Kwa Zulu, 7 January 1975.
2. Modikwe Dikobe, *The Marabi Dance* (London, Heinemann, African Writers Series, 1973). References are to this edition.
3. *Umteteli wa Bantu*, 17 October 1925.
4. ibid., 11 August 1934.
5. 26 January 1924. For an interesting example of middle-class appeal one might look at the Ovaltine advertisement which appears in *Bantu World*, 19 June 1937. Piet says to Johannes, 'Johannes, you are looking fine'. Johannes replies, 'Yes Piet, now I feel as strong as a lion because I drink "Ovaltine" every day'. Piet is on foot, carrying a stick, wearing a cloth cap and a rough jacket. Johannes has a bicycle, and is wearing a felt hat, a posh blazer (with outside pocket handkerchief) and a tie. Incidentally, the bicycle is a common feature of contemporary painting.
6. *Umteteli wa Bantu*, 1 November 1924.
7. Lovedale Press, Lovedale, 1930.
8. 10 October 1930.
9. *Umteteli wa Bantu*, 1 November 1930.
10. ibid., 10 October 1930.
11. *Sjambok*, 25 October 1929.
12. *Ilanga Lase Natal*, throughout 1944.
13. *Umteteli wa Bantu*, 18 February 1928.
14. Lovedale, 1928, pp. 16–19.
15. *Bantu World*, 7 August 1937.
16. *Umteteli wa Bantu*, 28 April 1934.
17. 21 December 1923.
18. *Ilanga Lase Natal*, 26 May 1933.
19. *Bantu World*, 28 September 1936.
20. This is one of the favourite words used by T. D. Mweli Skota in his important book *The African Yearly Register: A Black Folks' Who's Who*, published in the early thirties.
21. *Umteteli wa Bantu*, 17 March 1934.
22. See *Umteteli wa Bantu*, 5 May 1934.
23. Dr A. B. Xuma papers, University of the Witwatersrand archives, Johannesburg.
24. *Umteteli wa Bantu*, 22 July 1933.
25. *Tell Freedom* (London, 1954), pp. 192, 197.
26. *The Bantu Are Coming* (Student Christian Movement Press, London, 1930), pages 148, 150. 'Si Dakwa' was Charlie Chaplin, 'the little drunken man'. This mediating (possibly ameliorating, but certainly conflict-avoiding) role of the early liberals is also evident in the following report on 'Native Domestic Servants' which appeared in *Umteteli wa Bantu*, 26 October 1929: 'The following is the "Star" report of the proceedings at the annual meeting of the Helping Hand Club for Native Girls held last Saturday: "Mrs Bridgman referred to the great increase in the number of young Native girls coming into Johannesburg of recent years. She emphasized that proper provision should be made for them so that they could be controlled and properly trained."'
27. For a full list, see Ray Phillips, *The Bantu in the City* (Lovedale Press, Lovedale, 1938(?)), pp. 315–27.
28. *Umteteli wa Bantu*, 31 May 1924.
29. ibid., 5 December, 1925.
30. Interview with K. E. Masinga, Umlazi, Kwa Zulu, 7 January 1975.

31. See, for instance, the letters on the subject in *Ilanga Lase Natal*, 8 March 1950.
32. *Umteteli wa Bantu*, 11 April 1931
33. *Bantu World*, 7 August 1937.
34. *Umteteli wa Bantu*, 19 May 1934.
35. *Bantu World*, 4 March 1944.
36. ibid., 20 May 1944.
37. *Umteteli wa Bantu*, 14 October 1933.
38. ibid., 19 May 1934. For a copy of the programme, see the Rheinalt Jones papers, University of the Witwatersrand archives, Johannesburg, Box 47(b).
39. ibid., 9 June 1934.
40. *Bantu World*, 14 November 1936.
41. *Ilanga Lase Natal*, 10 February 1933.
42. Interview, Riverlea, Johannesburg, 30 December 1974.
43. See, for instance, *Umteteli wa Bantu*, 10 September 1932.
44. ibid., 11 February 1933.
45. ibid., 11 November 1933.
46. See W. M. B. Nhlapo, 'Reviews and Comments on City's Activities', *Bantu World*, 19 April 1941.
47. Interview, Riverlea, Johannesburg, 30 December 1974.
48. *Bantu World*, 19 April 1941.
49. Interview with Peter Razant, Riverlea, Johannesburg, 30 December 1974.
50. loc. cit.

# Transition

# Problems of a Creative Writer in South Africa

▼▼▼▼▼▼▼▼▼▼▼▼▼▼▼▼▼▼▼▼▼▼▼▼▼▼▼▼▼▼▼

## T. T. MOYANA

THIS is an introductory study of the problems that confront a literary artist in South Africa. The basic problem of course, is apartheid. Since the country is strictly divided and people live and operate within the narrow confines of their racial or tribal enclaves, I will try, where possible, to examine problems peculiar to writers in the different racial groups. The African writer, of course, suffers the most. For he, with other Africans, is the direct target of racial oppression. If he seems to receive more attention than others in this paper, it is because of this very fact. And it is only because oppression always destroys something in the oppressor that English and Afrikaans writers also suffer.

No attempt shall be made to review particular works of any writer. My concern is rather with the study of the legal, social, and psychological climate for literary production. I shall try to show that South Africa's totalitarian laws are, in effect, legislating literature out of existence. This is extra tragic when one realizes that the cultural climate for literary production in South Africa would most likely have remained poor even if these laws had not been passed. It will be necessary to draw analogies with other countries where protest literature was or is being successfully written: Soviet Russia, and France during the Enlightenment.

Finally, a theory of the nature of effective protest literature will be suggested.

A common sense thesis bandied about by casual literary theorists is that conditions of political, economic, and social repression in a country offer excellent material for vigorous literary activity. And quite a few famous writers – Voltaire, Rousseau, Dickens, Dostoevsky, Pasternak, Orwell, Richard Wright, to mention only a few – wrote in the circumstances or in the tradition of protest against an unjust order. Some of the best productions of the modern African literary scene – *A Grain of Wheat, A Man of the People, The Beautyful Ones Are Not Yet Born* – were conceived as protest literature. Why then should the South African writer not thank his luck for having in his hands readymade themes and plots in the persistent turmoil of oppressive racism he lives under?

Yet South African literature, both black and white, abounds in mediocrities. As late as 1965 Lewis Nkosi writing on fiction by black South Africans could say:

> With the best will in the world it is impossible to detect in the fiction of black South Africans any significant and complex talent which responds with both vigor of the imagination and sufficient technical resources to the problems posed by conditions in South Africa.[1]

Nkosi was particularly critical of what he called 'journalistic fact parading outrageously as imaginative literature', which abounds in most of the fiction. This, he thought, showed a lack of stylistic skills which other writers on the continent had long mastered. The South African black writer was working in a vacuum, writing as if Dostoevsky or Joyce had never lived. He ended by presenting concrete reality with cinematic accuracy but untransmuted by the creative imagination into art. Wilfred Cartey referred to the same weakness as 'an objective literary intellectualism that fails to produce a subjective emotional involvement'.[2] Nadine Gordimer explains the predominance of biographical writing in South Africa by the need to satisfy curiosity.[3] And this may also explain these writers' preoccupation with the concrete – in a society where the concrete is a revelation of man's inhumanity to man. Black poetry also displays a similar thinness of perception. There is too much surface anguish and bitterness; too much of what Dennis Brutus calls the 'raw experience' untransmuted into art.

Both Afrikaans and English writers display strange aberrations of vision. There is escapism into fantasy like those writing in the Haggard school. Some opt for mystic primitivism like Van der Post. Others take to lyrical evocation of natural beauty of the countryside, like Olive Schreiner, Percy Fitzpatrick, Carey Slater, Eugene Marais, J. D. Du Toit, and Uys Krige. And some take to the safe haven of historical themes. So successful has escapist literature been among the Afrikaners that up to 1972 no Afrikaner book had been banned and a sympathetic critic could write: 'While English and African writers unendingly examine and analyse the life around them, very little has been done in Afrikaans that admits the real difficulties of our racial situation.'[4] This literature cannot be about real people, for under South Africa's totalitarian laws, people live racially. And it speaks much for the self-imposed blindness of most white intellectuals in that country that a critic like Randolph Vigne would cast aspersions on Paton and Gordimer by calling them 'race relations writers' who are 'turning away from the human situations that first gave them the incentive to write'.[5] He does not say which situation in South Africa can be classified as human. But the whole thing is more farcical than that. Vigne's criticism of Gordimer is that 'much of what happens [in her stories] does so because this is South Africa and not because this is life'[6] (whatever that means). Gordimer speaks contemptuously of certain novelists whose works are 'propaganda with a story', apparently Paton being one.[7] Dennis Brutus, on his part, finds that Gordimer 'lacks warmth, lacks feeling, but can observe with a detachment, with the coldness of a machine'.[8] Apparently, none of these writers and critics have risen above the all-encompassing witchweed of the apartheid 'laager'. And they are all at different stages of calling their particular slavery freedom.

The worst aberration of the white South African novelist's vision shows itself in his characterization of blacks, which arises from his sense of guilt. Silent black faces or servants often appear at convenient places to be recipients of white charity, real or verbal. The African characters themselves are distorted to suit the white man's quest for forgiveness – as in Paton's *Cry the Beloved Country*. Often the whites present a strange psychopathic condition which is exacerbated by the presence of black men.

Above all, both black and white literature in South Africa is one-eyed literature; concentrating on one section of the racial spectrum. The artist has no choice. He knows his clan or tribe or race more than he will ever know others. The state presents him with a racial referant with which to interpret what he sees, hears, and thinks. The conclusion of Ezekiel Mphahlele is unavoidable:

> . . . as long as the white man's politics continue to impose on us a ghetto existence, so long shall the culture and therefore literature of South Africa continue to shrivel up, to sink lower and lower; and for so long shall we in our writing continue to reflect only a minute fraction of life.[9]

One should never look at the formidable list of censorship provisions in South African laws as the only impediments the government imposes on the creative writer. All repressive legislation in South Africa impedes the work of the artist. But that as many acts as listed here would carry some censorship provision of one form or other shows how determined the South African government is to destroy freedom of expression. The following carry the most restrictive provisions: the Bantu Administration Act (1927), Riotous Assemblies Act (1956), Entertainment (Censorship) Act (1931), Suppression of Communism Act (1950), Criminal Law Amendment Act (1953), Customs Act (1955), Extension of University Education

Act (1959), Prisons Act (1959), Unlawful Organizations Act (1960), Publication and Entertainments Act (1963), General Law Amendment Act (1963), Criminal Procedure Act (1965), Terrorism Act (1967), General Law Amendment Act (1969).[10] And there are more.

The total effect of these acts is to create an inescapable web around the proposed publication. The Publications Control Board, formed in 1963 amidst a storm of protest, decides what is to be published. But in addition to considering if the contents of the book are objectionable, it must also check if the writer is listed as a member of the Communist Party, or any banned organization, or if he is prohibited from attending public gatherings. The reason for stopping one from attending public gatherings might not at all be connected with one's work as a writer. In other words, the banning of a book may not in any way be connected with its contents. Even if the Board acted with unwonted faithfulness to reasonable common sense, and decided to judge a book upon its contents, still it would be caught in the inescapable net of those elastic phrases that virtually allow the interpreter of the law to be the law-giver. How could one ever write a book which, in the South African context, may be interpreted as innocent of promoting 'feelings of hostility between Natives and Europeans', or 'engendering feelings of hostility between the European inhabitants of the Union on the one hand, and any other section of the inhabitants on the other', or 'representing antagonistic relations between capital and labour, or making reference to controversial international politics, or carrying scenes of intermingling between Black and White or of pugilistic encounters between them' or furthering 'any of the aims of communism' or unlikely to cause someone to contravene 'any law by way of protest' or free of anything the Board could consider 'on any ground whatsoever objectionable'.[11] I have deliberately quoted phrases from these acts at such length just to show that when it comes to censorship, South Africans think it such a serious business that they do not mind subjecting themselves to the most stultifying redundancy. It is clear too from these phrases that most people in the country have broken some provision of the censorship regulations. In fact, if these laws were enforced by an independent and impartial juror, the Hansards of the South African Parliament would certainly be banned. The writer in South Africa publishes only by the grace of the government.

The operation of these censorship laws had led to the banning of an estimated 15,000 books by March 1971.[12] Booksellers are failing to keep up with the rate of the bannings and Dr Peter Garlick, while on a tour of the country in 1973, found a businessman making money from printing an up-to-date list of the latest banned titles for the benefit of the booksellers. The writings and speeches of 750 persons, including all the best-known

African and coloured writers, have been banned under the Suppression of Communism Act.[13] All the best-known African and coloured writers live in exile. These include Ezekiel Mphahlele, Dennis Brutus, Lewis Nkosi, Mazisi Kunene, Bloke Modisane, Alex La Guma, Peter Abrahams, Alfred Hutchinson, Arthur Nortje, Todd Matchikiza, Noni Jabavu . . . Some English and Boer writers too have left, among them well-known names like Roy Campbell, William Plomer, Laurens van der Post, Dan Jacobson, and C. J. Driver. Many writers have committed suicide in desperation: including three Afrikaner poets, according to one source,[14] and at least twice as many black writers, among them the journalists Can Themba and Nat Nakasa. The leading and prize-winning Afrikaner writer Breytenbach (now imprisoned) has lived in exile in Paris, because he married a Vietnamese, thus breaking the 'tribal' morality of the Boers. The authorities seized Alan Paton's passport in 1962; after a showing of his play *The Blood-Knot* in London in 1967, the playwright Athol Fugard also lost his passport. Every single writer worth the name has had to suffer in some way from the heavy hand of the law, because he is a writer.

This is where the analogy between the writer in South Africa, and either Soviet Russia or the French Enlightenment, breaks down. It is true that men like Voltaire and Rousseau, or Dostoevsky and Pasternak, experienced as much torture, imprisonment, and even flogging and exile, as Dennis Brutus or Alex la Guma. But in the days of Voltaire or Dostoevsky, censorship had not yet been developed into such a viciously meticulous science with a well-trained and permanent bureaucratic corps to enforce it. Even in Soviet Russia there are still some mitigating factors which permit Russians to create under repression in a way a South African writer cannot.

Most outstanding among these factors is the fact that the South African situation is racial. The ultimate logic of all racial repression is either mass extermination of a people or their permanent enslavement. Because of the economic necessity to keep at hand a vast human reservoir of cheap labour, the ruling Boers have not as yet committed themselves to Hitler's methods of mass extermination, but they are already committed to a course of slow but equally murderous economic genocide. There is mounting evidence of the extraordinarily high infant mortality in the impoverished homelands. One report puts the figure at 50 per cent.[15] One missionary found the graveyard in a new settlement 'so full that [he] gave up the attempt of trying to count the more recent graves at 200'.[16] Malnutrition claimed 40,000 African lives in 1967.[17] According to a 1972 UN report, 'a coloured child dies of malnutrition every 35 minutes and two African children die during the same time'.[18] Cases of tuberculosis rose to 63,787 among Africans compared to 824 among Europeans in 1970. And in the city, where according to the London *Financial Times*, black miners' wages were no higher than they were in 1911, the government census put infant mortality among blacks at 102·2 per 1,000 in 1960, as compared to 21 per 1,000 among whites.[19] Since 1960 the South African government has refused to issue any statistical data on the infant mortality and related matters among Africans. These facts must be remembered when one tries to analyse the plight of a black writer in South Africa. He is a member of the oppressed masses who live under the murderous sword of a white tribe sworn to a perpetual enslavement and mass slaughter of the black race. Where, for example, does the black writer belong in this statement of policy by the late Prime Minister, Henrik Verwoerd, to Parliament in 1953?

> ... if the native in South Africa today, in any kind of school in exis-
> tence is being taught to expect that he will live his adult life under a
> policy of equal rights, he is making a big mistake. There is no place for
> him in the European community above the level of certain forms of
> labour ...[20]

It is not entirely because of what he writes that the writer is persecuted in South Africa, but perhaps even more importantly, because of who he is. An educated black man, with a sensitive perceptive insight into men and their affairs, is the very embodiment of revolt to the apartheid mentality. Hence, the black writer is not always just banned from writing against the government; he is often banned from writing at all. The very act of putting pen to paper can be outlawed, as Dennis Brutus and Can Temba ultimately found out.[21] Perhaps no country in the world has used this form of censorship before.

The South African writer also lacks the mitigating influence of a popular literary tradition to soften the harshness of the ruler. In spite of their persecution, men like Rousseau and Voltaire were patronized and fêted by despotic monarchs like Catherine the Great, Frederick the Great, and Joseph II. Princesses dressed themselves like shepherd maids to affect the Rousseauist fad of a return to nature. One historian says: 'When Voltaire appeared at a reception, fashionable ladies turned pale and threw them-selves into his arms, while at the sight of Rousseau they burst into tears...'[22] Compare that with the case of Breytenbach. When his translation of *Hamlet* was being produced in South Africa, the public clamoured for the removal of his name from the programme because he had committed the unpatriotic act of marrying a Vietnamese girl. Dennis Brutus admits that he had no literary comrades all the time he was writing in South Africa, and that his only inspiration came from the students to whom he was teaching creative writing.[23] And Lewis Nkosi shows how the literary few in the African township are an alienated minority ridiculed even by gangsters.[24] The Jewish community that he extols as custodian of literary culture in South Africa is perhaps too small and too far removed from the seat of power to diffuse its graces into the basic fibres of South Africa's spiritual philistinism. The South African writer cannot make this profession of faith made by Alexander Solzhenitsyn in his Nobel Prize speech: '. . . . the convincingness of a true work of art is completely irrefutable, and it forces even an opposing heart to surrender'.[25] Such faith must have grown out of daily experiences with thousands of Russians who read and love good literature – people like the 14,000 Muscovites who gathered in the Luzhniki Sports Stadium in November 1962, to hear even their less-approved poets read their works.[26] What would a writer devoted to his craft not dare to write in such a country?

Solzhenitsyn's profession of faith would in fact sound ludicrous if it were made by a South African writer. What another writer has called the apartheid mentality of the Boers is in fact a variant of the same psychopathic condition displayed by rulers like Stalin and Hitler. And I know of no more accurate definition of this phenomenon than the one made by the American psychoanalyst, Lawrence Kubie:

> The measure of mental health is flexibility, the freedom to learn through experience, the freedom to change with changing internal and external circumstances, to be influenced by reasonable argument, admonition, exhortation and the appeal to emotions; the freedom to respond appropriately to the stimulus of reward and punishment, and especially freedom to cease when sated. The essence of normality is flexibility, in all these vital ways. The essence of illness is the freezing of behaviour into unalterable and unsatiable patterns. It is this which characterizes every manifestation of psychopathology whether in impulse, purpose, act or feeling . . .[27]

The Afrikaners are indeed a strange breed of men, produced by a tempestuous history of wars, hardship, and poverty. Clinging together like frightened men on a raft in a storm, they seem to have had their sensibilities atrophied into a fatalistic blind imperviousness to common sense and normal human feeling. They would not be moved by the literary word however high the level of artistry. For a Pasternak or a Solzhenitsyn, the international public might make significant noises that might save them from prison. But it is the 5,818 million rand of foreign investment that prevails in South Africa. And when the chips are down, a predominantly white world is not going to spill much sweat on the fate of a black writer who is arrested for denouncing their kith and kin.

One must pay tribute to so many South Africans who have continued to write under a system so calculated to eliminate their craft.

The cultures of South Africa are seriously impoverished. The country's history has been too much one of cataclysmic wars and perennial migrations: the wars and migrations of the Mfecane, the treks and attendant wars of the Boers, the perennial movements of Boer and African populations into the cities in search of livelihood, and the uprooting and replanting of African populations prescribed by apartheid laws and that is still going on. Added to this has been the compartmentalization of ethnic groups into exclusive units. The total result has been to destroy the cohesiveness of old African communities without the development of a new culture enriched by a diversity of constituent influences, yet expressing a unified and proudly accepted outlook of a South African nation. 'And it is out of culture', writes Gordimer, 'from which man's inner being is enriched as the substance in an integrated community grows fuller, that a literature draws its real sustenance in the long run.'[28] Great literature generally operates through the stable vision of a traditional outlook, steeped in the illuminating symbolism of a rich past. South African society is sadly lacking in these graces, and a writer tends to work in a vacuum.

Many critics have remarked on the extreme state of alienation in which characters in many South African novels and short stories are presented. Few perhaps realize that many of these characters come from South Africa's bastard cultures. The country is, in fact, built upon the principle of bastardization. The ruling Boers speak Afrikaans unrecognizable by speakers of the original Dutch; they believe in a Christianity that is the very antithesis of the parent religion; there are Africans that can speak no African language at all; and others who are so alienated from their traditional cultures that they search desperately for literary heroes with whom they can identify.[29] In the compounds of the mining towns one meets a diverse congregation of peoples from all over southern Africa, with no common language of their own, but communicating through an obscene tongue called Kitchen-Kaffir, developed in the master-servant dealings of Boers and their black workers. Worst of all, these city workers are often forbidden to bring their families with them. The Deputy Minister of Justice had among his top priorities in 1969 the repatriation into the reserves of 3,800,000 dependants of African city workers.[30] In Langa Township in 1965, the ratio between men and women was 8 to 1.[31] When you add to a society so composed the predatory raids of the police, the irritants of curfew laws, pass laws, low wages and overcrowding, the result is explosive. Lewis Nkosi writes:

Drinking, violence and sex bound people together as nothing else did, for even murder was a form of affirmation of one's presence and vitality; the desperate tsotsi finally striking out, attempting to feel or assert his own sense of being in a cruel and unthinking environment.[32]

Such is the raw material out of which the creative artist is expected to write his great novel, poem, or short story. But the black writer in South Africa does not, unlike in other countries, belong to a bourgeois class of detached *élites*, that can come to observe the masses and return to the tranquillity of their refined suburbia to write. They live these violent experiences day and night. Lewis Nkosi rightly sees this as a major impediment to writing:

> It is not so much the intense suffering (though this helped a great deal) which makes it impossible for black writers to produce long and complex works of literary genius as it is the very absorbing violent and immediate nature of experience which impinges upon individual life. Unless literature is assumed to be important in itself, for its own sake, unless it is assumed to be its own justification, there was no reason whatever, why anyone in our generation should have wanted to write. It seems to me that literature begins where life fails; in Johannesburg; there was much too much of this direct experience to be had; there was no privacy in which to reflect . . .[33]

The actual logistics of writing a work of creative literature thus constitute a problem for one living in a township in South Africa. Ezekiel Mphahlele, however, did write. But he agrees with Nkosi that the amount of extended concentration required for a full-length novel is difficult to maintain. 'The short story, therefore, serves as an immediate intense concentrated form of unburdening yourself, and you must unburden yourself', he writes. But the mere act of unburdening oneself of feelings of anger, frustration, and bitterness cannot amount to a literature of any artistic value. It has resulted in too much journalism and too little art.

The South African cultural scene is certainly not conducive to the flowering of creative literature. Frontier societies generally are not. The government's repressive laws are killing off a literature that would probably have had little potential for greatness even under a liberal regime.

Alexander Solzhenitsyn would probably disagree with all this. To Brutus's statement that Nadine Gordimer's lack of warmth and feeling illustrates how the South African situation dehumanizes even the artist himself, Solzhenitsyn would probably point to his own experiences as an example of how artistic vision cannot be destroyed by adversity. He writes, 'And in misfortune, and even at the depths of existence, in destitution, in prison, in sickness, his [the artist's] sense of stable harmony never deserts him.'[34] There is a paradox here: the paradox embodied in the work of that other Russian poet, Sinyavsky, for whom twelve years of prison 'brought him face to face with his own ideas, and with a world that intellectuals as a rule know little about; and most important of all, they taught him to sit still'.[35] To sit still, to be reduced to the four walls of a prison cell and just *sit still* . . . This extreme form of human torture became a blessing in disguise, and Sinyavsky was later able to say: 'To me a sheet of paper is like a forest to a fugitive.'[36] He had turned into himself and discovered a new world.

On the other hand, Dennis Brutus was imprisoned in South Africa for only eighteen months. Unlike Sinyavsky he was not permitted pen and paper, although he did some scribbling on toilet paper. Unfortunately, he lost all those poems and tried later to reconstruct them while under house arrest. The result was what he himself has called 'jagged bits' of emotional turmoil, with all the raw anguish of a fighter, but little art. It was his personal feelings, his anger, fear, frustration, bitterness that he was expressing. Sanyavsky observes: 'To write something that would stand the fullness of time you need to be altogether empty.'[37] Brutus was still too self-conscious, too full of himself to let the Muse have its way. Eddison Zvobgo, the Rhodesian poet-politician, after seven long years in prison was able to bring a whole wealth of symbolic associations from geography, space travel, to scenes of simple domestic love into one artistic cosmos, in a poem on one brick in his prison cell. 'The Bare Brick in my Prison Cell'[38] is not a cry of raw anger, bitterness, or fear; it is symbolism that illuminates the realities of human suffering everywhere. Alex la Guma also wrote his highly artistic novella, *A Walk in the Night*, while under house arrest, and after years in prison. His artistic achievement is much higher than that of writers like Mphahlele, who never went to prison.

The paradox we are confronted with can perhaps be resolved by an analysis of this statement by one prisoner in Solzhenitsyn's *The First Circle*: 'You only have power over people so long as you don't take everything away from them. But when you've robbed a man of everything, he is no longer in your power – he is free . . .'[39] Extreme deprivation, leaving a man only with himself, might be, and quite often proves, a blessing to creative art. The human spirit quite often blooms in such desolation and repression often defeats its own purpose. But where the oppressor has not taken away everything; in a situation where a Gordimer is permitted to operate in the half-light of spurious freedom, or in a situation where the black writer is permitted to operate piecemeal in occasional moments of repose from the grinding tortures of the law, the human spirit does indeed wither, the creative imagination drying with it. That is the lesson of the South African situation for art.

One disastrous effect of apartheid on the black writer is to reduce him to what one critic called a mental case. Many South African writers actually admit this. Bloke Modisane, hankering after a political 'climate where [he] could *humanize* himself', writes of a friend now in exile, 'Ezekiel Mphahlele had been writing me some letters which implied that he was on the road to a human recovery.'[40] The trouble arises from the necessity to live lawlessly in South Africa if one is to live at all. Nat Nakasa's case is most illustrative. While he was still editing the *Classic*, he received numerous letters from his friend in exile, all miserable, because:

After a lifetime of illegal living in the republic's shebeens, the exiles are suddenly called upon to be respectable, law-abiding citizens. Not a law to break in sight . . .
For my part, it would be an act of providence if I survived under such circumstances . . .[41]

In fact, when Nat Nakasa went into exile he committed suicide within a year.

The psychological crises of the African writer are amply illustrated by the tortuous, anguished, and violent mental states revealed in both style and content of the autobiographies of Nkosi, Modisane, and Mphahlele. Plagued by nightmarish encounters with the police, confined in every endeavour by pass laws, curfew laws, job reservation laws, drinking laws, public convenience restrictions, etc., and above all being sensitive, perceptive men who can understand the machinations of the oppressor, much more than others, the black writer is in fact a sick man, who should be congratulated for ever having written at all.

An additional difficulty to the creative artist in South Africa, especially the black writer, is that life itself is too fantastic to be outstripped by the creative imagination. Nkosi calls the theme of the absurd a theme of daily living in South Africa. Indeed, many writers of the absurd school would find their plots too realistic to startle anybody into serious questioning of their deeper meaning. How would the quarrel over a bench in Edward Albee's *Zoo Story* startle anybody in a country where thousands of people have been daily quarrelling over who should sit on a particular park bench, and the country's parliament has had to legislate on the matter? That's much more startling than Albee's little quarrel between two men. And Kafka himself would not have bettered the case told by Lewis Nkosi. He was arrested by a policeman who then phoned his superior to ask, 'What shall I charge him with?'[42] Or the incident of a white man and a coloured woman who were tried for being caught kissing. The court got bogged down over the question of whether the kiss was 'platonic or passionate'. One white reporter who covered the case for a local paper wrote: 'Lawyers and laymen are certain that the Minister of Justice will now have to consider an amendment to the law which will define the various degrees of kissing from the platonic to the passionate.'[43] Or what would Camus do with the story of a wife who did not mourn her husband when he died because the two had sworn not to mourn each other should either die. At least Meursault and his mother, in *The Stranger*, had not been reduced to such hopelessness as to make such vows to one another.

It seems to me that artistic creation in a situation like this should be extraordinarily difficult. A writer creates heroes who live a life he himself only dreams of. His heroes do the living and experience the trials he himself only dreams of. He may have lived part of these experiences in the past, or will perhaps live them in the future, but during the period of creation he is away from them. Hence, all the potential virility, lyricism, terror, ecstasy, joy, and sorrow in his being pour out into one integrated universe of creative imagination. But if he actually lived these fancies of the imagination his work would tend to turn into mere reportage, operating within circumscribed limits of real fear, real frustration, real ecstasy, and real joy, instead of flowing freely into the more limitless avenues of imaginary fear, imaginary frustration, imaginary joy, and imaginary sorrow.

Furthermore, the process of artistic creation involves a painfully beautiful psychical birth of an integrated artistic symbol that illuminates reality. The delivery is a kind of foetal purgation, that leaves the writer empty for a while. But the newly born artistic foetus cannot return to plague the writer again. In the South African situation it seems to me that the fantastic nature of daily living effects a daily purging of that 'protoplasmic' stuff which would otherwise grow into this artistic foetus. For the fantastic and absurd event with which to illuminate life is itself the lived-in reality.

Although creative literature is so clearly being killed by the South African government, one should never rule out the sudden and unexpected appearance of an exceptional talent. Such a welcome apparition would do well to mend the errors of contemporary writers by re-directing his creative vision to the celebration of life through love that we so often read of in passages like this:

> Whatever else Sophiatown was, it was home; we made the desert bloom; made alterations, converted half-verandas into kitchens decorated the houses and filled them with music. We were house-proud. We took the ugliness of life in a slum & wove a kind of beauty; we established bonds of human relationships which set a pattern of communal living . . .[44]

It is this indestructible human spirit, blooming through love, friendship, and zest for living even in a slum, that even protest literature must celebrate. The reader must identify himself with something heroic, noble, and almost sacrosanct in the lives of characters presented. He must be made to fall in love with intensely human characters, tenaciously clutching at each other as invaluable objects of love and personal concern. The protest should thus be expressed indirectly by showing how apartheid interferes with this rich life.

One of the bitterest criticisms ever made against a regime is summed up in those off-hand but icy two sentences that report the death of Lara in *Dr Zhivago*. They kill a Lara whom the reader has come to love as an extremely beautiful soul. Pasternak had marshalled all his literary genius to building up that image of his heroine. He had demonstrated the intensity of passion between Yury and Lara, ennobled by an almost divine visitation of poetic creativity in the former. But then comes the cruel truth:

> One day Lara went out and did not come back. She must have been arrested in the street, as so often happened in those days, and she died or vanished, somewhere, forgotten, as a nameless number on a list which later was mislaid in one of the innumerable mixed or women's concentration camps in the north.[45]

After what had gone on in the book, those lines present the reader with an outrage that he can't forgive. The protest is complete. But it is the affirmation of human values that made it effective, and the political system appeared only as a desecration of something rich, human, and noble.

If our extraordinary literary genius emerges in South Africa, and somehow triumphs against those factors I have presented as impediments to literature, it is hoped that he might produce a work that would stand as a literary masterpiece as well as a protest against an anti-human system.

### Notes and References

1. Lewis Nkosi, *Home and Exile* (London, 1965), p. 125.
2. Wilfred Cartey, *Whispers from a Continent* (New York, 1969), p. 112.
3. Nadine Gordimer, 'The Novel and the Nation in South Africa', in *African Writers on African Writing*, ed. G. D. Killam (London, 1973), p. 45.
4. Randolph Vigne, 'The Literature of South Africa', in *The Commonwealth Pen*, ed. A. L. McLeod (Ithaca, 1961), p. 91.
5. ibid., p. 96.
6. ibid., p. 96.
7. Nadine Gordimer, 'The Novel and the Nation in South Africa', p. 38.
8. Dennis Brutus, 'Protest Against Apartheid', in *Protest and Conflict in African Literature*, ed. Cosmo Pieterse and Donald Munro (London, 1969), p. 97.
9. Ezekiel Mphahlele, *The African Image* (London, 1962), p. 109.
10. Frene Ginwala, *The Press in South Africa* (Unit on Apartheid, UN No. 24/72) pp. 24–9.

11. ibid., p. 26.
12. *Books Banned in South Africa* (Unit on Apartheid, UN Publication No. 13/71), p. 1.
13. Unit on Apartheid No. 16/72, UN, August 1972, p. 44.
14. Bahadur Tejani, 'Prison Poems of Dennis Brutus', in *Standpoints on African Literature*, ed. Chris L. Wanjali (Nairobi, 1973), p. 325.
15. Julian R. Friedman, in Unit on Apartheid No. 5/72, UN, February 1972, p. 5.
16. Cited in William J. Pomeroy's *Apartheid Axis* (New York, 1971), p. 22.
17. op. cit.
18. *Unit on Apartheid*, No. 16/72, UN 8/72, p. 29.
19. ibid., p. 28.
20. Cited in Pomeroy, p. 19.
21. Dennis Brutus in *Conflict*, p. 94. Lewis Nkosi, 'Can Temba,' *Transition*, ed. Rajat Neogy, Kampala, Uganda, Dec./Jan. 1968, VII, 3, p. 40.
22. Gaetano Salvemini, *The French Revolution 1788–1792* (New York, 1954), p. 52.
23. Dennis Brutus, interview with the author, March 1974.
24. Lewis Nkosi, *Home and Exile*, p. 18.
25. Alexander Solzhenitsyn, Nobel Lecture in Literature in *Quest 81, Journal of Ideas*, March–April 1973, ed. V. V. John and G. D. Parikh, (Bombay), p. 20.
26. Patricia Blake, 'New Voices in Russian Writing', in *Encounter*, December 1962, ed. Melvin Lasky, London.
27. Lawrence S. Kubie, *Neurotic Distortion of the Creative Process* (New York, 1970), pp. 20–1.
28. Nadine Gordimer, in *African Writers on African Writing*, p. 36.
29. Lewis Nkosi, *Home and Exile*, p. 8.
30. *Unit on Apartheid* No. 16/72, UN, August 1972, p. 9.
31. ibid., p. 10.
32. Lewis Nkosi, *Home and Exile*, p. 17.
33. ibid., p. 17.
34. Alexander Solzhenitsyn, *Quest*, p. 20.
35. Henry Gifford, 'Andrey Sinyavsky,' in *Encounter*, February 1974, ed. Melvin Lasky, London, p. 36.
36. op. cit.
37. op. cit.
38. Eddison Zvobgo (c) 1972 for *Black Lanes*, ed. Tafirenyika Moyana (unpublished anthology).
39. Alexander Solzhenitsyn, *The First Circle*, cited in *Quest*, p. 31.
40. Bloke Modisane, *Blame Me on History* (New York, 1963), p. 250.
41. Nat Nakasa, 'Castles in the Air', in *The Classic*, Joubert Park, Johannesburg, South Africa, II, 1, 1966, p. 26.
42. Lewis Nkosi, *Home and Exile*, p. 36.
43. ibid., p. 38.
44. Bloke Modisane, p. 16.
45. Boris Pasternak, *Doctor Zhivago* (New York, 1958), translated Max Hayward and Manya Harari, p. 503.

# English-Language Literature and Politics in South Africa

▼▼▼▼▼▼▼▼▼▼▼▼▼▼▼▼▼▼▼▼▼▼▼▼▼▼▼▼▼▼▼

## NADINE GORDIMER

PEAKING of South Africa, the association of politics with literature produces a snap equation: censorship. But is that the beginning and end of my subject? Indeed, it may be the end, in a literal sense, of a book or a writer: the book unread, the writer silenced. But censorship is the most extreme, final, and above all, most obvious effect of politics upon a literature, rather than the sum of the subject. Where and when, in a country such as South Africa, can the influence of politics on literature be said to begin? Politics, in the form of an agent of European Imperialism – the Dutch East India Company – brought the written word to this part of Africa; politics, in the form of European missionaries who spread, along with their Protestantism or Catholicism, the political influence of their countries of origin, led to the very first transposition of the indigenous oral literature to the written word. When the first tribal praise-poem was put down on paper, what a political act that was! What could be communicated only by the mouth of the praise-singer to the ears of those present, was transmogrified into a series of squiggles on paper that could reach far beyond his living physical presence, beyond even the chain of memory of those who came after him. With that act a culture took hold upon and was taken hold upon by another.

Doesn't the subject begin quite simply, right there? And doesn't it extend – not simply at all – through the cultural isolation of whites who left their Europe over three centuries ago as the result of political events such as the revocation of the Edict of Nantes, the Napoleonic wars, the pogroms of Eastern Europe; does it not extend through the cultural upheaval of blacks under conquest; and the cultural ambiguity of the children one race fathered upon the other? The relationship of politics to literature in South Africa implies all of this, just as it does the overtly political example of writers forced into exile, and the subsequent development of their writings within the changed consciousness of exile. For some books are banned, and so South Africans never read them. But all that is and has been written by South Africans is profoundly influenced, at the deepest and least controllable level of consciousness, by the politics of race. All writers everywhere – even those like Joyce who can't bear to live in their own countries, or those like Genet who live outside the pale of their country's laws – are shaped by their own particular society reflecting a particular political situation. Yet there is no country in the western world where the daily enactment of the law reflects politics as intimately and blatantly as in South Africa. There is no country in the western world where the creative imagination, whatever it seizes upon, finds the focus of even the most private event set in the overall social determination of racial laws.

I am not going to devote any time, here, to outlining or discussing how the Publications Control Board, the censorship system, works in South Africa. I take it that anyone interested in South African literature is familiar with the facts. But lest it be thought that I pass over that matter of censorship lightly, let me remark aside that personally, although I myself have continued and shall continue to bang my head in protesting concert against that particular brick in the granite wall, my fundamental attitude is that South Africans cannot expect to rid themselves of the Publications Control Board until they get rid of apartheid. Censorship is an indispensable part of an interlocking system of repressive laws.

There are other forms of censorship in South Africa. Anyone under a political ban may not be published or quoted; which means that the books of a number of white writers in exile, and those of a number of black writers in exile and at home, are automatically banned, no matter what their subject or form. Through this kind of censorship, the lively and important group of black writers who burst into South African literature in the 'fifties and early 'sixties disappeared from it as if through a trap-door. A young black writer, Don Mattera, went the same way in 1973. Only those of us who care particularly for literature and writers remember; by the time the newspaper has been left behind on the breakfast table, most people have forgotten the banned authors and books listed there – the ultimate triumph of censorship.

I have said that South African literature was founded in an unrecorded political act: the writing down in Roman characters of some tribal praise-song. But the potted histories in academic theses always set its beginning with the writings of a white settler, an Englishman, Thomas Pringle. He was born the year the French Revolution started and came to South Africa in 1820, under the British government scheme of assisted immigration resorted to because of the agricultural depression in England that followed Waterloo. For we white South Africans may somewhat unkindly be called, as Norman Mailer did his fellow Americans, 'a nation of rejects transplanted by the measure of every immigration of the last three hundred and fifty years'. Pringle led a Scottish party to settle on the border of the so-called Neutral Territory of the Cape from which the Xhosa people had been driven. Thus far, he is a classic white frontiersman; but this Scottish scribbler of album verse at once felt the awkward necessity to adapt his late Augustan diction and pastoral sentimentality to the crude events of Africa:

> First the brown Herder with his flock
> Comes winding round my hermit-rock
> His mien and gait and vesture tell,
> No shepherd he from Scottish fell;
> For crook the guardian gun he bears, . . .
> Nor Flute has he, nor merry song . . .
> But, born the white man's servile thrall,
> Knows that he cannot lower fall.

Pringle was never quite to find the adequate vocabulary for what moved him to write in Africa (Coleridge deplored his archaisms) but he anticipated, astonishingly, themes that were not to be taken up again by any writer in South Africa for a hundred years, and longer. Unlike the majority of his fellow frontiersmen he refused to regard the cattle raids carried out by the Xhosa as proof that they were irredeemable savages. In a poem entitled 'The Caffer' he asks awkward questions of the whites:

> He is a robber? – True; it is a strife
> Between the black-skinned bandit and the white,
> (A Savage? – Yes, though loth to aim at life,
> Evil for evil fierce he doth requite.
> A heathen? – Teach him, then, thy better creed,
> Christian! If thou deserv'st that name indeed.)

He foreshadowed the contemporary South African liberal view – obliquely comforting to the white conscience, but none the less true – that any form of slavery degrades oppressor as well as the oppressed:

> The Master, though in luxury's lap he loll
> . . . quakes with secret dread, and shares the hell he makes.

Pringle was one of the first and is one of the few whites ever to grant that black men also have their heroes. He wrote a poem about the Xhosa prophet Makana who led an army of 10,000 tribesmen on the British settlement at Grahamstown in 1819:

Wake! Amakosa, wake!
And arm yourselves for war.
As coming winds the forest shake,
I hear a sound from far:
It is not thunder in the sky,
Nor lion's roar upon the hill
But the voice of HIM who sits on high
And bids me speak his will ...
To sweep the White Men from the earth
And drive them to the sea.

Pringle even wrote of love across the colour-line, long before miscegena-
tion laws made it a statutory crime and the Immortality Act provided the
theme of so many South African novels and stories. A young Boer speaks:

Our Father bade each of us choose a mate
Of Fatherland blood, from the *black* taint free
As became a Dutch Burgher's proud degree.
My brothers they rode to the Bovenland,
And each came with a fair bride back in his hand;
But *I* brought the handsomest bride of them all –
Brown Dinah, the bondmaid who sat in our hall.
My Father's displeasure was stern and still;
My Brothers' flamed forth like a fire on the hill;
And they said that my spirit was mean and base,
To lower myself to the servile race.

The young Boer asks:

Dear Stranger, from England the free,
What good tidings bring'st thou for Arend Plessie?
Shall the Edict of Mercy be sent forth at last,
To break the harsh fetters of Colour and Caste?

Pringle himself was back in England after only six years in South Africa,
hounded out of the Cape Colony by the English Governor, Lord Charles
Somerset, for his fight against press censorship. This had been introduced
to protect the British colonial regime against any mention of those controversial issues of the time, slavery, the condition of the black, and the anti-
British feelings of the Boers.

After Pringle had been packed off 'home' in 1826, a long colonial silence
fell. Diaries were kept, chronicles were written by white missionaries and
settlers, but no soundings were put down to the depths reached only in
imaginative writing until Olive Schreiner wrote *The Story of an African
Farm* in the 1880s. It is a very famous book and one that, as a South
African remembering it as a mind-opening discovery of adolescence, one
tends to think of as all-encompassing: that is to say, that final accomplish-
ment, the central themes of South African life given unafraid and yet

non-exhibitionist expression by a writer whose skill is equal to them. But reading it again – and it is a book that stands up to re-reading – one finds that of course it isn't that at all. It is one of those open-ended works whose strength lies at the level where human lives – our own and the book's characters' – plunge out of grasp. The freedom that Lyndall, one of the two extraordinary main characters, burns for, is not the black man's freedom but essentially spiritual freedom in the context of the oppression of women through their sexual role; yet the passion of revolt is so deeply understood that it seems to hold good for all sufferings of oppression. The society Lyndall rejects is the shallow white frontier society; yet the rejection questions societal values that gave rise to it and will endure beyond it. It is a book whites in South Africa like to think of, also as transcending politics; I have never met a black who has read it, with – ironically – the important exception of Richard Rive, who has just completed a book about Olive Schreiner's life and work. Certainly no black could ever have written *African Farm*. The alienation of Lyndall's longing to 'realize forms of life utterly unlike mine' is attempted transcendence of the isolation and lack of identity in a white frontier society; in the final analysis, this is a book that expresses the wonder and horror of the wilderness, and for the indigenous inhabitant that wilderness is home. The novel exists squarely within the political context of colonialism. Olive Schreiner's conscience was to reject colonialism, and her creative imagination to disappear in the sands of liberal pamphleteering, many years later. Perhaps she would have written no more imaginative work, anyway. But perhaps she took the conscious decision that Jean-Paul Sartre, in the context of the Pan-African struggle, has said any writer should make – to stop writing if he is needed to do any other task that, as he sees it, his country requires of him. It is certain that political pressures, in the form of a deep sense of injustice and inhumanity existing within their society, can cause certain writers to question the luxury value of writing at all, within a country like South Africa.

The establishment of South African literature in English and (so far as it existed) in African languages as a literature of dissent came in the 1920s and early 'thirties. The white man's military conquest of the blacks was over. The war between the whites, Boer and Briton, was over; the white man's other war, in which Boer and black had fought under the British flag along with the Briton, was over. In the State of Union of the four South African countries, the British Cape Colony and Natal, the Boer republics of the Orange Free State and Transvaal, blacks had been deprived of such rights as they had held at the pleasure of the more liberal of the separate governments. The black man's trusting willingness to identify his destiny with the white man's is expressed in the victory praise-song-cum-poem of

Samuel Mqhayi, a Xhosa poet of the time, who assumed a common black–
white patriotism after the 1914–18 war: 'Go catch the Kaiser, Let the
Kaiser come and talk with us/We'll tell him how the Zulus won at Sandl-
wana/Of Thaba Ntsu where the Boers were baffled . . .' The assumption
was met with rebuff and betrayal; only white men could be heroes, at home
or in Valhalla.

Then William Plomer, aged 19, published in 1925 a work of genius, a
forced flower fertilized upon an immature talent by reaction against the
racialism which had by then become entrenched under the name of a
union of the best interests of all people in South Africa. *Turbott Wolfe*
(Plomer's hero as well as the title of the novel) trails the torn umbilical
cord of colonialism; Wolfe is not a born South African but an Englishman
who plunges into Africa from without. But he understands at once: 'There
would be the unavoidable question of colour. It is a question to which
every man in Africa, black, white or yellow, must provide his answer.'
The colonial cord is ruptured, early on and for ever, for South African
literature, because Plomer's novel does not measure Africa against the
white man, but the white man against Africa. With it, a new literary
consciousness was born: that no writer could go deeply into the life around
him and avoid some sort of answer. Laurens van der Post's *In a Province*
is awake to it, concerned with modern Africans in conflict with white-
imposed values rather than Africans as exotic scenic props in the white
man's story. So, fighting against it all the way, is Sarah Gertrude Millin's
*God's Stepchildren*. This extraordinarily talented novel begs the question,
as a kind of answer, by revealing the morality South Africa has built on
colour and the suffering this brings to people of mixed blood, but nowhere
suggesting that the sense of sin suffered by Barry Lindsell, play-white
grandson of a white missionary and a Hottentot woman, is tragically,
ludicrously, and wastefully misplaced, until Barry Lindsell confesses to his
young English wife that he has black blood and she says in surprised relief:
'Is that all?'

Meanwhile, the novel has shown that it is, indeed, everything, in the life
around her from which the author drew her substance.

Roy Campbell was the third of the famous triumvirate – Plomer, Van der
Post, Campbell – who began in the 'twenties the tradition of exile, often
self-imposed, that has afflicted South African literature ever since.
Although accepted and anthologized as one of those who (in his words
about William Plomer) 'dared alone to thrash a craven race/And hold a
mirror to its dirty face', Campbell provides a fascinating example of the
strange and complex mutations brought about by the effect of politics upon
writers and literature in South Africa.

Campbell was a writer whose work may be lifted like a transparency to show against the light certain dark and tangled motivations where politics and the psyche struggle to accommodate one another in the South African personality. It is there that South African defence mechanisms are made. We shall see them reflected in the work of other writers, too, subconsciously producing work in answer to the need for various justificatory myths of political origin. It is believed, certainly Campbell believed, he left South Africa because the colour bar was abhorrent to him. In his poetry, he made biting and elegant attacks on white complacency. He wrote sensuously incomparable poems about blacks. But he dismissed political and social aspirations with indiscriminate contempt as 'the spoor and droppings of . . . the crowd emotions'. The attributes of the brave black hunter with which he identified were élitist rather than humanitarian, let alone egalitarian. In the context of a white man's life the hunting spirit is employed only for play, in blood-sports which are not dictated by hunger; for tribal Africans themselves, hunting is a means of existence.

I would say that Campbell left South Africa out of vanity – he did not think the whites capable of appreciating his genius. It was true; they were not. But his work did not ally itself in any way with the destiny of the blacks, either, in whose hands the culture of South Africa must ultimately become definitive. The brilliant satirical poet South Africa has never replaced ended as the last colonial, romanticizing himself as 'African' abroad, and irrevocably cut off from all but the white minority he rejected at home.

Campbell's justificatory myth was tailored to an individual need. But Pauline Smith, living in the 'twenties in the isolation of the Karoo as Schreiner did before her, created a justificatory myth of the Afrikaner people that continues to answer, in literature, to certain political pressures to this day. (I use the word 'myth' not in its primary dictionary sense of a purely fictitious narrative, but in the sense the anthropologist Claude Lévi-Strauss does, as a psychologically defensive and protective device. A myth is an extra-logical explanation of events according to the way a people wishes to interpret them.)

Pauline Smith, a writer of Chekhovian delicacy, was not an Afrikaner and she wrote in English. She wrote of rural Afrikaners, in whom her stories see poverty as a kind of grace rather than a limiting circumstance. Why? I believe that she was faithfully reflecting not a fundamental Christian view, but the guilt of the victor (British) over the vanquished (Boer), and also the curious shame that sophistication feels confronted by naivety, thus interpreting it as 'goodness'. One of the main points represented by her characters is their total unfitness to deal with the industrial society that came upon them after their defeat by the British. Her story 'The Pain' shows an old man and his dying wife terrified even by the workings of a hospital; the husband's humbleness is emphasized almost to the point of imbecility. This virtue in helplessness, in the situation of being over-whelmed by poverty, drought, economic depression, was to become a justificatory myth, in literature, of the Afrikaner in relation to the develop-ment of his part in the politics of domination. Based on it, at least in part, is the claim of Afrikaners to be a white African tribe. From Pauline Smith's stories in *The Little Karoo* through the long series of stoic novels in Afrikaans that André Brink has called 'a literature of drought and poor whites', to the tender and witty stories of an Afrikaner writing in English, Herman Charles Bosman, are Afrikaners not shown living as close to the earth and natural disasters as any black man? The measure of poverty as a *positive value* and the romanticizing of pre-industrialism into a moral virtue are important aspects of Athol Fugard's plays, when these are about whites. His white characters are the children of Pauline Smith's rural Afrikaners, forced to the towns by drought and economic depression, and their virtues lie in their helplessness, their clinging to the past, and their defeat by an 'English'-dominated industrial society. The myth poses the question: how can such people be held responsible for the degradation that racialism imposes upon the blacks? And also they themselves represent victims within the white supremacist society; are they then not in the same boat as blacks? But we know that these are the people who (like English-speaking South African whites) conquered the blacks; who built a national pride out of their defeat by the British; these are the people whose votes gained political power and legislated, once and for all, the white man's will to overlordship.

It is an ironic illustration of the effect of South African politics upon literature to remark that while, in the 'twenties, Plomer and Van der Post were writing novels exposing the colour-bar, they probably were not so much as aware of the existence of two remarkable fellow novelists of the time. The novelists were black. Thomas Mofolo's *Chaka*, written in Sesuto about 1910, was published in English in 1931, and is as extraordinary an achievement in terms of the writer's background, if not his age, as Plomer's *Turbott Wolfe*. It is, of course, a very different novel, in a way that was to be significant of the difference between white liberal or radical writings and the work of black writers themselves. It is written not *about* blacks, but reflects the identity of a black man. It is both an historical and political novel, based on fact and legend about the King Chaka, and its theme is dealt with in accordance with the author's own sense of the innate conflict in invoking Christian values to interpret an African power struggle. Mofolo, writing for original publication in a missionary journal, tried to approach the life of Chaka, the great despot, the Black Napoleon, as whites have called him, in the light of the Christian text: *What shall it profit a man, if he shall gain the whole world, and lose his own soul?* But although Mofolo presents Chaka's brutal conquering excesses against his own people as sinful blood-lust, they also represent the neurotic paroxysm of a dying nation, turning to rend itself before colonial conquest. When the spears of fratricidal assassins are meeting in Chaka's body, Mofolo has him cry: 'It is your hope that by killing me ye will become chiefs when I am dead. But ye are deluded; it will not be so, for uMlungu [the white man] will come and it is he who will rule and ye will be his bondmen.'

The guns of white conquest are cocked over Mofolo's novel, but there are no white characters in it. In Sol Plaatje's *Mhudi*, also based on historical events, and set slightly later in the nineteenth century, uMlungu makes his entry for the first time in South African black literature. The Boers appear, trekking north: 'travelling with their families in hooded wagons and driving with their caravan their wealth of livestock into the hinterland in search of some unoccupied territory to colonize and to worship God in peace'. 'But', asked Chief Moroka, 'could you not worship God on the South of the Orange River?'

'We could', replied Cillier, 'but oppression is not conducive to piety. We are after freedom. The English laws of the Cape are not fair to us.'

'We Barolong have always heard that, since David and Solomon, no king has ruled so justly as King George of England!'

'It may be so', replied the Boer leader, 'but there are always two points of view. The point of view of the ruler is not always the viewpoint of the ruled.'

Despite its stylistic crudities, the novel skilfully explores the white man's double standard slyly posited here. Barolong and Boer find a temporary identity of interest in military alliance against the armies of another African tribe, Mzilikazi's Matabele; but once the battle is won, the white man expects to dictate the sharing of spoils, that is, keeping the land for the Boers and handing over the captured cattle to the Barolong. 'What an absurd bargain', says the Chief, 'will cattle run on clouds, and their grass grow on air?' Similarly, although the white men will fight alongside the blacks, they want no personal relation with them. Juxtaposed with the power struggle between white and black there is in this book the sort of dream of its resolution in non-military, non-revolutionary, non-political terms that was to become the particular justificatory myth given expression by white liberal writers thirty years after Plaatje: a friendship between a young black and a young white. It is the literary wish-fulfilment of what South African society could be, would be, if only the facts of the power struggle conveniently could be ignored. The proposition cancels itself out. Ignored, the facts remain; they are not to be changed by turning to loving without changing the balance of power – to paraphrase Alan Paton's prophetic dictum in *Cry the Beloved Country* that by the time the whites have turned to loving, the blacks will have turned to hating. Perhaps the vision of black–white brotherhood reached its symbolic apotheosis in Athol Fugard's tragedy as *The Blood-Knot* between two men who are *actual* brothers, the skin of one reflecting the white side of their ancestry, the other the black. This friendship is a justificatory myth that embodies the yearning of many whites – and even some blacks – to escape the ugly implications of a society in which such apparently transcendental private relationships are in fact pretty meaningless, trapped in political determinism. Several of my own books explore these implications. In *Occasion for Loving* a young Englishwoman destroys a black man by indulging in a love affair with him. His flouting of the power of segregation laws leaves him, once she has gone back to England, exactly where he was: carrying a pass and drinking himself to death in the black ghetto. The prototype friendship of Ra-Thaga and Viljoen, Barolong and Boer boys in Sol Plaatje's novel survives until Viljoen sincerely offers Ra-Thaga all that a white man can, in a white-orientated society: 'I will catch Mzilikazi alive, and tie him to the wagon wheel; then Potgieter will make me his captain, and you will be my right-hand man.' And Ra-Thaga sincerely rejects the hand-out: 'Oh no! . . . what would my children think of me if I were to be the right-hand man of a wifeless youth?'

South African literature seems to have developed by curious fits and starts; the explanation lies close to political developments in the country. In the 'thirties and 'forties, of those writers whose work had been the most innovative in the 'twenties, Plomer and Van der Post were in exile, and Millin had turned her attention mainly to the domestic dramas of Pauline Smith's poor whites, now becoming industrialized in the towns. There were no more novels from Mofolo or Plaatje. Nor did any black writer emerge to follow their bold example of how black writers might (as Claude Wauthier suggests in *The Literature and Thought of Modern Africa*) reaffirm their origins, and use their present position.

For an explanation of this situation we have to look to the position of black intellectuals at the time. With General Hertzog's 'final solution' to the 'native question', as exemplified in laws such as the Land Act of 1936, blacks were beginning to realize that in South Africa, the Booker Washington faith in education as a means of gaining acceptance and a share in a common society was getting them nowhere. The eloquence of a scholarly leader like Dr Jabavu had not succeeded in gaining a recognition of civil rights for blacks when the constitution of the South African Union had been drawn up more than twenty-five years before. The eloquence of a Benedict Vilakazi, outstanding Zulu poet of the 'thirties and 'forties, did not succeed in rousing the white man to recognition of the black man's humanity, although he had the courage to tackle subjects such as the condition of black labour. A creative apathy took over among blacks, born of frustration; not for the last time.

By way of comparison, for Afrikaner writers, this was a period of consolidation, through literature, of the importance of their possession of a mother tongue distinct from those imported from Europe. In a movement that finds its parallel with the négritude movement among Caribbean and American Negroes, and Africans outside South Africa, Afrikaners were engaged in affirming their political claim through a cultural identity. Afrikaans had been a patois; it rose to become rich enough to be literary language, hand over fist, so to speak, with the climb to political power. Fine Afrikaner poets, such as Langenhoven, made it so; others, such as Van Wyk Louw and Uys Krige, internationalized it by bringing consciousness of the literary developments of the world outside into its orbit, in the field of poetry. The novelists continued to sing the saga of the rural Afrikaner, dealing with the black man as with the elements.

From the English-speaking population, little came but some poetry, sometimes fine, but often widely generalized in emotion – rather boring ontological thoughts on the Second World War. The war years had the effect, inhibitory to the development of an indigenous literature, of throwing the country back upon cultural links with Europe.

So far it had become a literature of dissent, although it was soon to build up to its strongest impetus ever, South African literature began again, after 1945, at a position somewhere behind that of William Plomer's *Turbott Wolfe*. It made a new beginning with Alan Paton's *Cry the Beloved Country*, which suggested the need of a Christian solution to the political problem of racialism. It was a book of lyrical beauty and power that moved the conscience of the outside world over racialism and, what's more, that of white South Africa, as no book had before; *Turbott Wolfe* had been too radical for them. No piece of writing was to have this effect again until the advent of Athol Fugard's plays, *The Blood-Knot* and *Boesman and Lena*, in the late 1960s and early seventies.

The decade-and-a-half through the fifties to the mid-sixties produced a paradox between English-language literature and politics. The Afrikaner Nationalists, who were to codify and implement a long-entrenched colour prejudice as apartheid, had come to power in 1948, and yet it was while this final processing of racialism was in progress that a wave of new South African writers, white and black, suddenly appeared to dig deep into the subsoil of South African society and give expression, in the dimensions of the creative imagination, to the kind of answers that 'every man, black, white or yellow' had given to Turbott Wolfe's 'question of colour'. Peter Abrahams, whose talent was given early encouragement by white leftists – for so many years the only whites prepared to take seriously the possibility of a black writer being more than a sort of quaint freak, a literary albino – wrote the first proletarian novel, *Mine Boy*, story of a black man confronted with the twin experience of industrialization and race discrimination in a city. My first novel, *The Lying Days*, published in 1953, was essentially about an experience many young white South Africans have shared. They are born twice: the second time when, through situations that differ with each individual, they emerge from the trappings of colour-consciousness that were as 'natural' to them as the walls of home and school. In his brilliant first novel, *A Dance in the Sun*, Dan Jacobson returned South African Literature to the Karoo, making of the old colonial wilderness the stony ground of self-deception, doubt and questioning. The emphasis is on what happens to whites as oppressors. White Fletcher's attitude to black Joseph, whose daughter has had a brat fathered on her by Fletcher's brother-in-law, is shown as the whole process of action and interaction between the personality of a man and the morality within which it exercises itself. The old woman in Alan Paton's *Too Late the Phalarope*, a later novel exploring the same moral theme, this time through a variation of Thomas Pringle's prophetic 'Brown Dinah' story, states a conclusion: 'We are not as other people any more.' Jack Cope, in a novel called *Albino*, made an ingenious attempt to side-step the white writer's problems of politically decreed isolation within his white skin; this is a novel about a young white boy brought up as a Zulu – in the words of one of the characters, 'a white with a black mind'.

In this period, black South Africans were beginning again to write about themselves, not in terms of the epic past but in direct terms of the present.

The central experience of urban life on the dark side of the colour-bar was bringing to paper 'the stench of real living people', as one of those writers, Lewis Nkosi, has said. The short stories of Ezekiel Mphahlele, Can Themba, Casey Motsisi, carried in Mphahlele's case by a sullen force, and in those of Themba and others jigged with a jaunty wit and self-lacerating humour, reflected survival characteristics developed by the nature of life in those human conglomerations, neither city nor suburb, now called black 'townships'. The 'townships' had in the past been more accurately called 'locations', sites chosen by whites to dump blacks outside the city limits, after work, just as they choose sites well out of the way for the city trash heap. Lewis Nkosi, in *Home and Exile*, a book of essays and literary criticism unique in South African literature, where literary criticism can scarcely be said to exist, wrote from the audacious, acrobatic position peculiar to African intellectuals in the fifties: simultaneously he is a young black who has a foot in the white liberal world, while holding his place in the black proletariat of the 'township'. Though their boldness was a reflection of confidence stemming from the existence of such movements, none of these writers gave direct expression to the black liberatory movements that drew mass support at the time, the African National Congress and Pan-Africanist Congress. Subconsciously their writings were aimed at white readers and were intended to rouse white consciousness over black frustration. Even in the writings of the most talented black novelist since Peter Abrahams, Alex la Guma, who was a political activist, and the poetry of Dennis Brutus, both later to be political prisoners on Robben Island, there was no overt commitment to a particular political line, nor did they use the vocabulary of political clichés. La Guma's moving novel *A Walk in the Night*, like his short stories set in prisons, backyards, and cheap cafés, presents men and women who don't talk about apartheid; they bear its weals, so that its flesh-and-blood meaning becomes a shocking, sensuous impact. Few South Africans have been exposed to it, however; La Guma was a banned writer before it was ever published abroad. As the black–white political tension rose, exploded at Sharpeville and culminated in mass imprisonments and the outlawing of black political movements, all these writers and more, with few exceptions, were forced into exile.

Work by white writers who tried to trace, through imaginative insights, in terms of political, social, and spiritual options open to South African whites, the motivation of the young whites who turned to sabotage against the regime in the late sixties, was banned. My novel *The Late Bourgeois World*, Mary Benson's *At the Still Point*, Jack Cope's *The Dawn Comes Twice*, C. J. Driver's *Elegy for a Revolutionary* – none of these has been read by South Africans themselves, who lived through the experience of that period. It all happened; it certainly exists within their memory; it does not officially exist in South African literature.

Again, by comparison, how was writing in Afrikaans developing in the sixties? The changes were regarded as so fundamental that their decade provided a generic term for the writers who emerged: the 'Sestigers'. In the words of one of them, André Brink, 'a conscious effort was made to broaden the hitherto parochial limits of Afrikaans fiction', to challenge certain cultural taboos in Afrikanerdom, especially the Calvinist taboos on uncompromising religious exploration, and the challenging of old moralities, especially on sexual matters. Against the background events of a country that seemed on the brink of a revolution, the Sestigers preoccupied themselves with just precisely these things, and with William Burroughs-inspired experiment in literary form. They challenged with sexual candour and religious questioning, taunting the church and the Afrikaans Academy of letters; but the evidence that not one of them published anything that was banned shows how they turned away, astonishingly, from the deepest realities of the life going on around them. The Sestigers' outstanding prose writer, and indeed the most sweeping imaginative power in South African literature as a whole, Etienne le Roux, makes the lofty claim that his trilogy, *Towards a Dubious Salvation*, is a 'metaphysical' novel; but if a writer is part of the creative consciousness of the society in which he lives, is it not a form of betrayal, of creative as well as human integrity, to choose to turn away from the messy confrontation of man with man, and address oneself to God? In fact, reading this dazzling book, you sometimes have the feeling that Etienne le Roux *is* God, an infinitely detached Olympian observer, amusing himself by recording all those absurd and dirtily flamboyant little battles and copulations way, way down on earth.

In 1974, for the first time, a book by an Afrikaans writer was banned. André Brink has written a novel that breaks the *political* taboos answering the challenge he himself published in a newspaper five years ago: 'If Afrikaans writing is to achieve any true significance within the context of the revolution of Africa (of which we form part) . . . it seems to me that it will come from those who are prepared to sling the "No!" of Antigone into the violent face of the System.' Not unpredictably, his novel suffers from the defiant exultation and relief of that cry, coming so belatedly from the Afrikaans novel, looting a newly seized freedom of expression on whose validity the seal of 'banned' was almost sure to be set. Perhaps it was inevitable that this novel should demand of its creator that it encompass all that is forbidden in the ninety-seven definitions of what the Censorship Act finds 'undesirable'; that it should roll up pell-mell all the forbidden themes and many of the cliché situations written about already by others. It follows that this novel cannot do André Brink justice, as a writer. Yet its exaggeration, its stylistic piling-up of words, images, events, like a series of blows – Take that! and that! and *that*! – remind one of the works of certain black South African writers, in which the truth is in the excesses and even absurdities because *this is the fantasy bred by our society*, it is the truth as evidence of the kind of nightmares that grow out of our kind of daylight.

That 'No!' of Antigone has come out loud and clear from Afrikaans literature only once before, and from a poet, Ingrid Jonker. Somehow she managed, without compromising her great gifts, to write a poem of the sixties that sets the era's events in a perspective that takes in past and present and projects the future as no writer, black or white, has done after her. The poem refers to the pass-burning campaigns of the African National Congress and Pan-Africanist Congress, when women and children were killed in the course of police and military action:

> The child is not dead
> the child lifts his fists against his mother
> who shouts Afrika! shouts the breath
> of freedom and the veld
> in the locations of the cordoned heart
> The child lifts his fists against his father
> In the march of the generations who are shouting Afrika!
> shout the breath
> of righteousness and blood
> in the streets of his embattled pride
> The child is not dead
> not at Langa nor at Nyanga
> nor at Orlando nor at Sharpeville
> nor at the police post in Philippi
> where he lies with a bullet through his brain
> the child is the dark shadow of the soldiers
> on guard with their rifles, saracens and batons
> the child is present at all assemblies and law-giving
> the child peers through the window of houses and into the
> hearts of mothers
> this child who wanted only to play in the sun at Nyanga is
> everywhere
> the child grown to a man treks on through all Africa
> the child grown into a giant journeys over the whole world
> without a pass.

What is the position of South African literature in the mid-seventies, the era of Bantustan independence within the country while former guerrilla movements become constitutional governments in countries round about; the era of dialogue on black–white federalism; of streaky, if not exactly thoroughly mixed sport; and of the re-emergence of mass black action in the form of striking labour forces? The series of blood-lettings over the years – writers going into exile – emphasizes the enormous influence of politics on literature not only in the obvious way – that so many writers *are* in imposed or self-imposed exile – but also in the state of South African society as reflected in their work if they continue to live here in South Africa, as opposed to the vision of the place held by writers now removed

from the actual scene. A writer as immensely gifted as Dan Jacobson, after
a series of novels rooted 'from memory', so to speak, in South Africa, has
begun to write novels thematically remote from it. Perhaps this is a liberation. Alex La Guma, in the gentle, beautifully written *In the Fog at the
Season's End*, writes, like so many black exiles, as if life in South Africa
froze with the trauma of Sharpeville. Since he is a good writer, he cannot
create at the newspaper-story level, and cannot, from abroad, quite make
the projection, at the deeper level, into a black political milieu that has
changed so much since he left. Ezekiel Mphahlele's novel *The Wanderers*
also suffers from this lack of connection. Only the poet Dennis Brutus
seems to have drawn strength from the 'bitter bread of exile' and to have
developed his gifts fully, if perhaps differently from the way he might
have at home. In a collection of poems that places him perhaps higher in
achievement than any of the younger generation, Arthur Nortje, exiled
and dead before his book *Dead Roots* was published in 1973, writes the
spiritual autobiography of exile on the most harrowing level. In the end,
he who has had to make do with crumbs from the white man's table at
home may find no stomach left for Europe's bounty: 'I drag my shrunken
corpulence/among the tables of rich libraries./Famous viands tasted like
ash . . .' These are the terrors of exile, for a writer; and the extinction of a
literature.

At home, significant South African drama in English has been created,
single-handed, by Athol Fugard. The obvious major influence of Beckett
on his work is a fascinating example of an esoteric mode, in which character
is sacrificed to symbolic abstraction, and dialogue largely disembodied,
returned to flesh and the individual involved rather than alienated. This is
an interesting example of a writer's methodological response to his socio-
political situation.

Of the new novelists – few and far between – who have emerged lately,
a black one, Bessie Head, in exile but still on the continent of Africa,
expresses an indiscriminate repugnance for *all* political aspirations in *all*
races, and a white one at home, Sheila Fugard, takes into the arcane realm
of Buddhist mysticism the old white liberal justificatory myth of the power
of love to melt racialism. One of the two most interesting newcomers,
J. M. Coetzee, with his two-part novel, *Dusklands*, links the behaviouristic
conditioning of peoples by other peoples as a congenital flaw in human
nature. His first narrative, that of a South African working in 1970 as a
United States government official on a 'New Life Project' for the people of
Vietnam, posits the choice offered by the anthropologist Franz Boas: 'if we
wish to take over the direction of a society we must either guide it from
within its cultural framework or else eradicate its culture and impose new

structures'. It does not require much insight to understand where the reader's eyes are being turned: to that other society, in South Africa, where both these techniques of socio-political manipulation have been tried upon the indigenous population. And this could lead us obediently to a conclusion: if white South Africans are no better, they are merely just as bad as other people with the will to follow up military with psychological conquest. Like them, they run the risk of losing their own souls in the contest – the narrator retreats into madness in which he has 'high hopes of finding whose fault I am'.

The second narrative is a superbly written attempt of a dubious kind to which South African white writers are beginning to turn, it seems, in unconscious search of a new justificatory myth: the explanation of the present in terms of the past; and therefore, does it not follow, a present as helplessly inexorable as the past? The narrator in this story set in 1760 goes hunting elephant and falls ill among hostile Hottentots. With a putrefying backside as the sum of his pain and humiliation, he enters the old Conradian heart of darkness. In order to survive, he must live as the people he despises as savages manage to live; he must admit, in himself, hideous instincts that he had attributed only to them. The final irony of some of his reflections would seem to make them those of a twentieth-century Coetzee, rather than an eighteenth-century one: 'To these people [the Hottentots] for whom life was nothing but a series of accidents, had I not been simply another accident? Was there nothing to be done to make them take me more seriously?' And again, 'I am an explorer. My essence is to open what is closed, to bring to light what is dark. If the Hottentots comprise an immense world of delight, it is an impenetrable world, impenetrable to men like me, who must either skirt it, which is to evade our mission, or clear it out of the way'. After his recovery and return to white settlement he goes back with a punitive expedition to the Hottentots who had both succoured and tortured him. He wipes them out in 'the desolate infinity of my power over them'. The fatalism, the detachment borrowed from history in this novel are best signified by the choice of epigraph for the second narrative, a quotation from Flaubert: 'What is important is the philosophy of history.'

Another newcomer, D. M. Zwelonke, apparently a member of Poqo, the underground wing of the Pan-Africanist Congress, has written a first novel in exile after a spell on Robben Island. His book takes its title from and is set on that prison island where once Makana, the prophet who wanted to drive the white man into the sea, was also imprisoned. Much of the writing is naïve and sometimes even nonsensical, but where he deals with the dreams and nightmares that spring from spare diet, solitary confinement, and the repetitious labour of endless stone-breaking, no polished 'imagining' of the situation by anyone, even a black writer, could achieve his branding-iron impact. As for the book's vision of the white man, here it is another new myth-making:

> We have seen the mole and a curse has befallen us. There is a time-old legend that he who sees the mole shall hear of a friend's relative's death. An evil omen was forecast: we have seen the colonial monster in his bathroom, naked, playing with his penis and anus. In consequence he was enraged. He caught us and dragged us to Makana Island, and there we were his prisoners. A curse has fallen on us. He is like the mole because he cannot see. He gropes in the blind alley of the tragedy of history.

All this is a long, long way from the world of the black writer Lewis Nkosi in the fifties, the mixed parties where black and white argued politics, arms around each other's necks, glass in hand. And it is the vision, too, that hovers in incantation over the resurrection of black writing after the apathetic post-Sharpeville silence induced by censorship and the relentless equation, in the minds of the security police, between black articulateness and subversion. I believe these new young black writers instinctively attempt poetry rather than prose because poetry is the means of literary expression least accessible to the rules-of-thumb employed by the Censorship Board. The deracination of their predecessors of the fifties does not attract them; they are street-corner poets whose work reflects an affirmation of black identity aimed at raising black consciousness rather than rousing white consciousness to the black man's plight. Blacks have seen white culture, naked, for what it has proved to be, *for blacks*: posited as an absolute value, and eternally withheld from them. These writers are interpreting the assertion of a particular kind of black separatism which exists concurrently with, if discounted by, the official kind accepted in dialogue between Bantustan leaders and white leadership in and outside the South African government. Mongane Wally Serote makes the black claim to the right to dictate terms:

> White people are white people
> They must learn to listen.
> Black people are black people
> They must learn to talk.

Oswald Mbuyiseni Mtshali takes hold of the everyday intrusion of horror into his people's lives, unafraid to write the elegy of the black prisoners who suffocated to death in a van that had broken down on the route from prison to court:

They rode upon
the death chariot
to their Golgotha –
three vagrants
whose papers to be in Caesar's Empire
were not in order.
The sun
shrivelled their bodies
in the mobile tomb
as airtight as canned fish.
We're hot!
We're thirsty!
We're hungry!
The centurion
touched their tongues
with the top
of a lance
dipped in apathy:
'Don't cry to me,
but to Caesar who
crucifies you.
A woman came
to wipe their faces.
She carried a dishcloth
full of bread and tea.
We're dying!
The centurion washed his hands.

Irony is perhaps the best literary mode of expression, where passionate assertion will not pass the censors. James Matthews' book of poems, *Cry Rage!*, plumbs with passion not always matched by skill the hollowness of high-sounding apartheid terms such as 'separate development' and 'surplus people', and is banned. Another of these young poets, Don Mattera, has recently been declared a banned person; one wonders how long the better-known Adam Small, who (like Mattera) has taken the decision of many people of mixed blood to see themselves now as blacks rather than half-whites – will go on being published if along with that abandoned half-white status, he also abandons the idea of love always acceptable to whites, as a weapon of a struggle. Judging from some of his statements lately, I do not think he will again be writing in terms such as these:

You can stop me
goin' to Groote Schuur
in the same ambulance
as you
or tryin' to go Heaven

from a Groote Kerk pew
you can stop me doin'
some silly thing like that
but O
there's somethin' you can
never never do:
true's God
you can stop me doin'
all silly things of that sort
and to think of it
if it comes to that
you can even stop me hating'
but O
there's somethin' you can
never never do –
you can't
ever
ever
ever stop me
loving
even you!

In conclusion, to return to the situation in which all South African writers find themselves. Black or white, writing in English, Afrikaans, Sesuto, Zulu, even if he successfully shoots the rapids of bannings and/or exile, any writer's attempt to present in South Africa a totality of human experience within his own country is subverted before he sets down a word. As a white man, his fortune may change; the one thing he cannot experience is blackness – with all that implies in South Africa. As a black man, the one thing he cannot experience is whiteness – with all that implies. Each is largely outside the other's experience-potential. There is no social mobility *across* the colour-line. The identification of class with colour means that breaching class barriers is breaking the law, and the indivisible class-colour barrier is much, much more effective, from the point of view of limiting the writer's intimate knowledge of his society, than any class barrier has ever been. The black writer in South Africa writes from the 'inside' about the experience of the black masses, because the colour-bar keeps him steeped in its circumstances, confined in a black township and carrying a pass that regulates his movements from the day he is born to the status of 'piccanin' to the day he is buried in a segregated cemetery. The white writer, aseptically quarantined in his test-tube *élite* existence, is cut off by enforced privilege from the greater part of the society in which he lives; the life of the proletariat, the 19 million whose potential of experience he does not share, from the day he is born *baas* to the day he is buried in his segregated cemetery.

The black writer would seem to have the advantage here; there are only 4 million whites. But this compartmentalization of society works both ways. The black writer is extremely limited in his presentation of white characters – witness the frequency with which his are no more than cardboard or caricature. What he cannot know about the white man's life because of those large areas of the white experience he is excluded from by law, he supplies out of a fantasy distorted by resentment at the exclusion. The very force of the accusation he feels he must make against the white man sometimes loses the strength it should have. So it happens that you come across, in the work of a talented black writer, a white character so clumsily presented that he seems to have no place in the work. A black South African, in exile in a near-by territory I visited recently, challenged my assertion that the presentation of white characters in work by black writers is *limited* by caricature: on the contrary, he countered, this is the way whites are, so far as blacks are concerned. I think he makes an interesting point. Caricature under these circumstances is perhaps not a deliberate distortion of the subject but a form of truth about those who see the subject that way. The idea relates to my own observation about André Brink's novel.

In the work of white writers, you often get the same gap in experience between black and white lives compensated for by the projection of emotions about blacks into the creation of a black typology. Guilt is the prevailing emotion there; often it produces cardboard and unconscious caricature just as resentment does.

Professor Harry Levin defines cultural identity as 'nothing more nor less than the mean between selfhood and otherness, between our respect for ourselves and our relationship with our fellow men and women'. The dilemma of a literature in South Africa, where the law effectively prevents any real identification of the writer with his society as a whole, so that ultimately he can identify only with his colour, distorts this mean irreparably. And cultural identity is the ground on which the exploration of self in the imaginative writer makes a national literature.

## Selected Works and Studies

*Works*
Thomas Pringle, *African Sketches* (London, 1834).
Olive Schreiner, *The Story of an African Farm* (London, 1883; Penguin, 1972).
Sarah Gertrude Millin, *God's Stepchildren* (London, 1924; 1951).
Pauline Smith, *The Little Karoo* (London, 1925; 1952).
William Plomer, *Turbott Wolfe* (London, 1925; new edn with introduction by Laurens van der Post, 1965).

Roy Campbell, *Collected Poems*, 3 vols (London, 1949–61).
Sol Plaatje, *Mhudi* (Grahamstown, 1930; new edn with introduction by T. J. Couzens, Johannesburg, 1975).
Thomas Mofolo, *Chaka*, translated by F. H. Dutton (1931; London and New York, 1967).
Laurens van der Post, *In a Province* (London, 1934; 1953).
Peter Abrahams, *Mine Boy* (London, 1946; 1969).
Dan Jacobson, *A Dance in the Sun* (London, 1956).
Ezekiel Mphahlele, *Down Second Avenue* (London, 1959); *In Corner B* (Nairobi, 1967); *The Wanderers* (New York, 1970).
Lewis Nkosi, *Home and Exile* (London, 1965).
Herman Charles Bosman, *Unto Dust* (London, 1963).
Athol Fugard, *The Blood Knot* (Penguin, 1968); *Port Elizabeth Plays* (London, 1975).
André Brink, *Looking on Darkness* (*Kennis van die Aand*) (London, 1974).
Nadine Gordimer, *Occasion for Loving; The Lying Days; The Late Bourgeois World* (London, 1963, 1958, 1966).
Jack Cope, *Albino; The Dawn Comes Twice* (London, 1964, 1965).
Can Themba, *The Will to Die* (London, 1972).
Alex La Guma, *A Walk in the Night; In the Fog of the Season's End* (London, 1967, 1972).
Mary Benson, *At the Still Point* (Boston, 1969).
C. J. Driver, *Elegy for a Revolutionary* (London, 1969).
Etienne le Roux, *Towards a Dubious Salvation* (London, 1973).
Dennis Brutus, *A Simple Lust* (London, 1968).
Oswald Mbuyiseni Mtshali, *Sounds of a Cowhide Drum* (London, 1972).
Bessie Head, *Maru* (London, 1972).
Mongane Wally Serote, *Yakhal N'komo* (Johannesburg, 1972).
James Matthews, *Cry Rage!* (Johannesburg, 1972).
Benedict Vilakazi, *Zulu Horizons*, translated by D. M. Malcolm and J. Mandlenkosi Sikakana and rendered into English verse by Florence Louie Friedman (Johannesburg, 1973).
Arthur Nortje, *Dead Roots* (London, 1973).
Sheila Fugard, *The Castaways* (London, 1973).
D. M. Zwelonke, *Robben Island* (London, 1973).
J. M. Coetzee, *Dusklands* (Johannesburg, 1974).

*Studies, Anthologies*
Ezekiel Mphahlele, ed., *African Writing Today* (London, 1967), contributions by Casey Motsisi and others.
Jack Cope and Uys Krige, ed., *The Penguin Book of South African Verse* (London, 1969), poems by: Ingrid Jonker; Uys Krige; C. J. Langenhoven; N. P. van Wyk Louw; Samuel Mqhayi; Adam Small; and others.
Rowland Smith, *Lyric and Polemic: the Literary Personality of Roy Campbell* (Montreal, 1972).
Harry Levin, Essay in *Comparative Literature Studies*, 10 (1973; University of Illinois).
Claude Wauthier, *The Literature and Thought of Modern Africa*, translated by Shirley Kay (London, 1966).

# Black Poetry in Southern Africa: What it Means

▼▼▼▼▼▼▼▼▼▼▼▼▼▼▼▼▼▼▼▼▼▼▼▼▼▼▼▼

## OSWALD MTSHALI

IS there anything like black poetry in South Africa, as divorced from Jewish poetry, Afrikaans poetry, and English poetry? Are there ethnic poetry differences in our society? My answer to that is a big 'yes'.

The reason why I give an affirmative answer is because a black man's life in South Africa is endlessly a series of poems of humour, bitterness, hatred, love, hope, despair, and death. His is a poetic existence shaped by the harsh realities and euphoric fantasies that surround him.

Every day is a challenge in survival not only in the physical sense but also spiritually, mentally, and otherwise. It is hard for people who live in 'free' societies to comprehend a black man's life in this strange society. If you do not share my environment and my culture it is hard to understand what I am talking about.

I can only explain this life that generates and inspires black poetry by making an example of a typical black child's life from birth to death. Perhaps this illustration will clarify what I mean.

Jabulani Moya was born at Baragwanath Hospital in Johannesburg. His parents live at Zola Township, where they occupy a four-room house. Jabulani has to get a birth certificate from the hospital which is issued through the Bantu Commissioner. This certificate must be presented to the township superintendent who then authorizes Jabulani to legally join his parents when his name is put on the house permit. If the parents fail to follow this onerous procedure, it does not augur well for Jabulani's entrance into this world.

When Jabulani reaches school age, he registers in an ethnic school for Zulus because that is what his parents are. His schoolmates and playmates are supposed to be Zulus. Jabulani will be taught in Zulu by Zulu teachers until standard 3. If he does not drop out before then, he can continue his education in English and Afrikaans.

After going through high school, he will enrol in a Zulu university, where he will come into a more direct contact for the first time with white people. Like the township superintendent, the university authorities wield enormous power over the life of Jabulani. And when he graduates he will take a job that is tailored only for his qualifications as a black man. He comes into more contact with a white man, who is his employer.

When he has saved enough money he will marry a Zulu girl, who also must have been born in Johannesburg. If he fancies a girl from Springs or Pretoria he must forget her because they will not be allotted a house in Soweto. His life is restricted to Soweto and he must only work in Johannesburg. Even if he is offered a more remunerative job, say in Bloemfontein, he cannot take it. When he dies he will be buried at Doornkop Cemetery, where other Soweto residents are buried.

In this brief outline I have sketched the life of Jabulani Moya, but if we gave him a pen and paper and asked him to write about himself and his experiences, what would we get? Black experience.

If an artist is shaped by his environment and society, then Jabulani Moya would be no exception. I am using the word 'artist' in its broadest sense. What Jabulani would produce would be black art.

Black art, of course, has its different fields like visual arts, drama, music, and literature. If Jabulani Moya is a poet, then his poetry will depict his life and the people around him. It will describe stokvels, shebeens, police vans, prisons, churches, hospitals, trains, murders, rapes, robberies, night vigils and funerals – in short, all aspects of a black man's life.

If a black artist uses his paint and brush or pen and paper to depict these scenarios of his life, his work is given the name of 'Township Art' by the white critics. I cannot go into the merits and demerits of that tag which has been attached to our works, except to say that to me it smacks of patronizing, if not downright contempt.

It is for that reason that I will restrict myself to what I believe is black poetry or Township poetry if anyone wants to call it that. As I have said before, black poetry depicts the black man's life as it is shaped by the laws that govern him. He has no hand in the making of these laws, but he must abide by them. Black poetry is the mirror that reflects black man's aspirations, his hopes and disappointments, his joys and sorrows, his loves and hates.

A poet, or for that matter any artist, cannot contrive his subject matter or themes. He must know what he is writing about. If he does not, he will come up with something unnatural, unrealistic, and downright phony. Only a Jewish poet can write about barmitzvah. Only an Afrikaner poet can describe Nagmaal.

I, as a black man, can tell you how I slaughter a black goat for my ancestors. The rest is as remote and foreign to me as the changing of the Queen's Guards at Buckingham Palace.

Poetry is the language of emotions. Only words can convey the meaning of this language to the heart, where emotions are said to be situated. These emotions are only existent in human beings with the result that creatures other than homo sapiens are said to be devoid of love, hate, fear, despair, and hope. Consequently, every person should, because he has emotions, understand and appreciate poetry; otherwise he is no different from a brute or a stone.

Like people all over the world, we black people of South Africa have emotions. We love, we hate, we fear, we despair, we aspire. I do not exaggerate if I say to a certain extent we do these things to a higher degree than other people. For instance we have hope in our hearts which through centuries has come to cease to be a virtue and has turned into a vice. The reason being simply that we seem to have been hoping against hope. Whether this has had a stultifying effect on our other emotions and feelings is very difficult to say.

In recent times, within the past few years to be exact, our feelings as black people have become more and more vocal. For too long we have been muffled by our unfounded fears which we cannot contain any more. Of course there have been real fears of being lynched, murdered, and imprisoned if we dared to raise our voices to what we knew for a long time to be wrong and expected to be righted. Our fears have been compounded by the teachings of missionaries about heaven and hell. Acceptance of the injustices perpetrated on our lives would be rewarded with heavenly bliss, and the opposition of this oppression would lead to perdition; so we were taught to believe. Of course now we have seen through this smokescreen and we know the truth.

Before I elaborate on the poetry movement amongst the black people in South Africa, I want to describe and analyse the racial setup in my country, which is South Africa. I want to do this so that, I hope, you will get a clearer picture of my position and that of my fellow black men.

At the last census taken in 1971 there were about 21 million people living in South Africa. About 16 million Africans like myself; then 3 million whites, a million and a half of coloureds or mulattoes, and less than a million people of Indian descent. We Africans have lived in Southern Africa since time immemorial, that is according to our indisputable black historical facts; the other version, namely that we came to South Africa from the Equator at the same time as the Honourable Mr Jan van Riebeeck in 1652 is nothing else but fiction.

I have been fortunate enough to have been taken, by a friend of the family before she died, on a tour to a row of caves in the Lebombo Mountains in the northern part of Zululand. That guide was an old woman of about 90 or more and I was about 10 years of age then. She told us (my oldest brother was there too) that the caves were there when she grew up. They were used as hiding places during the wars and endless battles that were fought amongst Zulus and Swazis, and also during the wars that followed later between whites and Zulus. Some of the dwellers in those caves were my ancestors who fled Shaka's wrath and vengeance after he and his army invaded Ntabankulu (Big Mountain), the ancestral home of the Mtshali clan. Later on some of my forbears settled in northern Zululand and Swaziland.

Though I was quite young when I was told this exciting bit of my history, I still remember it as vividly as if that old crone had related it to me only last night. I remember seeing the timeless relics of my past, like claypots, crude iron tools and kiln where iron was smelted to forge assegais (imikhonto), battle axes (izizenze), hatchets (ocelemba), and of course hoes (amageja) for tilling the soil. As can be expected archaeologists and excavators have discovered some of these caves which stand in a somewhat long row from the village of Ngotshe (Louwsburg) and Magudu to the Lebombo Mountain side of Swaziland.

I have digressed from the topic on black poetry in South Africa. I have given you the background to my culture which will provide you with an insight into my timeless existence and civilization in southern Africa before the advent of the so-called refined and much-vaunted western civilization.

Our existence having been established beyond any doubt, I wish to propound the fact that we had and in some parts of the country still have the remnants of a beautiful culture, which makes my heart bleed when I see it raped, prostituted, and destroyed since the first contact the black man has had with the followers of Jan van Riebeeck. Wherever I go I try to collect the debris of my shattered culture and try to immortalize it in my poetry. That is why I have now more than once before let the Muse dictate to me in English and Zulu. I write in English for my present state of reality or unreality and I write in Zulu to establish my identity which will be translated by posterity. Only then will my past heritage be accorded its right and respectful position. For me that will be absolute and the most highly cherished freedom anyone can endow me with.

The greatest tragedy that ever befell the black man in the southern part of Africa is not that he did not invent the wheel, but that he could not write. Otherwise if he could, I would be reading to you today poetry that was written long before the birth of Jesus Christ. I call this a tragedy because this inability to record our civilization has contributed to the gross misrepresentation of our culture as far as the written word is concerned, but the redeeming factor for which the black is eternally grateful, is the preservation of the paintings of the Abathwa people in mountain caves in some parts of southern Africa. We are also grateful to the black sculptors who recorded our culture through their works which are found all over the continent of Africa. But the most important contributors and preservers of our civilizations are the musicians whose musical instruments are in great evidence in many parts of Africa. The songs, though passed from mouth to mouth and not scored, are as fresh as ever. I am thinking of the war songs, and the war cries of the people, say, the Zulus. My grandmother used to sing them to me as freshly as her grandmother used to sing them to her. Hence from what she told me I could learn what an artist like a poet could and should do for our society.

The role that can be played by a singer or a poet is a great one indeed. To us, black people of South Africa, Miriam Makeba is a goddess of our struggle to be free because she has articulated our feelings and immortalized our wretched lives, thus proclaiming that every black man wants freedom in the land of his birth. This is an obligation I have taken upon myself to carry out, in my own modest way through my poetry, for the liberation of my people.

I have purposely not dwelt on the political side of my country because this is too well known for me to mention. I have only mentioned the results of the contact with the white man since 1652 which, with dire consequences, has denuded the black man of his dignity because of the destruction of his civilization and culture. Through my poetry I am trying to gather the scattered pieces of my culture, and this is not only my goal, but it is also that of the crop of other poets who have sprung up like mushrooms in the stormy life of the black man. It is dictated by the political ideology pursued by the government of South Africa. This political policy is known to the outside world under the insidious name of apartheid. In South Africa it is respectfully called Separate and Equal Development.

One may ask then what has poetry to do with this political setup that separates the black man from the white, and is imposed on a voteless black majority by a white electorate? The answer is that black poetry, like every art form, describes the life of the black people in this type of society. It portrays the lives of the people who find themselves helpless victims in vicious circumstances not of their own making. The black poets who have sprung from seemingly nowhere are the oases in the bleak desert of black man's life from where he will drink the waters of liberation as he forges his way to the green pastures of complete freedom. The poetry of twenty years ago is far less strident in its feeling than that of the present day. The reason is that the political events in the African continent have given the situation in South Africa a sense of urgency. This momentum is rising to a feverish pitch from both sides, the white man's side and the black man's side. In this dramatic stage of our development I find that to keep pace with the latest events one needs a very objective mind. Some time ago I attended a memorial service in Soweto for Mr Abram Ongkopoetse Tiro, a 27-year-old black leader who was killed by a parcel bomb in Botswana where he was living in exile from South Africa. A very large crowd of black people, young and old, attended this church service. And one of the most remarkable sights to observe was the lack of emotionalism and hysterics which is very common in our funerals. Instead there was a calm and a grim determination to continue where Mr Tiro had left off. Indeed if ever there was a people who knew their destiny, those were the people.

Another contributory factor to the urgency and potency of the black poetry movement is the increase in the number and the harshness of the laws that govern the black man. This has been brought about by the impetus of the ever-increasing strikes by Zulu workers around Durban and the events which are happening beyond the borders of our country. Thus one can see that the poems of Bloke Modisane and Can Themba in the early fifties were more subtle and humorous than that of the current poets like Mongane Serote and James Matthews whose poetry is the reflection of ever-growing, fast proliferating black awareness, black consciousness, and its end result, black power. This spirit of self-assertion has been sinisterized purposely by the white press, even by our so-called liberal press, because the white people are horrified that the black man, that is the African, the coloured and the Indian, are coming together to form a single united block that will confront and demand freedom from white domination. The classic example of what I mean is the banning of *Cry Rage!*, a book of poems written by James Matthews and Gladys Thomas. There was no outcry when this book was banned, there were no petitions signed by the white intelligentsia, there were no vociferous shoutings by the white liberal press, and no fund was established to help the proscribed writers by taking the matter to court. The book was, I suppose, justifiably banned for being black power propaganda. But now an Afrikaner writer had his work banned, the first time in the history of white literature that a thing like this ever happened, and the noise that has followed has deafened the whole world. I, as a black man, am not surprised by the duplicity that every black man has come to expect from the whites. It is these double standards practised by the whites that the black poets are questioning, condemning, and rejecting as pernicious and retarding to the black man's struggle.

You may wonder why there is this upsurge of black poetry in South Africa. I have given part of an answer at the beginning of this essay. And I have explained the emotional strings played by poetry in the black man's heart. Other forms of writing will follow just as night follows day. In fact two plays are a pointer to this direction. They tell how a black man finds himself caught up in the cobweb of the multifarious laws that govern him, especially the much-detested pass laws that restrict every black man.

In the near future I do not foresee any novelist coming out of South Africa because the urgency of the situation does not allow time to sit down and pen a lengthy piece of writing as demanded by a novel. Another factor against a novel is that poetry, music, and drama can be shared with many other people at the same time. But a novel can only be read alone. I suppose it's the black man's gregarious instinct to share the bitter and the sweet or, as one black sage once said, 'A sorrow shared is a sorrow lessened, and a shared joy is a joy increased a hundredfold.'

Now why do black poets in South Africa write in English if they are proud of their culture? I will quickly point out that I write in English and Zulu as I have said before. But the answer to this question I have given already. I will only amplify it by saying that the English that we use in our poetry is not the Queen's language that you know as written by say Wordsworth and Coleridge. It is the language of urgency which we use because we have got an urgent message to deliver to any one who cares to listen to it. We have not got the time to embellish this urgent message with unnecessary and cumbersome ornaments like rhyme, iambic pentameter, abstract figures of speech, and an ornate and lofty style. We will indulge in these luxuries which we can ill-afford at the moment when we are free people. Only then shall we write about bees, birds, and flowers. Not the harsh realities that are part and parcel of black man's life.

# Today

# Pictures of Pain:
# The Poetry of Dennis Brutus

▼▼▼▼▼▼▼▼▼▼▼▼▼▼▼▼▼▼▼▼▼▼▼▼▼▼▼▼▼▼▼

R. N. EGUDU

ACRITIC has recently observed that the poetry of Dennis Brutus of South Africa shows that for him (Brutus) there are 'no reserves of energy, no courage of beliefs from deep within, no conflict, no fortitude to buoy him against the hostile environment'; that 'Brutus's strength in dealing with experience is uncertain'.[1] A similar charge had earlier been made against Brutus by another critic who said that 'a little less shouting for more silence and mime might not only make for manly dignity but also command attempts at rescue and action'.[2] These two critics have at least accepted that Brutus is not unaffected by the realities of his society; they are only quarrelling against the method of his response to those realities.

The issue of the relationship between the artist and his society with regard to his reaction to social problems is one which has always been discussed in respect of writers all through the ages and in many parts of the world. For several obvious reasons, it seems especially relevant to the African situation. Thus says Louis James: 'In situations as explosive as that of Africa today there can be no creative literature that is not in some way political, in some way protest. Even the writer who opts out of the social struggles of his country and tries to create a private world of art, is saying something controversial about the responsibility of the artist to society.'[3] Of special significance in James's observation is his objectivity in recognizing that there are different ways in which creative literature can be 'political' and 'protest', and this will be relevant to the discussion of the nature of protest Dennis Brutus is engaged in.

Another objective assessment of the African writer's plight, especially with regard to South Africa, is that made by Paul Theroux. After quoting Albert Camus as saying that a writer living in this world 'cannot hope to remain aloof in order to pursue the reflections and images that are dear to him', Theroux says: 'The South African writer is in a very special position. With Britain, the United States, Germany, Japan and countless other countries pouring money and industrial schemes into the country, it takes a strong voice and a skilful hand to unravel the gorgeous South African travel brochure, shout in the faces of the Great Powers and touch the brutalized nerves beneath it all.'[4] Theroux recognizes the difficult nature of the task, and credits Brutus with a considerable amount of success in dealing with the situation.

Similarly, Gerald Moore fully appreciates the difficulty which the writer in South Africa faces. Moore remarks that 'in an environment where everyone has been to some extent dulled to the full impact of cruelty and injustice by sheer familiarity' the poet should not be noisy:

> Though he must be angry, he must never be shrill. His must be a quiet voice where there is already too much shouting. For it is not so much the call to action that he is uniquely qualified to give, as the call to see, to hear and to know. The coloured poet Dennis Brutus has measured the difficulty of this task . . . he has achieved in some poems a control which masters horror without diminishing its impact.[5]

Moore sees the need for the South African poet to react to the social situation, but does not think that this reaction has to be the rabble-rousing type. For Moore further remarks that 'unlike the tortured prisoner, the poet may talk, but at least he will not squeal'.[6] Thus, as another critic has observed, 'it is natural that a South African poet with an a "open" sensibility should react to the horny police regime that operates in his country' and Brutus 'reacts with vigour, integrity and defiant hopefulness'. It is Brutus's 'temper, intellect and imagination that save his protest from sounding merely strident, from degenerating to blubbering emotionalism or mawkish self-pity or naïve malice'.[7]

Brutus himself is fully alive to his social responsibility as a South African poet. He once said: 'I think it is simply true that an artist, a writer, is a man who lives in a particular society and takes his images and ideas from that society'.[8] This is tantamount to saying that 'the nature and magnitude of a person's behavioural response i.e. what he says, thinks or does, is some function of . . . the stimulus situation in which he is placed and of . . . the nature of his personality': 'R = F (S.P)':[9] Where 'R' stands for 'response', 'S' for 'stimulus situation', 'p' for 'personality', and 'F' for 'function', the position with regard to Dennis Brutus will be as follows: 'S' is apartheid in its various ramifications, R is Brutus's poetry, and 'P' is Brutus's personality, an idea of which Abasiekong has given us as indicated above. And his poetry, being his response, is of course the product of the interplay of the socio-political situation and his personality. The present study is concerned with the nature of this response and how it has been effected in terms of artistic rendition.

The poetry of Dennis Brutus is the reaction of one who is in mental agony whether he is at home or abroad. This agony is partly caused by harassments, arrests, and imprisonment, and mainly by Brutus's concern for other suffering people. Thus Brutus feels psychically injured in some of his poems. When he traverses all his land as a 'troubadour',[10] finding wandering 'motion sweeter far than rest', he is feeling the pinch of restiveness resulting from dislodgement. All the factors that make life uncomfortable are assembled in the poem: banning of 'inquiry and movement', 'Saracened arrest', and 'the captor's hand', and against them Brutus takes to roaming in freedom, 'disdaining', 'quixoting' (i.e. pursuing an ideal honour and devotion), singing all the time. His fight is purely psychological, not physical, for he puts up an attitude which his oppressors would least expect and which would disconcert them.

The emotional tension is palpable: to find 'motion' sweeter than 'rest' is in fact to have no rest. The conceit is as effective here as that used by John Donne when he wrote 'Until I labour, I in labour lie', in the poem 'Elegie: Going to Bed'. Like W. B. Yeats, Brutus is pursuing his mask, his anti-self or that which is least like him. His expression of love emotions towards the land is a pathetic dramatization of his want of love. Thus instead of a 'mistress-favour' he has 'an arrow-brand' to adorn his breast. Brutus is therefore seeking for 'something that is dear to him, but something that is out of reach'.[11] Tejani, however, has missed this point for he argues that Brutus's reference to himself as a 'troubadour' is an 'archaic description of himself, more relevant in the sunny non-racial climate of the Mediterranean,' and that this description and the mood of the poem show that the poet listens to the outside voices with a decisiveness which is his weakness.[12] This is of course in consonance with Tejani's former view that Brutus lacks the strength to engage in a physical action against apartheid, not realizing that the kind of action Brutus is concerned with is more psychological than physical.

But Brutus shows no weakness in the poem. He is fighting the forces of oppression with that 'tenderness' which, though it is 'frustrated, does not wither' (*SL*, p. 4). As in the previous poem, the agents of pain here touch the mainstay of the mind. There are the 'investigating searchlights'; there is the 'monolithic decalogue/of fascist prohibition', and above all there are 'patrols' which, like snakes, 'uncoil along the asphalt dark/hissing their menace to our lives'. These forces have organized that 'terror' with which 'all our land is scarred' and which 'rendered [it] unlovely and unlovable'. The fact that Brutus emphasizes his use of 'tenderness' and not malice or even physical action as a fighting weapon does not mean that he is not appreciative of the ugliness of his situation. He clearly states in 'I am the exile' (SL, p. 137), that although he is 'gentle' and 'calm' and 'courteous to servility', yet

> ... Wailings fill the chambers of my heart
> and in my head
> behind my quiet eyes
> I hear the cries and sirens.

And this goes to emphasize the point that his pain is mental rather than physical.

For this kind of pain, Brutus devises a mental weapon, as he indicates in 'Off The Campus: Wits' (SL, p. 12):

> So here I crouch and nock my venomed arrows
> to pierce deaf eardrums waxed by fear ...
>
> and from the corner of my eye
> catch glimpses of a glinting spear.

In warfare it is the nature of attack that determines the type of weapons to be employed by the attacked for defence. In South Africa, it is not so much the physical destruction of the blacks and coloured by the whites, as the dehumanization of these people, the dementing process of dehumanization, that is painful to Brutus. Even the 'shouts' of 'Nordics at their play', 'pursuing us like intermittent surf' make the blacks 'cower in our green-black primitive retreat'. The use of 'cower' and later 'crouch' indicate the presence of terror, and both words naturally lead up to and link with that 'fear' which 'waxed' people's 'eardrums'. To fight this terror and fear Brutus uses, not a gun, but the 'venomed arrows' and 'glinting spear' of his poetry.

That fear is the 'enemy' to fight is an insistent motif in Brutus's poetry. 'A letter to Basil' (SL, p. 74) is entirely on this. Fear is a deadly enemy; it 'seeks out the areas of our vulnerability/and savages us'. If we do not appreciate how fear can reduce one to a bestial level, we tend in reaction 'to resort to what revolts us and wallow in the foulest treachery'. But

> To understand the unmanning powers of
> fear and its corrosive action
> makes it easier to forgive.

Here the humanity of Brutus, that tenderness of his, is shown not to the perpetrators of fear, but to its victims. He is as ready to show tenderness to injure his oppressors as to forgive his compatriots who, under the influence of fear, are tempted to be treacherous.

When in prison, one of his most harassing problems is fear – fear that is generated by memory and forethought. In 'Letters to Martha' Nos 1–13 (*SL*, pp. 54–63), Brutus delineates the unnerving impact of fear in a prison-situation. In 'After the Sentence' we hear of 'the load of the approaching days' and 'the hints of brutality'; and we are told that the only tempering factor is 'the knowledge of those/who endure much more/and endure . . .' No. 2 of 'Letters to Martha' shows the effect of the prisoner's merely hearing 'that nails and screws and other sizeable bits of metal/must be handed in' which forms part of that 'mesh of possibilities' that give rise to 'notions' cobwebbing 'around your head' and 'tendrils' sprouting 'from your guts in a hundred directions' ('Letters', No. 3). Or it may be 'whispers of horrors/that people the labyrinth of self' ('Letters', No. 5), or such intimations as 'At daybreak for the "isle"', and 'Look your last on all things lovely' – it could be these that constitute 'this crushing blow' ('Letters', No. 13). Fear thus destroys the 'man' in man before the arrival of the possible actual death.

In addition to this consciousness of fear, Brutus felt much the separation from ordinary physical nature while he was in prison, and the pain resulting from this is as mentally torturing as that caused by fear. In 'Letters' No. 17 (*SL*, p. 65), clouds and birds become rare things and therefore 'assume importance' because they are cut off from view by the 'walls/of black hostility':

> The complex aeronautics
> of the birds
> and their exuberant aerobatics
> become matters for intrigued speculation
> and wonderment;

also,

> – the graceful unimpeded motion of the clouds
> – a kind of music, poetry, dance –
> sends delicate rhythms tremoring through the flesh.

The plight of the poet in prison, who lacks freedom and motion, is the direct opposite of the condition of the birds and clouds which are free and moving; and this is implicit in the poem. The fact that 'clichés about the freedom of the birds' now 'become meaningful' to the poet underscores his consciousness of his lack of this basic need – the need to be free. One therefore wonders why Tejani, referring to those lines quoted above about the free movements of the birds, should doubt that there is 'poetry' in those lines, and say that 'the sense of distance which we need when thinking of the cloud or the bird [is] not present in the poem'.[13] If the two beautiful and powerful images contained in the first and third of those five lines are not 'poetry', then one is at a loss to say what else is 'poetry'.

The same critic for a different reason attacks some other lines from another poem of Brutus – 'On the Island', No. 1 (*SL*, 71):

> Cement-grey floors and walls
> cement-grey days
> cement-grey time
> and a grey susurration

Commenting on these lines, Tejani says that one must question 'the repetitions' in Brutus's verse; that 'everything' Brutus says 'seems so strikingly familiar'; that his 'verse . . . contains no surprises'; that 'the lack of compression is remarkable, the total effect prosaic, undermining the very mood it seeks to create'; and therefore that Brutus has not effectively communicated the idea of being in 'solitary confinement'.[14] It is perhaps because the critic has misunderstood the mood and idea Brutus seeks to communicate, and also the very essence of poetry, that he made those remarks. Brutus is not simply telling us about his being in 'solitary confinement', though this is part of the fact; he is talking of the bleakness, boredom and death-like coldness of a prison situation, all of which result from the stagnant, monotonous life in that situation. The repetition of the double-barrelled modifier 'cement-grey', far from constituting 'lack of compression', concretizes and emphasizes this theme in a dramatic way, especially the monotonous (or repetitive) nature of the actual situation; and it enhances the music of the dirge which in fact the poem is. The notion of cold motionlessness and monotony is underscored in the last two lines of the poem: 'and one locked in a grey gelid stream/of unmoving time'. Finally, to say that what the poet says 'seems strikingly familiar' does not of course mean that the way he says it is not unfamiliar. Poetry after all is a 'miracle' of the commonplace; the poet's business is to prepare a new (unfamiliar) wrappage for a familiar idea, which is 'what oft was thought but ne'er so well exprest', according to Alexander Pope.

It is necessary here to refer to the poem 'Prisoner' by the Nigerian Wole Soyinka[15] to see the same word, 'grey', used repeatedly to generate an effect similar to that produced by Brutus's use of the word. This poem sees every man as a prisoner-victim of life from birth to death. The 'grey' 'wet-lichened wisps' breed 'the grey hours/And days, and years'. We shall build 'grey temples' to 'febrile years'. Man in his loneliness is caught in a 'sandstorm' in the 'desert wildness' where he lies, a 'stricken/Potsherd . . . disconsolate'. And then in the last stanza:

> . . . time conquest
> Bound him helpless to each grey essence.
> Nothing remained if pains and longings
> Once, once set the walls; sadness
> Closed him, rootless, lacking cause.

Man's prison cell is one whose walls are made of 'pains and longings' and whose roof is made of 'sadness'. What can be more 'grey' than this, especially when the whole situation is made all the more dreadful by the existentialist notion of 'lacking cause'? Incidentally, the word 'grey' is used four times in the poem.

Another dimension of the injury which caused pain to Brutus is that which is expressed in terms of somatic images. Brutus would want us feel with our mind as well as with our body the nature of his agony, just as he does. For ordinarily, the pain on the body registers on the mind. In some of Brutus's poems therefore images of bruise, sore, scar, and complete crushing are used. In 'More terrible than any beast' (*SL*, p. 7), the cannibal is 'the iron monster of the world' which 'ingests me in its grinding maw'. The notion of a toothed stomach is quite frightful; and the harsh, hard word 'grinding' is enough to send a shiver through the body of the reader whether we conceive it as 'crushing' or oppressing and harassing with exaction; or in terms of toiling monotonously, in which case Brutus has transferred the epithet from himself to the 'maw'. The nature of this toiling is brought out clearly in the last stanza by the image of a 'ballet-dancer/fragile as butterfly' who does 'eggdance with nimble wariness' to 'stave off my fated splintering'. This last word continues and echoes the impact of 'grinding'; and the plight of the poet is underscored by the sharp contrast between the hardness of the 'iron monster' and his own fragility.

The plight is no less mitigated in the poem 'This sun on this rubble after rain' (*SL*, p. 9), in which the body is 'bruised' and 'our bones and spirits crunch' under the weight of 'jackboots', and are 'forced into sweat-tear-sodden slush'. Here somatic and psychic injuries are brought together to exacerbate the poet's pain. But as in many of the poems dealing with body injuries, grief is counterbalanced by hope for reaction from nemesis and relief from pain, which (hope) the poet needs for his continued struggling. Thus as we hear in 'Time, ordinary Time' (*SL*, p. 10):

> – these sores –
> unhealed and unattended
> that bleed afresh each day
> under the horny ministrants of law
> must, under impulse of augmented streams

explode in gouts and swish
these papered clerks and all
into a messy bloodied waste

The clinical atmosphere shows South Africa to be one vast hospital in whose Casualty Section the wounded are carelessly left untreated; and still the patients do not despair! The country is thus 'a sickly state' in which victims are 'succumbing to the variegated sores/that flower under lashing rains of hate'. ('For a Dead African', *SL*, p. 34). John Nangoza Jebe, in whose memory the poem was written, was 'shot by the police in a Good Friday procession in Port Elizabeth 1956'. And as the last stanza shows, Jebe is one of 'these nameless unarmed ones [who] will stand beside/the warriors who secured the final prize'. Even in the face of 'impartial death' (to use Soyinka's expression),[16] there is still the hope that the 'final prize' will be won.

The police regime in South Africa, however, remains a force to be reckoned with for it fathers forth all the injuries done to the victims of apartheid. Thus in 'The sounds begin again' (*SL*, p. 19), the police 'siren in the night' and the 'thunder' of their 'boots at the door' cause 'the shriek of nerves in pain' and 'the keening crescendo/of faces split by pain', both of which constitute that 'wordless, endless wail/only the unfree know'. Though this 'wail' is noiseless, we still can hear the piercing sound of the alliteration in 'keening crescendo' and the sound made by the axe of pain as it splits faces like dry firewood. A little relief is brought about by the 'wraiths [that] exhale their woe' (i.e. curse) over the agents of oppression; but the sounds, which have now become the poet's, begin again! According to Gerald Moore,

> Brutus lets the night-sounds of a South African city yield their own secretion of terror, yet the single word 'my' which qualifies them in the last stanza, by bringing the living and suffering poet directly into the poem, somehow *diminishes* that terror just a little; it makes the impact of the sounds more intimate and almost humanizes them. For to assert ownership of anything in a system that denies your humanity is to assert that humanity also.[17]

One may disagree with some aspects of this view. The immediate effect of the word 'my' in the poem is to demolish the sense of distance which is created by the article 'The' in the opening line of the poem, and which tends to make the poet appear so far removed from the effect of the sounds as to become a mere spectator-commentator not directly involved. By removing this illusion of distance through the use of 'my', Brutus shows that he is not only directly involved like any other victim, but also is the representative victim whose vicarious suffering, like that of

Christ, is for the rest of the people. This Christ-figure, a kind of traditional 'scapegoat', features prominently in another poem of Brutus, 'Being the mother of God',[18] the last stanza of which reads as follows:

> So I must beg you to excuse
> any inattention and neglect of you
> in the midst of what is really your event
> and hope that you will accept my anxious thought
> and planning for the joy of others
> as something which is really yours.

It is because Brutus is suffering for the rest of the oppressed humanity in South Africa that the sounds can rightly be called his own. Furthermore, the point here is not so much that the terror is diminished as that because of his altruism and 'self-sacrifice' for the 'joy of others', the poet has shown himself to be superior to the terror to the extent that its impact appears to be totally nullified.

It is this concern for the suffering of others more than for his own suffering that is one major source of Brutus's pain. Those poems dealing with homosexuality in the prison, which is one of the worst human aberrations, are pathetic. Brutus in 'Two men I knew specifically' (*SL*, p. 57), feels particularly touched by the plight of a prisoner who 'sought escape/in fainting fits and asthmas/ and finally fled into insanity'. In 'Perhaps most terrible are those who beg for it' (*SL*, p. 58), we are told that the 'agonies' the 'prisoners have endured' are 'fierce', that sodomy is 'regarded as the depths/of absolute and ludicrous submission' and is 'one of the most terrible/most rendingly pathetic/of all a prisoner's predicaments'. And in the climactic poem on this theme, the 'Blue champagne' piece (*SL*, pp. 58–9), we notice the depth of the degradation of man, and according to the poet, the young boy turned 'girl' who 'would sleep with several/each night' 'had become the most perverse among/the perverted'. The sight and knowledge of this bestial plight of the prisoners is a crushing experience for Brutus.

It is perhaps with regard to these poems that one rightly feels, as Bahadur Tejani wrongly feels in respect of other poems,[19] that Brutus can be prosaic and let poetry escape him at times. But it can be argued in his favour that the weight of sorrow was so heavy upon his heart that he became unsettled mentally and could not pay the necessary attention to his art. The pressure of the matter was too oppressive for the manner of its expression to be attended to. And like Christ, Brutus could justly proclaim: the thought of your (prisoners) plight has eaten up my heart!

For it is the thought about those blacks who were attacked by the white crowd ('The mob', *SL*, p. 48) that has made him moan in words echoing those of Christ. It is the white crowd that perpetrate those 'faceless horrors/that people my nightmares'; theirs also are the 'fear-blanked face-lessness/and saurian-lidded stares/of my irrational terrors'. Here again the word 'my' makes the suffering the poet's. And so he wails:

> O my people
> What have you done
> and where shall I find comforting
> to smooth awake your mask of fear
> restore your face, your faith, feeling, tears.

Commenting on oppression in South Africa and on how Brutus consis-tently raises a condemning voice against it, S. Okechukwu Mezu quotes from this poem. He points out the similarity between the first three lines of the stanza just reproduced above and the words of the 'Good Friday' song: 'O my people, O my people! What have I done to you? Please answer me'. And Mezu observes that the 'people in question' in Brutus's poem 'is humanity at large but more especially the white world'.[20] But curiously it is in the light of this very poem that Tejani accuses Brutus of taking sides with the whites: 'It is legitimate to ask who are the poet's people and if they deserve his sympathy. The mob that attacked those who struggle for the minimal freedom in South Africa are literally faceless, faithless, and ... without the gift of human tears. Yet the poet's refrain, 'O my people', gives his heart to them.'[21]

Here as in the other cases of his accusation, Tejani has, it seems to me, got it all wrong. In the first instance it is obvious, as indicated above, that the action of the white mob caused Brutus a lot of mental and heart ache. In the second place Brutus sees the mob as erratic and shameless, without fear of doing evil, or faith in humanity, or human feeling, or ability to shed tears; they are simply as brutal and callous as the Jewish captors of Christ. Thus Brutus addresses them with the moral tone of a superior being who reads and understands the hearts of the mob better than the mob them-selves, recalling to the reader's mind the words of Christ: 'Father, forgive them; for they know not what they do' (Luke, 23:34). It is a mark of triumph for Brutus to seek to restore in those whites the human qualities they have lost. Finally, at a purely literary level, there is a note of irony and satire in Brutus's addressing the oppressors as 'my people'; for by so doing he attacks their failure to understand the bond of unity holding mankind together, and their lack of humanness. The poem, therefore, far from showing Brutus as giving his heart to the mob, is a quiet corrective condemnation more effective than a noisy vitriol. And above all, it is quite clear that by taking this stand, Brutus has taken upon him the burden of those that were attacked.

Even when in exile, Brutus is also seriously concerned about the sufferings of his people at home. I think it is Earnshaw in *Modern Writers* who says that an Irish exile often takes with him the consciousness of the moral disposition in his country. In the same way, Brutus went into exile with a full load of this type of consciousness. Thus in the title poem of his major collection, 'A simple lust is all my woe' (*SL*, p. 176) he says:

> only I speak the others' woe:
> those congealed in concrete
> or rotting in rusted ghetto-shacks:
> only I speak their wordless woe,
> their unarticulated simple lust.

And so he wishes that he could be 'armed with such passion, dedication, voice',

> that every cobblestone would rear in wrath
> and batter down a prison's wall
> and wrench them from the island where they rot.
> ('Shakespeare winged this way . . .', *SL*, p. 127)

His feeling of distress for those suffering back home is intensified by his thought of the apparent contrast between his life now that he is 'free' in exile, and that of the prisoners still denied their freedom. In the poem 'In the dove-grey dove-soft dusk' (*SL*, p. 101) there is the 'agonizing poignant urgent simple desire/simply to stroll in the quiet dusk.' Though Brutus could satisfy this desire in the land of his exile, he feels sad that his compatriots at home could not satisfy theirs: 'as I do now, and they do not'. Nor does Brutus derive any meaningful joy from 'the soft spring rain', 'the street lights [that] gild the flowering trees', and 'the late light breaking through patches of broken cloud'. These pleasant natural phenomena from which he was shut off when he was in prison but which are now placed at his disposal in England are ineffectual, for they are now overwhelmed by the memory of 'the men who are still there crouching now/ in grey cells, on the grey floors, stubborn and bowed' ('I walk in the English quick silver dust', *SL*, p. 102). A similar experience is depicted in 'Here' (*SL*, p. 126) in which the moon or a 'blurred Orion' watched by Brutus on the island of New Zealand reminded him of his own people on another island (Robben Island?) who were lying 'on the cold floor/between cold walls' in the 'long endless night' of the prison world. Thus, like the man who dreamed of the fairy land in W. B. Yeats's poem of that title, and who could not find peace in the grave,[22] Brutus could not find rest in his exile. For instance, for him, the loveliness of England is 'tainted by disease'; and so 'I must be faithful to a land/whose rich years unlike England's, lie ahead'. ('It is hers . . .', *SL*, p. 104).

This is that hope at its strongest which, as noted earlier, is the mainstay of Brutus's spirit of struggle. Hope is the basis of his determination, the 'anger and resolution' which 'yeast in me'. It is hope that enables him wait patiently 'for the time of achievement/which will come if God wills/ when I flog fresh lashes across these thieves' ('And they know I will do more', *SL*, p. 91). Therefore he rightly prays in 'Prayer' (*SL*, p. 94) for a 'steadfast wing' for soaring, protection from the 'slightest deviant swoop' and from being 'ruffled or trifled, snared or power misspent', so that he may swiftly and unerringly soar

> hurling myself swordbeaked to lunge
> for lodgement in my life's sun-targe –
> a land and people just and free.

It is Brutus's ever-buoyant hope which makes him not 'question that further power/waits for a leap across gulfs of storm', and which assures him 'that pain will be quiet, the prisoned free,/and wisdom sculpt justice from the world's jagged mass' ('Now that we conquer and dominate time', *SL*, p. 95). So in the final analysis,

> Peace will come
> We have the power
> the hope
> the resolution
> Man will go home
>                          ('Above us, only sky?' *SL*, p. 96)

A poet who shows this kind of resolution cannot be reasonably described as 'a dog holding up a mauled paw' or 'a child in a fit of convulsion', as J. P. Clark has described Brutus.[23] Nor can one who understands Brutus's method of struggle and attack agree with Tejani that he (Brutus) reaches 'simplistic conclusions of hope without struggle'.[24] Paul Theroux, incidentally, fully appreciates the nature of Brutus's struggle when he says: 'Brutus is whipped and he lashes back furiously. It is true that sometimes his punches are wild, sometimes he misses, but he swings enough times for us to see what he is aiming at.' And, in Theroux's view, Brutus has succeeded in detaching himself from 'metaphysics' in order 'to exist among the most miserable and unhappy' in his country, 'identifying with all the injustice and lust and criminality'.[25]

It is true that in his struggle Brutus has not used a machine gun; that would be the proper duty of one who is literally soldiering. But he has used a powerful weapon that befits the province of his operation: poetry. He has employed in most of his poems language that is effective for its poetic vigour and beauty. He 'has escaped from the decayed language of revolt, the clichés of the man oppressed',[26] and rather embraced the living language of poetry which he has used for creating 'those images that yet/ Fresh images beget'.[27] As Abasiekong has observed and as evidenced in most of the poems discussed above, Brutus's success in his poetry results from 'the brilliant intensity of his imagery' and 'the way he presses language urgently and aptly into service ... The sense of Brutus's poetry ... is a sense tried upon the pulses rather than merely spelled out by cold reasoning. The poet impresses his *thoughts* upon us by way of *feelings* induced by apt images.'[28]

Thus in his intellectual protest without malice, in his mental agony over the apartheid situation in South Africa, in his concern for the sufferings of the others, and in his hope which has defied all despair – all of which he has portrayed through images and diction that are imbued with freshness and vision – Brutus proves himself a capable poet fully committed to his social responsibility. What he has said of Albert John Lutuli in 'So the Machine breaks you' (*SL*, p. 171) can equally be said of him (Brutus):

> Yet your great soul
> asserts a worth –
> transcendent humanity.
>
> There is a valour
> greater than victory:
>
> Greatness endures.

## References

1. Bahadur Tejani, 'Can The Prisoner Make a Poet? A Critical Discussion of *Letters to Martha* by Dennis Brutus', *African Literature Today*, No. 6 (1973), pp. 134–5.
2. J. P. Clark, 'Themes of African Poetry of English Expression,' *Présence Africaine*, XXVI, 54 (1965), p. 80.
3. 'The Protest Tradition: *Black Orpheus* and *Transition*', in *Protest and Conflict in African Literature*, ed. Cosmo Pieterse and Donald Munro (London, 1969), p. 109.
4. 'Voices Out of the Skull: A Study of Six African Poets', in *Introduction to African Literature*, ed. Ulli Beier (London, 1967), pp. 110–11.
5. *The Chosen Tongue* (London, 1969), p. 210.
6. ibid., p. 211.
7. Daniel Abasiekong, 'Poetry Pure and Applied: Rebearivelo and Brutus', *Transition*, V, 23 (1965), p. 45.
8. 'Protest Against Apartheid', in *Protest and Conflict in African Literature*, p. 100.
9. See Raymond B. Cattell, *The Scientific Analysis of Personality* (Harmondsworth, 1965; rev. edn 1967), p. 25.
10. 'A troubadour, I traverse all my land', in: *A Simple Lust* (London, 1973), p. 2. Subsequent references to this collection will be embodied in the essay with the abbreviation '*SL*'.

11. Theroux, op. cit., p. 111.
12. Tejani, op. cit., p. 133.
13. ibid., p. 137.
14. ibid., p. 138.
15. See *Idanre and Other Poems* (London, 1967; repr. 1969), p. 44.
16. 'Civilian and Soldier', ibid., p. 53.
17. Moore, op. cit., p. 211 (my italics).
18. Contained in: *Seven South African Poets*, ed. Cosmo Pieterse (London, 1971), p. 29.
19. See Notes 13 and 14 above.
20. 'Poetry and Revolution in Modern Africa', in *African Writers on African Writing*, ed. G. D. Killam (London, 1973), p. 99.
21. Tejani, op. cit., p. 140.
22. See *Collected Poems*, p. 49.
23. Clark, op. cit., p. 80.
24. Tejani, op. cit., p. 142.
25. Theroux, op. cit., pp. 112–14.
26. ibid., p. 113.
27. Yeats, 'Byzantium', in his *Collected Poems*, pp. 280–1.
28. Abasiekong, op. cit., p. 46.

# The Plot Beneath the Skin:
# The Novels of C. J. Driver

▼▼▼▼▼▼▼▼▼▼▼▼▼▼▼▼▼▼▼▼▼▼▼▼▼▼▼▼▼▼▼▼▼▼

ROWLAND SMITH

MANY writers have developed an instinctive revolutionary sympathy when the social conditions around them appear intolerable. During the 1930s a whole group of young English writers persistently jeered at the culture of their age. That capitalist world, with its middle-class values, appeared to them to be flawed beyond repair, decadent, absurd, shuddering along to its final collapse. The fact that they themselves came from the insular world of the professional middle class, wrote for the young intellectuals in that class, and were limited by the experiences of a middle-class upbringing, made all the more dogmatic their sneers at the foibles of the culture they knew from the inside. The revolutionary element in their work is thus curiously interwoven with coterie jokes about coterie taste.

While Auden was giving assent to 'New styles of architecture, a change of heart', he was also giving the house captain's moral advice, 'Prohibit sharply the rehearsed response/And gradually correct the coward's stance.'[1] Even his sympathy for the working class in a typical poem such a 'A Communist to Others' is coloured by an extraordinarily tweedy view of social differences. The ruling classes are:

> Those who in every county town
> For centuries have done you brown,
> But you shall see them tumble down
> Both horse and rider.

While the working classes are the antithesis of the school prefects:

> We do not know how to behave
> We are not beautiful or brave
> You would not pick our sort to save
> Your first fifteen.[2]

This curious mixture of revolutionary ideals and bourgeois instincts is particularly evident in the obsession with the 'leader' that is reflected in the writing of the left-wing authors of the period. The aim of much of the public-school education which they hated was to produce 'leaders'. And in their reaction against public-school values it is often not clear whether they are simply sneering at the concept of the perfect subaltern (as the aim of most public-school education) or conjuring up a revolutionary anti-hero who still has the traits of a character out of *Journey's End*. Auden and Isherwood are defeated by this basic confusion in their verse-play *The Ascent of F6*. Their attempt to show a noble, selfless individual crushed by the jingoism of his peers and the devouring will of his mother is at odds with their own stereotyped, public-school image of what makes the hero-mountaineer an exceptional individual. The central figure is really a kind of Rupert Brooke, as cliché-ridden as the presentation of his mother complex.

The white South African revolutionary in the 1960s found himself in a situation similar to that of the bourgeois revolutionary writers of the 1930s. He too was as encapsulated in his privileged white world as they in their middle class. The obvious injustices of the society are those which, by and large, the white activist sees as an observer rather than as a victim. Even as an object of police harassment he enjoys privileges denied to his black revolutionary ally. So too the liberal premise underlying most white political reaction against the monolithic racist state is inappropriate to an effective black revolutionary programme. These confusions have been delicately incorporated into certain novels about white South African life. However, they choke the work of the young novelist C. J. Driver. Like so many of the socially committed writers of the thirties, he makes political action itself the ostensible centre of his interest. And, like many of them, he balances political motivation against the unconscious drives that arise from dark psychological depths. The result is very similar to that achieved by the writers of the thirties. Their revolutionary-psychoanalytical, guilt-ridden platform is the prototype of his, even though 'liberal' rather than Marxist values form its foundation in Driver's case.

C. J. Driver's four novels have been well received.[3] They are: *Elegy for a Revolutionary* (1969), *Send War in Our Time, O Lord* (1970), *Death of Fathers* (1972), *A Messiah of the Last Days* (1974). The first two deal with revolutionary groups in South Africa, which the author left in 1964; the third with relations among masters, parents and pupils in a British school; the fourth with a revolutionary movement in Britain. The themes of guilt, parental influence, and betrayal recur in all four.

Betrayal provides the link between political and psychological worlds in

*Elegy for a Revolutionary.* The novel is based on real events: the formation and demise of a group of white saboteurs in 1963 and 1964. In the novel, the group sets out to sabotage installations without harming people. They do, however, blow up a night watchman by mistake. Once they are rounded up, the leading personality amongst them agrees to turn state witness, and gives evidence against the group. Most of the fictional events closely parallel historical events, and the characters in the novel bear resemblances to real people. This is one of the strongest points of the book. Driver has an easy narrative style, and his early descriptions of the formation of the sabotage group ring true even when he overexplains the situation for the uninitiated reader. To a certain degree, the interest in at least part of the book is that of seeing in the fiction how the real events could have taken place. But the surface truth is not Driver's concern. His real interest is psychological. Instead of creating a vivid revolutionary character in the person of Jeremy, the betrayer, Driver ponders the wider issues raised by that betrayal. His questions have the ring of the school housemaster about them: in what way is Jeremy a born leader; how does he attain psychological ascendancy over his followers; are they not all capable of his betrayal; who is really innocent? The inward nature of this debate highlights the absurd inefficacy of the revolutionary movement which is its *raison d'etre.* But this is not a created effect. It is as a by-product of the author's soul-searching that the white revolutionaries appear ponderous, dated, and provincial.

In her unfavourable review of *Elegy for a Revolutionary,* Jean Marquard argues that the novel is marred 'by the ambiguity of his [Driver's] attitude to his subject . . . one feels disturbed by the author's lack of clarity, this time on the internal or philosophical issues that the novel attempts to discuss.'[4] In his reply[5] Driver states that the reviewer had made the mistake of 'not recognizing the fundamental technique of the novel: the technique of the imperfect narrator'. He goes on to explain that he wanted to judge Quick, the journalist-saboteur, 'through his own mind'. Driver writes:

> most readers would have felt more comfortable if I had judged Quick directly, and had not attempted a stylistic and psychological judgement. But then I wasn't interested in writing a book about political theory or about the failings of young South African liberals; I was interested in a set of characters in a particular setting, primarily in the tragic and heroic James Jeremy and in Quick, who is incapable of understanding heroism or tragedy because he cannot bear to judge himself objectively.

One of the strange features in this 'stylistic and psychological' approach is that the book does not embody the horror of South African life. The need for revolutionary action, and the goodwill of those determined to topple the regime, are accepted more or less as the data of the story. The group of students among whom Jeremy moves is first described in these bland terms: 'Jeremy, though he could not be called popular at the university – he was too efficient, too ambitious – had a good many hangers-on, students who believed in the same things that he believed or who followed his fashion of thought.'[6] The uncertainty here is typical of the book. Jeremy is efficient and different from those around him. Many of his political allies are shallow. But are they all shallow? Are Jeremy's politics shallow? The remainder of the plot certainly casts doubt on the political *savoir faire* of the group. Towards the end of the book there are increasingly sardonic comments about liberal principles. Yet here Jeremy is exceptional and noteworthy, followed by those with genuine convictions like his as well as by those who are following his fashion. The blinkered, circumscribed student world is there, in the novel, all right, but it is often given assent as part of the glamour which surrounds the exceptional Jeremy. A few lines farther on, Quick is described as reacting to these friends or 'hangers-on' of Jeremy's:

> Quick didn't like many of them very much; he was himself a liberal but he was one by birth not conversion, and he was a pacifist as well, a pacifist who accepted revolution as inevitable, who almost believed in revolution, but who could not stomach what revolution meant. (p. 32)

The author cannot take cover under his theory of the imperfect narrator at this point unless his overt intention is to create confusion. For all their apparent subtlety, the distinctions here are arbitrary. In what direction is the irony (if it is irony) moving? Against Quick's watery beliefs about revolution? Against his congenital liberalism? But isn't the implication that to be a liberal by birth is what distinguishes Quick from Jeremy's converted liberal hangers-on? The ambiguity is not merely in Quick's mind, as Driver would have us believe. There is no centre of gravity to the debate and yet that debate is presented as significant, not as the mere ramblings of the deluded.

The trapped, entombed quality of life for white South Africans with humane values, their terrifying impotence, and the ghastly fact that humane values themselves are part of their privileged status, are all created aspects of Nadine Gordimer's novel, *The Late Bourgeois World*. The difference is marked between her sureness of touch and Driver's confused resonance. *The Late Bourgeois World* opens with a 30-year-old Johannesburg divorcee learning of her ex-husband's suicide. Like Jeremy, he had been a member of a sabotage group; like Jeremy, he had been dominated by prosperous parents; and like Jeremy he had turned state witness. (The public facts of the 1964 sabotage trials affected most white South Africans.) There, however, the similarity ends. As she lives through the rest of the day, the ex-wife wrestles with her own political conscience and her memories of the particular kind of failure her ex-husband was. She explains his suicide to her son: "'. . . he wasn't equal to the demands he . . . he took upon himself." I added lamely, "As if you insisted on playing in the first team when you were only good enough – strong enough for third."'[7] And later thinks: 'Max wasn't anybody's hero; and yet, who knows? When he made his poor little bomb it was to help blow the blacks free; and when he turned state witness the whites, I suppose, might have taken it as justification for claiming him their own man. He may have been just the sort of hero we should expect' (p. 21).

Nadine Gordimer's tone is thoroughly disinfected. She is not attracted to the futile political gesture. She is not trapped in the clichés of an irrelevant Forsterian liberalism implied by phrases such as 'speaking out', 'making a statement', 'taking a position'. And yet she is not scornful of those who hold Forsterian values. The values themselves are not empty. They are merely inappropriate in this situation. That is one of its most depressing features

In Nadine Gordimer's novel the trappings of the late bourgeois world are always in perspective. Part of its theme is the attempt of the central character to focus her world: the terror arising from her contacts with a member of the black underground, her ex-husband's futile political actions, and the bland Edwardian surface of her social life. The mixture is curiously South African, and the author's observation of it beautifully precise. In *Elegy for a Revolutionary*, however, the society itself is seldom the centre of interest. The student world with its parties, girl friends, rugby players, student meetings, merely provides a background for Driver's investigation of Jeremy's qualities of leadership, the nature of his betrayal, and hints of his mother's influence over him.

Driver does not look at the surface of his plot, but continually strives to explain its depths. The plans of his would-be revolutionaries are described at length, their arguments analysed, Jeremy's psychological manipulation of others marvelled at. Yet always the descriptions presuppose the seriousness of the group in which the 'tragic and heroic' Jeremy moves. The perspective is continually from within: 'As the evening went on, Jeremy who, perhaps because he was himself so secretive, never found it difficult to make other people talk about themselves, realized that all Devis's flamboyance covered not the emptiness of too much money and too little thought but the emptiness of despair' (p. 53). The earnestness of this description is typical of *Elegy for a Revolutionary*. Its house chaplain's tone contrasts strikingly with

Nadine Gordimer's elegant poise. In *The Late Bourgeois World*, the saboteur-husband makes a speech at his sister's society wedding, in which, instead of toasting the bride and groom, he lectures the assembled haute bourgeoisie on the dangers of 'moral sclerosis'. His ex-wife comments:

> Poor Max – *moral sclerosis*! The way he fell in love with that prig's phrase and kept repeating it: *moral sclerosis*. Where on earth had he got it from? And all the analogies he kept raking up to go with it. Like our old Sunday school lessons – the world is God's garden and we are all His flowers, etc. (The Blight of Dishonesty, Aphids of Doubt). And could there have been a more unsuitable time and place for such an attempt? What sort of show could his awkward honesty make against the sheer rudeness of him? *They* were all in the right, again, and he was wrong; and I could have kicked him for it. (p. 38)

Nadine Gordimer's scepticism about the effectiveness of white activists makes the situation more oppressive. She does not doubt their genuine dislike of the regime nor their courage. The monolithic brutality of the regime is brought out all the more clearly by her portrayal of a claustrophobic white world in which many of the few active opponents of the status quo are self-centred and woolly minded.

Driver does not create a sense of the quagmire in which his revolutionaries attempt, ineffectually, to act. He also fails to convey an impression of the violence of the regime his characters attempt to topple. The events of his first two novels are brutal. They involve, on one side, sabotage and terrorism, on the other, torture, solitary confinement, and execution. Yet very little horror is communicated. Scenes depicting police behaviour are included, but they have a mannered, literary ring to them. Early in *Elegy for a Revolutionary* the saboteurs are arrested and taken off into solitary confinement. As the security police search the flat of one of them, the following description occurs:

> The sergeant looked at him without replying again for at least ten seconds – he had a trick of doing this. It gives you the impression that he does not think that anyone outside him exists as an object, thought Arthur; except as far as it conforms to an image which he has already formed. Arthur realized suddenly that the sergeant would be a very dangerous person if your behaviour did not conform to the image. (pp. 20–1)

The weakness of this passage is largely caused by its lack of observation. It is almost all abstract; speculative, reflective. Its shallowness is all the more apparent when compared with a well-known passage from Alex La Guma's *A Walk in the Night*. The 'coloured' protagonist is stopped on the streets of Cape Town by two white policemen:

'Where are you walking around, man?' The voice was hard and flat as the snap of a steel spring, and the one who spoke had hard, thin, chapped lips and a faint blonde down above them. He had flat cheekbones, pink-white, and thick, red-gold eyebrows and pale lashes. His chin was long and cleft and there was a small pimple beginning to form on one side of it, making a reddish dot against the pale skin. 'Going home,' Michael Adonis said, looking at the buckle of this policeman's belt. You learned from experience to gaze at some spot on their uniforms, the button of a pocket, or the bright smoothness of their Sam Browne belts, but never into their eyes, for that would be taken as an affront by them.[8]

The superficial details here convey as much the feeling of a sensibility frozen by threat as do the abrasively alien features of the policemen's whiteness. The microscopic accuracy of the observations creates the chilling reality of rule by violence even more than the comment about enforced prudence with which the description ends. Driver never achieves such dramatic clarity in his writing. In spite of all the political material in his novels, he is not really interested in writing about politics or political action. Nor is he concerned with the outward or observable.

The denouement in *Elegy for a Revolutionary* involves Quick's seeing the real Jeremy for the first time. He has betrayed his friends in court, and is about to be shown to have betrayed his friend in bed, when that friend meets him for a man-to-man talk. Jeremy 'explains' that he is 'a special person' and Quick 'understands ... suddenly, for just a moment':

He saw what he had known about Jeremy from the start, he saw the enormous egocentricity which went with an equal distrust of self, a distrust of the privately heroic, a distrust which could only go with an egocentricity so certain that it could not be doubted – for if the self was the centre of the world, the touchstone of all judgements, the heart of light, then you could distrust it because it could not be destroyed. Quick saw, for just that one moment, that Jeremy had not broken, that Jeremy had not turned into anything – all he had done was to fulfil himself.

Apart from the confusion at the heart of this subtlety – that this is a momentary vision of something Quick had 'known ... from the start' – the extraordinary feature of the scene is its sense of revelation. The facts of the plot have repeatedly made it obvious that Jeremy is self-centred. His behaviour is arrogant and spoiled; his amateur's inability to follow professional sabotage instructions clearly irresponsible. The amazing element of the story is not that he should betray his friends, but that they should take him so seriously.

*Elegy for a Revolutionary* is based on real events. As a result it embodies an element of political and psychological reality which Driver's inward analyses cannot distort. In *Send War in Our Time, O Lord,* however, the plot is unconvincing. The widow of a noted white schoolmaster travels, after his death, to the mission settlement founded by an illustrious ancestor. She is on the verge of breakdown, and plans to overcome her grief with selfless toil. She becomes involved by accident with a black terrorist group; suffers anguish and collapse; her old-fashioned values offer no solace; she finally kills herself.

The black guerrillas remain shadowy figures throughout the book; their campaign incredible. Driver's interest is openly on the mixture of guilt and trauma in the central character, obsessed with the great men in her life: her husband and the legendary Dr Allen. From them she derives her idea of selfless leadership, implicit in her concept of 'service' on the settlement. Yet the reality of the decaying mission station is a continual denial of her unrealistic belief in the values and sacrifices involved in its establishment.

Mrs Allen's pride in the renowned Dr Allen is presented as a parody of imperial creeds: 'the founder of the Allen family, the founder of this settlement, the world-famous Doctor Timothy Xavier Allen, the enormous, larger-than-life hunter turned doctor and then missionary, one of the first men to see that the way to men's souls lay through proper care of their bodies'.[9] But the leader-mystique reappears in another form in the book; in this case without any irony. Simbele, the black teacher on the settlement, has been a political leader. His new identity as schoolmaster has been assumed after his release from imprisonment for political activities. On him, Driver focuses his debate on true leadership. Simbele is the link between the terrorist-guerrillas and the outside world, and he meets a heroic and tortured end at the hands of the police.

Not only does Simbele embody the traits of the true leader, which Mrs Allen sentimentally attributes to old Dr Allen; he is also the vehicle for an involved discussion on leadership among the guerrillas. He muses in this fashion on their leader: 'Well, thought Simbele, that is what being a leader means; that is what I am not. Once there was a time when a man whom I have now destroyed was that; but he is destroyed' (p. 80). The leader wins both Simbele's loyalty and that of Petrus, a boy member of the group. When the leader is gunned down by an unscrupulous rival from his own ranks, Petrus's horrified desire for revenge is presented in the most extraordinarily melodramatic terms: '. . . had he cried for the old leader? Yes, thought Simbele, it was probably mostly for the old leader, the man who had made Petrus start on the all-road, for Petrus would need a leader, would need to have one man to follow – and now he carried two empty shells in his pocket, to make him remember' (p. 149). Petrus finally kills the usurper and leaves the two cartridge cases with the body.

The tone and values here are just as stilted as those of Mrs Allen, and yet in these passages they are given authorial assent. Like Mrs Allen, Driver is himself obsessed with the concept of the dynamic leader or man of mystical influence. As with the left-wing writers of the thirties, his supposed interest in revolution and social comment often only provides the framework for a dramatic discussion of the ideal Head of School (who may well be marred by a Freudian mother or at least Freudian guilt).

Driver's third novel, *Death of Fathers*, would seem to clinch the comparison between his mode and that of the early Auden, Isherwood, and Warner. The setting is irredeemably that of the private school. No revolution is possible; no great injustices revealed. The plot hinges on concepts of betrayal (there are several kinds: fathers and sons, masters and boys, friends and wives), suggestions of the psychological burdens passed from father to son, and visionary glimpses of the awesome responsibilities that befall a born leader of boys. The setting is far removed from Cape Town and sabotage. But the tone and manner of *Death of Fathers* are the same as those of the earlier two novels.

In his latest novel, *A Messiah of the Last Days*, Driver has returned to almost all the themes of *Elegy for a Revolutionary*, although – once again – the setting is England. The novel deals with the emotional hold that a young radical has on his followers and the middle-class lawyer who defends him on a charge of murdering a police informer. Like *Elegy for a Revolutionary*, *A Messiah of the Last Days* dwells at length on the nature of its hero's influence. That hero, John Buckleson, is the leader of the Free People, a group who live communally in a warehouse and have a vision of an alternate society based on imaginative urban planning. Buckleson is fascinating and vital. A solicitor briefing the barrister-narrator explains in a piece of heavy-handed dialogue typical of the book: "'. . . but there's no denying the young man has charm. They don't call it that any more, do they? There's another word, a foreign-sounding one."/"Charisma?" I suggested./"That's the one. Same as we used to call charm, isn't it?"'[10]

The theme has announced itself: mystical influence in the man of vision. Tom Grace, the narrator, wishes to believe in Buckleson because the latter's rhetorical fervour captivates him. Grace retells in detail his many dreams (an interest he shares with writers of the thirties). One of them involves an ideal city. It is this dream which Buckleson makes real. Hence Grace's attachment to Buckleson in spite of his ruthless behaviour and his history of psychiatric illness. Because the significance of the Visionary Leader is so arbitrarily imposed on the plot, it has to be explained by the narrator: 'Was he deluded? Was the man who had made my dreams come alive on a summer's afternoon in a crowded park only a madman? A nutter? There was no answer to any question, only a sense of unease which was also curiosity' (p. 38).

For all its apparent chic; for all the trendiness of its comment on Britain in the seventies, *A Messiah of the Last Days* repeatedly reveals this kind of laborious issue-seeking. Not only is the leadership debate itself stilted, but also the psychiatric explanations of Buckleson's egomania are – to say the least – familiar. He has run away from an unhappy family with a crushing, pious mother and a successful, hard-hearted father. And the skeleton in the family cupboard is revealed by a portrait of his alcoholic grandfather. 'What made him turn to this wickedness?' asks Buckleson's mother. And the imperfect narrator has an answer which he is too polite to give: 'What could I say? That I did not understand myself? That the explanation lay in a household where an only son was watched every moment of every day for evidence he would repeat his grandfather's weaknesses, where his father did not care for his wife or son or home, where every time he walked down the passage he saw his drunkard of a grandfather staring with ironic intensity down from the wall . . .' (p. 218).

The circle is complete. *A Messiah of the Last Days* obviously returns to the debate on the Jeremy-type begun in *Elegy for a Revolutionary*, and the similarities are marked. However, the discussion on leadership, guilt, and betrayal has been the informing spirit in all Driver's novels, even in the second and the third. His real subject matter has not changed at all.

### References

1. 'XXX', *Poems*, 2nd edn, (London, 1940), p. 89.
2. Michael Roberts, ed., *New Country* (London, 1933), p. 210.
3. Two reviews by Jean Marquard in the South African journal, *Contrast*, are notable exceptions. Both are unfavourable, and raise serious questions about the books. They are: 'Personal Frustration', *Contrast*, 22 (1969), pp. 90–2 (a review of *Elegy*); and 'Not Stranger than Truth', *Contrast*, 25 (1971), pp. 90–1 (a review of *Send War*).
4. 'Personal Frustration', *Contrast*, 22 (1969), p. 90.
5. 'The Imperfect Narrator', *Contrast*, 26 (1971), pp. 94–6.
6. *Elegy for a Revolutionary* (Harmondsworth, 1971), p. 32 (first edn, London, 1969).
7. *The Late Bourgeois World* (New York, 1966), p. 20.
8. *A Walk in the Night and other stories* (London, 1968), p. 11.
9. *Send War in Our Time, O Lord* (London, 1970), p. 21.
10. *A Messiah of the Last Days* (London, 1974), p. 32.

# Arthur Nortje:
# Craftsman for His Muse

▼▼▼▼▼▼▼▼▼▼▼▼▼▼▼▼▼▼▼▼▼▼▼▼▼▼▼▼▼▼▼▼▼▼

## CHARLES DAMERON

WHEN Arthur Nortje committed suicide at Oxford in 1970 shortly before he was to be deported back to South Africa, he left behind a body of poetry which is remarkable for its flexible powerful diction, its piercing insight, and its reflection of the poet's intense self-examinations. Many of his poems were published posthumously in the collection *Dead Roots* (London, 1973); others are still in manuscript and are at present unpublished. Nortje wrote a number of these poems while in his early twenties, and he was only 27 at the time of his death. During the last five years Nortje lived in England and Canada in self-imposed exile. The bulk of his later work reflects his deep concerns as an exile and wanderer: with the turmoil in his distant homeland, with his experiences in new environments, and with the introspective demands of his poetic craft.

In the poems on South Africa written prior to his departure, Nortje laments the shackles on free speech that bind the outraged black dissident. His poem (Soliloquy: South Africa) poses the situation by using sharply ironic reversal:

> I have seen men with haunting voices
> turned into ghosts by a piece of white paper
> as if their eloquence had been black magic. (*DR*, p. 5)

It is the impersonal ban on public speech that black-magically turns these men into disembodiments of themselves. Furthermore, when language is gagged, and one can speak 'only in whispers of freedom/now that desire has become subversive', the relationship between man and country becomes strained and awkward. One is left to vent frustration and rage through mere soliloquy; the poet opens and closes the poem with the same line: 'It seems me speaking all the lonely time.' In 'Hangover', Nortje reiterates this notion when he says that 'Silence keeps me home, I'm lonely' (p. 9).

He breaks this silence through his poetry; his image for his creative work is one of isolated roaring, and appropriately reflects his situation:

> I am alone here now, here living
> with shoals of fragments, a voice hoarse like rubble
> shifted by currents.

Occasionally Nortje personifies South Africa. In 'Windscape' he depicts his homeland as a 'wild slut' who 'howls for rain/to soothe her caked and aching hollows' (p. 21). More often she is an estranged lover. In 'The long silence', written shortly before his departure from South Africa in 1965, Nortje again expresses the consequences of political repression:

> The long silences speak
> of deaths and removals.
> Restrictions, losses
> have strangled utterance.
> How shall I embrace your rhythms? (p. 24)

Temporal estrangement leads Nortje to ponder the matter of spatial estrangement. Has the former been nurturing the latter? Nortje suggests so in these lines which set up a metaphor of organic, inevitable growth:

> the loveless essence
> remains the empty
> nights and years, husks of the exile.

The exile grows ripe and ready for his personal harvesting. As the moment nears, Nortje speaks of his 'swelling dream' to his lover, who is presumably both a specific individual and his country in general:

> Parting of ways exposed
> love's tattered fabric
> but the world rose
> larger through the tears in bright enticement.
>                         ('Song for a passport', p. 30)

So Nortje chooses the rest of the world over South Africa. His ties of love with his homeland have frayed, though they still exist. But the poet demands his freedom, and in the poem's final lines he cries, 'O ask me all but do not ask allegiance'. He does not repudiate his people, but the conditions of repressive apartheid which limit his actions and artistic expression. In 'Transition', Nortje bids affectionate farewell to his struggling black countrymen:

> For your success, black residue,
> I bear desire still, night thing!
> Remain in the smoky summer long
> though I be gone from green-flamed spring. (p. 31)

Once in exile, Nortje recalls his homeland with sadness and a sense of helplessness before some overriding world fate. In 'Cosmos in London' he remembers three South Africans whom he admires – Brutus, Mandela, and Lutuli – then halts and speaks of the futility of these painful thoughts:

> – but the memory
> disturbs the order of the song, and whose
> tongue can stir in such a distant city?
> The world informs her seasons, and she,
> solid with a kind of grey security,
> selects and shapes her own strong tendencies.
> We are here, nameless, staring at ourselves. (p. 39)

This view of memory, as something which is disturbing and even insidious because it cannot be altered, echoes a vivid passage from the earlier poem, 'Soliloquy in South Africa'. 'In you/lies so much speech of mine buried/ that for memory to be painless I must knife it' (p. 6). But memories, unlike people, do not die; they absorb poetic knifings and merely wait for the inevitable resummoning.

As time passes in exile, Nortje feels the need to self-justify his decision to abandon South Africa. In 'Affinity (To Maggie)' he gives two reasons to justification – his lack of belonging and his artistic sensitiveness; on the latter he asks rhetorically, 'and why/should I deny them' (p. 62). In several other poems he elaborates on the notion of not fitting into the society by alluding to his mixed parentage. While speaking bitterly of a broken love affair in 'Casualty' he says, 'I shall be true eternally towards/ my father Jew, who forked the war-time virgins' (p. 35). In 'Waiting' he refers to the complexities of his mixed heritage when he reflects that 'Origins trouble the voyager much, those roots/that have sipped the waters of another continent' (p. 90). Much later he takes a sharply critical view of his paternal branch, identifying it with 'white trash/coursing through my blood/for all the unalienable seasons' ('Questions and Answers', p. 141). In 'Dogsbody half-breed', a brilliant poem written during his creative surge in the final year of his life, Nortje focuses on the agony of South Africa, which is similarly his personal agony – a mixed heritage caused by the 'Magnet of exotica . . . which brought blond settlers like a hex/into the heartland, oxdrawn, ammunitioned' (p. 104). This imposed a wearisome burden on the land: 'Maternal muscle of my mixed blood life/ with child were you heavy, with discontent rife.' After biting some injustices and cruelties that the blond settlers have inflicted on the indigenous black community, Nortje volunteers to reduce the friction between black and white, presumably through his poetry:

> and I hybrid, after Mendel,
> growing between the wire and the wall,
> being dogsbody, being me, buffer you still.

This passage suggests that the poet sees himself as a buffer who has absorbed the abrasions that the two surfaces cause as they rub at each other. This seems fanciful, as does Nortje's conclusion to 'Poem: South African', where he develops a transcending vision that emerges out of his poetry:

> The wind guillotines
>                     your correspondences
> but these broken sentences
>         stumble to heaven on the hill despite
>         the man with the ship who beats my
>         emaciated words back
>
> they die but
>         at last
> get us all together as a vision
>         incontrovertible, take me as evidence. (p. 114)

Though the words die, the images, ideals, and concepts for which they stand do not; those things which words merely symbolize are not mangled when language is, but can become a communal vision. The poet asks that we take him as evidence that this is so.

In his rich and complex attack on apartheid in 'Questions and Answers', Nortje demands vengeance and projects his role as avenger:

> I am no guerilla.
> I will fall out of the sky as the Ministers gape from their
>                                                 front porch
> and in broad daylight perpetrate atrocities
> on the daughters of the boss:
> ravish like Attila. (p. 139)

The passage is ambiguous – perhaps consciously so. Does the poet mean to become an active, bloodthirsty revolutionary upon his return to South Africa? Probably not; yet how his poetry would achieve such results is unclear also. The final lines of the poem continue the revenge motif, yet there is a sense of self-destruction here also:

> I bred words in hosts, in vain, I'll have to
> bleed: bleed for the broken mountains, lost
> Umshlanga, Hangklip, Winterberg,
> the starving rivers wait for me to plunge through
> to the forefront,
> the mud has hardened on my boots.
> Ancestors will have their graves uprooted,
> uncouth will be the interrogations and bloody the reprisals.
>                                                 (p. 141)

In these lines Nortje repudiates his poetry (while in the process of creating poetry) and adopts a rather suicidal stance that may or may not reflect the notion of returning to South Africa. He never did return, but died from a drug overdose shortly after writing 'Questions and Answers'.

A significant aspect of Nortje's poetry is the degree to which it reflects the work of a conscious prosodist using traditional English forms. With few exceptions, his poems are shaped in stanzaic patterns. Most repeat a pattern of a fixed length, ranging from three, four, six, seven, eight, to ten lines, although others are fashioned with stanzas of varying lengths. The collection also contains eight sonnets. Of the few poems which do not have stanzaic patterns, one depends on a visual pattern like some of E. E. Cummings' work while the others achieve form through line indentation. At another point Nortje juxtaposes the inhuman activities of Vietnam ('This is our napalm year, the year of the million lost illusions') with the remarkable but sterile technological achievements in space exploration:

> I admire our doings, yes, the shiny calyx
> holding the platinum petals reports the desert:
> transmitters bleep in the dry gardens of the moon.
> ('For Sylvia Plath II', p. 48)

The cosmonaut who returned to earth dead and the three astronauts who burned to death in training become the most sensational modern images of man's inevitable arrival at death's domain in 'My mother was a woman' (p. 73). Nortje speaks of death in an early poem as 'the final truth,/ Not malice and not love or magic spell./Whose past is black or white no glance can tell. ('Bitter fragment', p. 23). Death, the colour-blind final equalizer, reconciles the races. Nortje responds to one particular death, Gamel Abdel Nasser's, with a poem of lament. The process of grieving recalls other grounds for sorrow:

> I think of the sons of Africa sometimes
> and my heart bursts.
> When I think of Chaka or Christ the rebel
> my heart bursts.
> ('Nasser is dead', p. 131)

As an exile and wanderer, Nortje, a truly contemporary poet, drew upon his immediate environment and matters of global significance for many of his images and themes. He incorporated this material into his work in an integral way, and in doing so demonstrated the breadth and power of his poetic vision.

In a recent work on African writers, Nadine Gordimer notes the sharp differences in thematic concerns between European/American writers and their African counterparts. She argues that African writing does not reflect the 'hyperintrospective tendency of much of contemporary European writing. . . . European and American writers find themselves on the very edge of being' (*The Black Interpreters*, Johannesburg, 1973, p. 10). African writers, she suggests, are concerned with social and political developments in their respective countries. Gordimer's observation is generally accurate; Nortje, however, is an exception to this notion. Much of his work is, in fact, quite hyperintrospective, and the explanation to this is bound up in a large part with his exile and his ultimate allegiance to his Muse.

Nortje often expresses a strong sense of loneliness and separation in his work. In 'Exception' he says

> There are no people I can closely know.
> When passion stirs the spirit
> diffidence or apathy melts
> the urge to make the joy deliberate. (p. 15)

In the final stanza he suggests that his lover is an exception to this statement; the shift works within the poem, but doesn't seem to create a constant source of renewal in Nortje's personal life. For in 'Americans in town' he reflects on life and love with these words:

> It's what I like
>             now, my life, the world of birds, dusk, sequence
> without result, but purpose that can strike
> to bend her will at any moment. Once
> I thought of love as permanent, but since
> I've come to know the growing grey of absence. (p. 68)

These lines express a grave but calm resignation to life; at another time, however, the poet's sense of loneliness is traumatic:

> I suffer the radiation burns of silence.
> It is not cosmic immensity or catastrophe
> that terrifies me:
> it is the solitude that mutilates,
> the night bulb that reveals ash on my sleeve.
>                                         ('Waiting', p. 91)

Indeed, the solitude of darkness comes to obsess Nortje, and a number of his poems reflect the turmoil that seizes him at night. Diabolical images emerge again and again; in 'Notes from the middle of the night' Nortje begins by saying 'Untold anxieties through the dark/cannot at random exorcise themselves' (p. 121). The room seems to come alive and haunt the poet:

> Through the flow of silence, tenor of night,
> unlovely the butterfly guts that won't relax
> the brain that reeks with guilt feelings
> hearing a peripatetic devil
> in the cooling of a floorboard or a cat's tread.

But the dawn brings relief and breaks the grip of madness:

> I will lay me down to sleep in strong sunshine
> airing these fretful sentiments,
> with a sigh letting go these obsessions.

'The Near-mad' follows a similar pattern; Nortje speaks of delusions that 'haunt you to lunacy' and of the miraculous escape: 'A hair's-breadth from the edge of hell/you hug the miracle of dreamless sleep' (p. 69). The delusions that he speaks of represent, at least in part, the bitter disappointments and utter loneliness of life. Nortje wrote two poems to Sylvia Plath, the American poet who knew the grip of madness, in which he cites personal betrayal and the insane destructiveness of civilization as conditions for madness. Nortje's world at these moments is a bleak and excruciatingly painful one.

Nortje leans on drugs and alcohol to ease this pain and alter reality for momentary respite. In 'My mother was a woman' he notes that

> The milk that cannot permeate the blue
> steel existence, quietly in the glass
> syringe affords me some drab ecstasy. (p. 73)

Yet fixes and acid trips, like moonshots, inevitably return the traveller to this earth-framed reality, as this passage in 'Message from an LSD eater' affirms:

> Who has taken a fortunate trip
> beyond the moon, past violet stars, through luminous soundwaves
> invisibly travelling the years' kaleidoscope
> falls back into the sea of capture,
> is earthbound, banal, nauseous, sorry. (p. 78)

Besides plumbing his loneliness and indulging in drugs, Nortje gave his senses free rein to explore the gritty recesses of life. This led to feelings of self-disgust, at times, but increased his range of experiences. In a series of late sonnets Nortje defends his actions as necessary ones for him to take. In 'Natural Sinner' he recounts how 'I have preyed on my emotions like a mantis' and 'how the glut/of worms in meat has forced verse from my bones' (p 137). Nortje addresses a disturbed audience in 'Sonnet three' and speaks of his relationship to his art:

> Unpalatable beast, or you who think
> I revel in disgust, yourself are cloyed
> with chocolates and caviar, discreetly stink;
> in self-indulgence, secret self-abuse
> you wallow in self-same mud, know not the void
> I as a sycophant wander in, timeserver to the Muse. (p. 135)

Nortje could speak ironically of his world as a void and himself as a mere sycophant to his art, yet his intense devotion to his creative impulses allowed him to fashion his brilliant verse, with all its evidences of human warts and griminess. As Nortje notes about his subject matter in the beginning of this poem,

> What is mundane I wish to make sublime,
> What ordinarily moves upon the ground
> can rise and rainbow, shooting from the slime,
> can glow in revelation, can transcend.

The stuff of life is what Nortje fashioned into poetry. And in turn, Nortje seemed to believe that the creative impulse saved him from madness and allowed him to come to terms with himself and his experiences. The final stanza of 'Shock Therapy' sums up this motion vividly:

> Spreadeagled in the blue gore on the page
> or tightening the words to pearls of sweat
> that the busy brain fosters from a latent life,
> shock is the stilling therapy for the post. (p. 109)

Stilling therapy though it may often have been, Nortje's verse nevertheless records the disintegration process of a gifted, despairing young African exile. In one of his final poems the poet speaks in a moment of quiet, drained reflections:

> What consolation comes
> drops away in bitterness.
> Blithe footfalls pass my door
> as I recover from the wasted years.
>     ('All hungers pass away', p. 146)

Shortly afterwards, however, Nortje was dead, his voice silent, his recovery aborted. Yet his finely crafted, sensitive, compelling poetry remains, a gift from Nortje and his Muse.

# Politics and Literature in Africa: The Drama of Athol Fugard

## ROBERT J. GREEN

THE writings and practice of Julius Nyerere exemplify the intimate relationship between culture and politics that obtains today in Africa; they are parabolic of the unity of the continent's intellectual life. The author of three substantial volumes of theory, who has been described as one of the foremost political thinkers of our age, Nyerere is in addition a statesman of international stature, the translator of Shakespeare's *Julius Caesar* and *The Merchant of Venice*, and an educational theorist whose views are often considered alongside Ivan Illich's.[1] There is here a totality of vision, a remarkable holism, that recalls Marx's celebrated phrase in *The Critique of Political Economy* about 'the whole process of social, political and intellectual life'. Nyerere has, it is true, warned Tanzanian intellectuals against the uncritical acceptance of foreign socialist ideologies; he said that this would turn them into 'intellectual apes ... of the left'.[2]

And yet in his own refusal to bifurcate principle from practice or culture from society he is epitomizing the most vital legacy of Marxian thought. Although Nyerere has not yet addressed himself to any full theoretical statement about literary criticism – to the assumptions underpinning, for example, his two Shakespearean translations – his work contains a number of implicit ideas which, if developed, could prove valuable to African criticism.

One of Nyerere's essays deals explicitly with the relation between the intellectual and a developing nation. It is titled 'The Intellectual Needs Society' and this phrase offers us a serviceable summary of Nyerere's views here and in similar treatments of the same issue.[3] He always recognizes that the intellectual is objectively different from the farmer or the urban labourer: he is literate, articulate, and familiar with the deployment of abstract ideas. Yet at the same time the intellectual is dependent on the majority of society, on the less privileged who have financed his education, since a poor society provides him with the opportunity of relating his knowledge to the practical problems of 'help[ing] people to transform their lives from abject poverty – that is, from fear of hunger and always endless drudgery – to decency and simple comfort'.[4] The western intellectual Nyerere notes, doesn't possess this direct access to the levers of fundamental social transformation; the intellectual in Europe or America may discover with disappointment that his skills of analysis and celebration may only mean 'the difference between a coloured and a black-and-white television service – which is hardly calculated to give one mental or emotional stimulus!'[5] The intellectual in Africa has, then, privileges, of status and of mental sophistication, that must set him apart from his fellows. But he also has obligations, a contractual relationship with society which necessitates that he both harness his aptitudes to the transformation of his world and that he permit the practice of the majority, accumulated from a familiarity with the actual and concrete, to inform and enrich his theory.

These ideas are patently related to the wider discussion that has been conducted all over independent Africa about the nature of the intellectual's commitment. The literary critic is only one kind of intellectual, like the economist or the agronomist, and plainly his concerns are embraced by Nyerere's general propositions: this controversy is, however, all too familiar and I don't propose to allude to it further. In addition, though, it also seems that Nyerere's theory – of a dialectical relationship in the intellectual between his privileged mental autonomy and his social affiliations – has a further interest to the literary critic; the intellectual's existence can be seen, in fact, as paradigmatic of the existence lived by the work of art itself, the novel or poem that is the object of our professional attention. That is to say, like the critic/intellectual of Nyerere's essays, the work of literature is simultaneously blessed with a degree of luxurious autonomy and is also socially conditioned, externally receptive, and enriched. Nyerere's sustained recognition, both in his writings and in his political practice, of the delicacy of this relationship in so far as it concerns the intellectual, the understanding he has shown of the ease with which freedom may be abused and commitment trivialized, is, I am suggesting, paralleled by the sensitivity required by the critic as he seeks to unravel the complexities in the work of art's existence as an artifact, discrete and with its own verbal or plastic structure, and its genesis in an external, cultural and historical, reality.

This point seems worth making because examples abound of the balance being unachieved in recent critical practice. Even worse, we read articles and books on African literature that seem blind to the need for any such harmony, the obligation on the critic to recognize that there are countervailing pressures in a novel or poem – some centripetal, bearing inwards on the work's structural unity; others centrifugal, pulling outwards to the circumambient, 'real' world.[6] In the interests of critical health, which would result in the fullest, most sensitive elucidation of a work possible to the individual critic, neither of these two different tensions can lawfully be ignored. All that we can do, as critics and readers, is surely to welcome their complicating coexistence and to attempt to move alertly between the two, mindful both of the work's inner dynamics and of its social determinants.[7]

The first of these pressures leads to the desire to see the work of literature as absolutely free and unconditioned. (This is paralleled, perhaps, by the claim advanced by some students in Africa to the licence of total separateness from their impoverished environment.) Its critical methodology, formalist and structuralist in sympathy, has been exported to Africa by exponents of the Anglo-American 'New Criticism', a 'multinational corporation' which once enjoyed a virtual hegemony in western literary criticism. Frequently affiliated with political conservatism, its exponents have produced criticism which is often notoriously ahistoricist. Thus history was reduced to the aridities of a specious 'literary history' in which the determinants were limited to the explication of influences of 'genre' and 'tradition' totally divorced from any real, lived historical process. Literature is separated from life; personal divided from social relationships. It is true, of course, that critics of this persuasion have, at their best, produced illuminating studies of the textual densities, the harmonies of image and metaphor, in particular works. Nevertheless for us the essential point is that there is a deep-seated contradiction between a purist, orthodox 'New Criticism' and the actualities of African art, both today and in the past. It is well known that traditional African aesthetics, pre-industrial and pre-literate, could not have included any notion of art's being discrete and 'unapplied': art – plastic, ritualistic, or narrative – was embedded in practice, custom, and communal belief. Similarly today, in very different cultural circumstances, in an urban, cash-centred society, art is tightly bound up with the social polity, a unity evidenced by the biographies of many writers, in the East and West as well as, very sharply, in the chained South. It is difficult, then, to envisage how a New Critical methodology can, in its purest form, be of any relevance to the explication of African literature. For an African critic to write from these beliefs would, one might suggest, be equivalent to what Nyerere has described as the intellectual's treason when he frees himself in arrogance from public obligations.

There is, however, a second form of betrayal and one that is less easy
to write about if only because it appears better intentioned, more generous,
and superficially more 'committed'. Nevertheless, there is evidence that
recent criticism has been written which ignores the distinctions between
a work of imaginative literature and, say, a political manifesto or a socio-
logical critique. As a result, African artists have been castigated on the
grounds that their work is not explicitly 'progressive' in content or extractable statement. Such criticism might perhaps claim a line of descent from
Engels and Lenin, yet neither of these models encouraged such reductive
procedures. Engels, for example, detested Balzac's monarchism and his
anti-democratic instincts; V. S. Pritchett has recently told us how Balzac
saw the physical turmoil of the 1848 Revolution primarily as an opportunity for assuaging his 'bricabracomania' with some covert looting. Still,
for all this, Engels paid tribute to the 'triumph of realism' in the *Comédie
Humaine*. Lenin, similarly, was critical of Tolstoy's 'utopian socialism'
while remarking about *Anna Karenina* that one of Levin's metaphors in
the novel couldn't be bettered as a 'characterization of the period 1861/
1905'. Certainly we must attend to the question of a novel's social life – that
it is the product of an individual writing out of a concrete historical situation, and that it has the potency both to reflect that situation and to facilitate
its transformation – but these recognitions oughtn't to lead to literature
being reduced to what is programmatic and paraphraseable. An African
novel, thus, may superficially be 'counter-revolutionary', like Balzac's
enormous tapestry of Louis-Philippe's bourgeois monarchy, and in its
setting and characterization may seem to be advocating political reaction
or condoning an inert status quo. When we look again, however, with the
sensitivity required by literature's complexities, we may discover that the
fiction's most vital energies, its verbal harmonies and the rhythms of its
plot, are being employed in the service of political radicalism. In this way,
in Balzac's *Cousin Bette* (1846), a novel published by a reactionary on the
eve of revolution, Hulot's frenetic energy in philandering and in raising
money illicitly is evidence, alongside the implacable class-hatred of Bette
himself, of Balzac's deepest intuitions about the approaching political
convulsions.

What concerns us here, in the context of African literature and its bur-
geoning criticism, is the tendency for the politics of a work of art to be
seen as in some way extractable from its aesthetic formulations. For, if
there is a danger, as Nyerere has perceived, of the intellectual trivializing
the moral responsibilities he owes his society, so too, it seems, is there a
possibility that the critic will view the political ramifications of a poem or
novel in a mechanistic, philistine fashion. In fact, of course, art's political

impetuses can never be exposed for analysis and understanding by the use of a simplistic, reductive methodology, whether it be 'vulgar-marxist' or 'formalist'. In any work of literature that merits our discussion the relations between its political and aesthetic components will always be complex and dynamic. Indeed these two elements can only be separated provisionally and artificially, because they are in reality one and inseparable. Eugene Goodheart expressed this unity very lucidly in his recent book, *Culture and the Radical Conscience*. Politics, he wrote, is not 'a merely adventitious element' in the work of literature, nor should the critic's 'political attention to literature' ever be 'discontinuous with an aesthetic awareness of the literary process'.[8] Goodheart, it is true, was here addressing himself particularly to the American situation, yet his observations can scarcely be less relevant to Africa today, where the political and cultural domains are continuously overlapping and merging. The political thrust of African literature, I am suggesting – that is, our sense of whether this particular work is aligned with, is advancing the cause of reactionary or progressive forces in society – cannot be evaluated solely from what the author seems to be 'saying'. 'The way it is said' must also be considered: 'the political implication of a work is bound up with the imaginative disposition of the artist. His development as an artist, which includes matters of language, characterization, narrative method, may also be a matter of politics.'[9]

The plays of Athol Fugard offer an opportunity to explore some of the political and artistic tensions in the work of one of Africa's leading writers. Furthermore the nature of the society in which Fugard is writing, repressive and philistine, censorious and neurotically suspicious, lend to the tension innate in any literature a particular exigency and a singular sharpness. As an outsider reads any work of South African literature he is conscious of this underlying reality: art produced in such hostile circumstances must be vulnerable to political temptations and aesthetic dangers which are in equal measure aesthetic temptations and political dangers. Nadine Gordimer's latest novel, *The Conservationist*, is remarkable for the skill with which the illiberal views of its central character, Mehring, a rich industrialist scornful of political dissenters, are 'placed' and made worthy of our interest. But, as Fugard himself has said, 'there are several ideas I have for plays which I just know would not be allowed to reach the stage or, if they did, would be shut down very soon after opening'.[10] Drama is perhaps a more fragile, imperilled genre than fiction. In these forbidding circumstances, under the constant threat of censorship or closure, it is inspiring and remarkable that Fugard has created plays at all. Nor is our sense of the magnitude of his achievement lessened when we remember that this substantial body of work (beginning with *No-Good Friday* and *Nongogo* in the late fifties, leading on to *The Blood Knot, Hello and Goodbye,* and *Boesman and Lena* ('The Family Trilogy'), and now, most recently, the experimental *Sizwe Bansi, The Island,* and *Statements*) was done in a theatrical vacuum, with no effective tradition of 'western drama in' South Africa within which Fugard could place himself and learn his craft.[11] Fugard was once asked by a British interviewer whether his early experiences as a journalist had included meetings with South African playwrights. 'There were none around', he replied.[12] Eliot's celebrated phrase 'Tradition and the Individual Talent', would have, in this situation, only a mocking, ironic irrelevance: Fugard's talent is at work quite bereft of any sustaining tradition and, furthermore, it must nourish itself in opposition to an illiberal milieu.

His detestation of the policies of the Nationalist regime has never been ambiguous since the period in 1958 when he worked in Johannesburg's 'Native Commissioner's Court'. These months he has described as a 'traumatic' experience for him and led directly to his first play, *No-Good Friday*.[13] Fugard's commitment to change hasn't wavered in the intervening seventeen years, but what has undeniably altered is his sense of the relation between his work in theatre and his political engagement. The two introductory essays written for *Three Port Elizabeth Plays* and *Statements,* in conjunction with the plays themselves, constitute some fascinating evidence about the dynamics of literature's political life in contemporary Africa.

From 1961 to 1968 Fugard was at work on what he now sees as his 'Family Trilogy', his large reputation outside Africa being built on these three plays. During those years Fugard had been preoccupied with domestic, familial relationships, this stage of his work being summarized in a Notebook entry for September 1968:

> The thought today that *Boesman and Lena* is the third part of a trilogy, that together with *The Blood Knot* and *Hello and Goodbye* it should be called *The Family*.
>
> First [in *Blood Knot*] brother and brother, then child and parent [*Hello and Goodbye*], and now in *Boesman and Lena,* parent and parent, man and woman.[14]

The completed trilogy forms a powerful and moving exploration of the tensions generated from intimacy; it is, beyond doubt, a major theatrical achievement.[15] Racial injustice, the currency of daily human impoverishment under apartheid, is never far away from the action and dialogue of the trilogy, but is hardly presented explicitly. In these plays the reality of a statutory inhumanity is a ceaseless murmur at the level of their 'sub-text';

it is present only in the assumptions and perspectives of the characters: *Boesman and Lena* is sufficiently indirect to have nearly provoked a riot *against* Fugard during one ghetto production.

After completing *Boesman* – whose intentions were in reality *opposed* to apartheid – Fugard seems to have become dissatisfied with the domestic realism of the trilogy and his three later plays are marked by changes in content and in dramatic style. Fugard's themes have moved from the family outwards, to the various ways in which a harsh society impinges upon the individual's freedom. In *Sizwe Bansi Is Dead* it is the pass laws and their limitations upon the freedom of man as a worker; in *The Island*, the draconian penal system; and finally, in *Statements After an Arrest Under the Immorality Act*, the effect of sexual prohibitions upon man's erotic and emotional growth. Repression and barbarity are portrayed explicitly; these plays could never be misunderstood in the ghetto as succouring apartheid. This development in Fugard's art had been anticipated earlier, in a Notebook entry for December 1968:

> The social content of *Boesman and Lena*. Nagging doubts that I am opting out on this score, that I am not saying enough. At one level their predicament is an indictment of this society which makes people 'rubbish'. Is this explicit enough?[16]

The need expressed here so honestly for greater directness is met by the three plays in *Statements*, all of which confront injustice head-on.

Fugard's career can thus be viewed in terms of the changes in his subject matter, from presenting man as a unit in a family structure to the more recent portrayals of him as a citizen; in such a reading, the internally generated pressures of the home have been replaced by the external tensions of the statute book and law courts; familial abrasions become forensic assaults enforced by police and warders. Alone, though, an account of Fugard in these terms is incomplete, since it neglects to note how the forms and structures have also developed as a vehicle for political dissent. In the earlier plays, and particularly with *Hello and Goodbye* and *Boesman*, Fugard has recorded with characteristic overtness the difficulties he experienced with 'plotting'. In the former the images and characters of Johnnie and Hester were clear from the start, but the playwright was long exercised by the 'mechanics of the climax,' by the need to give verbal definition to a 'full and complete expression' of Hester's sense of the absurd.[17] Similarly with *Boesman and Lena*, the ideas and images were lucid and the problem again was how they were to be embodied: Fugard has written of his 'struggle to reveal the full carnal reality of [Boesman's hatred] in incident and dialogue'.[18] Incident and dialogue: these were at the heart of Fugard's creative blockages, and they had to be resolved because of the dictates of the form in which he had chosen to express himself. In the drama which derives from Ibsen and Chekhov, the verbalized and linear plot is the means by which the playwright embodies his intuitions. The word is here paramount and when the verbal, narrative vocabulary has been discovered, when the ideas and images have been given flesh, the resulting, complete text is the writer's security.

Simultaneously with the development from an indirect, implicit material to the explicitness of *Sizwe Bansi*, there was a growing feeling in Fugard that the whole *form* of the domestic plays was now no longer suitable: 'My work had been so conventional: it involved the *writing* of a play; it involved *setting* that play in terms of local specifics; it involved the actors *assuming* false identity . . .'[19] It is as if Fugard now felt, after *Boesman and Lena*, that all the battles he had fought to 'plot' those plays with lucidity were now irrelevant. And even, moreover, as if the earlier search for verbal clarity had, paradoxically, only led to an essential ontological falsity, an inauthenticity. The orthodox dramatic form now no longer seemed worth 'retailing'. The conventional modes of western realism, that had served so well in relatively open societies, appeared to Fugard inseparable from his own failure to give full expression to the living texture of life in a totalitarian state. And so, with the inspiration of Grotowski's theories and of his own practice since 1963 with the Serpent Players, Fugard abandoned the complete, 'prefabricated' text, conventionally offered to the actors at the outset of rehearsals, and began to work under no constraint from the exigencies of plot and sequential dramatic logic. In this new process, which was to result in *Sizwe Bansi* and *The Island*, plays of a startling polemical candour, the writer remains essential, because it is his images – 'at least an image, sometimes an already structured complex of images about which I, as a writer, was obsessional' – that are the seedbed of the play.[20] The process involves devolution and decentralization: not abdication. The writer, in other words, gives his actors what Fugard calls a 'mandate', which is not a plotted, structured text but a cluster of images on which they work. The actors created their own 'texts' in rehearsals and these were moulded and disciplined as if in the preparation of a conventional play. The result has been, in Fugard's account, 'as if instead of first putting words on paper in order to arrive eventually at the stage and a live performance, I was able to write *directly* into its space and silence via the actor'.[21] This, in summary, has been the collaborative genesis of *Sizwe Bansi* and *The Island*, and, in part, of *Statements*, which, though plotted conventionally, was rehearsed with similar techniques. The new political incisiveness of these three plays rests, therefore, upon formal and stylistic modulations in Fugard's art as well as upon a more publicly accessible group of themes.

The degree of political acuity won by Fugard's use of a dramatic form unconstrained by narrative demands, in which he can write 'into space and silence' without being diverted by the linear, temporal exigencies of episode, is exemplified in *Sizwe Bansi Is Dead* (1972). Of the three representatives of Fugard's new dramaturgy recently published in one volume, it is this play which most effectively blends the creativity of the players, John Kani and Winston Ntshona, with the writer's power of shaping, of plotting, the actors' own text of mime and reminiscence. The mimetic and reminiscential have always been large constituents of Fugard's theatre – as in, for example, the 'car-ride' scene of *The Blood Knot*. Indeed such passages, though potent in themselves, have sometimes threatened to absorb imperialistically the advancing narrative. Now, though, in the last three plays, Fugard seems able to view them more dispassionately, because they are the product not of his solitary creativity but of the communal pressures generated in the rehearsal room. Prolixity and verbal repetition had had to be controlled by the author alone in *The Blood Knot* and *Hello and Goodbye*, two plays with, we know, an autobiographical poignancy. Latterly, however, the altered, public genesis of the 'Political Trilogy' has enabled Athol Fugard to gain an objective, critical distance, the result of which is a new brevity and economy. The devolution involved in moving away from a complete, quasi-patristic text, for which the writer was solely responsible, to a theatre built from the unexpected catalysts which are then moulded by the writer, has furnished Fugard's company, as he has noted, with 'a much more immediate and direct relationship with [its] audience'.[22]

In a South African context the political implications of this loss of obliquity don't perhaps need to be spelt out in full. That articulation of verbal harmonies, the total effectiveness of dramatic realism for which Fugard had wrestled until *Boesman*, is seen only to lead to an art which was mediate and muffling. This modification has involved a radical reappraisal by Fugard of the effectiveness of realism, a form which since the fiction of the last century has been generally directed to political dissent, cultural agnosticism, and individual emancipation. (Lukacs' seminal *Studies in European Realism* is the classic exposition of this connection.) But to the artist working in a society which defiles semantics, which rewrites, for instance, the rich associative power of the word 'homeland', the cybernetics of realism, a mode rooted in historical and verbal confidence, must appear problematic. A society becoming increasingly repressive, despite its recent attempts to mouth the vocabulary of international docility, places strains upon the artist's viable forms of communication. It is not simply that the themes of literature change shape under these pressures: forms, and styles must also develop. The 'Family Trilogy' of the sixties, like Nadine Gordimer's monumental *A Guest of Honour* in an allied genre, had been founded on the paramountcy of the world:

> ZACHARIAH: Not as hot as last night, hey?
> MORRIS:   Last night you said it was too hot.
> ZACHARIAH [*thinks about this*]: That's what I mean.
> MORRIS:   So what is it? Too hot or too cold?[23]

The word – 'hot' or 'cold' – here serves as a way of mediating familial emotional shortcircuits. The trilogy's plots, too, had been diachronic, moving steadily from, say, Hester's sudden return in *Hello and Goodbye* to her parting from Johnnie at the conclusion. Now, though, in the later trilogy, the structure of the action is often flexibly synchronic. The word, similarly, is subordinate to the power of the images: the flashed photographs of interracial intimacies in *Statements*; the photo of the labourer in *Sizwe Bansi*, emasculated by the pass laws and snatching at dignity by smoking a pipe and a cigarette at the same time. Once again the parallels between Fugard and Nadine Gordimer are suggestive. Her last novel, *The Conservationist*, also develops synchronically and revolves obsessively around images – eggs, marbles – and gesture, the shredding of a letter, the burial of a nameless corpse.

In Fugard, then, as perhaps in Nadine Gordimer, we can discern a certain pattern of development from realism to a species of 'Imagist' art, much less concerned with the exfoliation of characters within a dense, fully rendered environment. Fugard has indeed recorded his interest in Pound's definition of the 'Image' as 'that which releases an emotional and psychological complex in an instant of time'.[24] The playwright's account of the genesis of the three plays in *Statements*, as well as the plays themselves, underline the similitudes between Fugard's recent work and the earlier Imagism of Pound and Ford. However, it is remarkable how the earlier aesthetics of Imagism, implicated with an élitist, apolitical ideology, has been transformed by Fugard into the vehicle of a progressive, deeply dissenting theatre. The kinetics of literature's political life is, we should recognize, complex and only to be established after attention to both form and content. These recognitions and attentions are, I would suggest, a fundamental necessity to the critic of a literature which is, north and south of the Caprivi Strip, so firmly plaited with the events and pressures of the political life. In its vocabulary and methodology literary criticism is enriched when it is in tune with the reciprocities within a 'social, political and intellectual life' indisputably a 'whole process'.

# References

1. Julius K. Nyerere, *Freedom and Unity : Uhuru na Umoja* (Dar es Salaam, 1966); *Freedom and Socialism: Uhuru na Ujamaa* (Dar es Salaam, 1968); *Freedom and Development: Uhuru na Maendeleo* (Dar es Salaam, 1973).
2. *Freedom and Development*, p. 198.
3. 'The Intellectual Needs Society' (delivered at the University of Liberia, 29 February 1968), *Freedom and Development*, pp. 23–9. See also, in this connection, these two papers: 'Relevance and Dar es Salaam University', *Freedom and Development*, pp. 192–203; 'The Role of Universities', *Freedom and Socialism*, pp. 179–86.
4. 'The Intellectual Needs Society', *Freedom and Development*, p. 25.
5. loc. cit.
6. I have attempted to exemplify this point elsewhere: 'Joyce Cary and Africa', *The Conch Review of Books*, II, iii (September 1974), pp. 214–16; 'African Literary Criticism: Limitations of a British Legacy', *Research in African Literatures* (forthcoming).
7. See further the illuminating recent study by a British critic, Jeremy Hawthorn's *Identity and Relationship* (London, 1973).
8. *Culture and the Radical Conscience* (Cambridge, Mass., 1973), pp. 81, 83.
9. ibid., p. 82.
10. Athol Fugard, *Three Port Elizabeth Plays* (London, 1974), p. xxv.
11. The evidence of this blight is assembled in Mervyn Woodrow, 'South African Drama in English', *English Studies in Africa*, XIII, ii (September 1970), pp. 391–410.
12. Christopher Ford, 'Life with a Liberal Conscience', *Guardian*, 24 July 1971, p. 14.
13. Introduction, *Three Port Elizabeth Plays*, p. viii.
14. ibid., p. xxiv.
15. See further my two essays on these plays: 'South Africa's Plague: One View of *The Blood Knot*', *Modern Drama* (February 1970), pp. 331–45; 'Athol Fugard's *Hello and Goodbye*', *Modern Drama* (September 1970), pp. 139–55.
16. Introduction, *Three Port Elizabeth Plays*, p. xxiv.
17. ibid., pp. xiii–xiv.
18. ibid., p. xx.
19. Introduction, *Statements: Three Plays* (London, 1974) unnumbered pages (italics in original).
20. loc. cit. See also, Mary Benson, 'Athol Fugard and "One Little Corner of the World"', *London Magazine*, XI, vi (February/March 1972), pp. 135–40.
21. Introduction, *Statements*. For an account of this creative process from the perspective of Fugard's players, see Peter Rosenwald's interview with John Kani and Winston Ntshona, 'Separate Fables', *Guardian*, 8 January 1974, p. 10.
22. Introduction, *Statements*.
23. *Three Port Elizabeth Plays*, p. 3.
24. ibid., p. xxiii.

# The Novels of Bessie Head

▼▼▼▼▼▼▼▼▼▼▼▼▼▼▼▼▼▼▼▼▼▼▼▼▼▼▼▼

ARTHUR RAVENSCROFT

IT is appropriate to begin with a brief passage from Bessie Head's third novel, *A Question of Power* (1974),[1] with a passage in which she uses a very homely, very South African plant to image the idea of settling organically into a new environment. It occurs as the long-drawn-out purgatory of Elizabeth the central character's inner life is approaching its climax, while her mundane life as a co-operative vegetable gardener is proving highly successful:

> The work had a melody like that – a complete stranger like the Cape Gooseberry settled down and became a part of the village life of Mota-beng. It loved the hot, dry Botswana summers as they were a replica of the Mediterranean summers of its home in the Cape. (p. 153)

Alas, not all South Africa's political and cultural exiles have found such replicas of climate, and perhaps it is not too extravagant to refer to those exiles as South Africa's post-1948 diaspora.

I think we can begin to talk of a new category of South African novel, which, in theme at least, may be termed the South African Novel of Africa, concerned certainly with the viciousnesses of South Africa's political kingdom, but seeing them in meaningful relation to South Africa's future, by means of present models for that future at hand for close observation in the independent countries of Africa. The first of these novels was Peter Abraham's *A Wreath for Udomo*, which appeared as long ago as 1956. But it was Nadine Gordimer's *A Guest of Honour* (1970), with its extraordinarily fine political perceptions, that made such a sub-division of the South African novel seem a possibility, and it was soon followed by Ezekiel Mphahlele's *The Wanderers* (1971). And then one looked with fresh eyes at Bessie Head's novels and, within the past year especially, at *A Question of Power*. Her novels strike a special chord for the South African diaspora, though this does not imply that it is the only level at which they work or produce an impact as novels.

They are strange, ambiguous, deeply personal books which initially do not seem to be 'political' in any ordinary sense of the word. On the contrary, any reader with either Marxist or Pan-Africanist political affinities is likely to be irritated by the seeming emphasis on the quest for personal contentment, the abdication of political kingship – metaphorically in *When Rain Clouds Gather*, literally in *Maru*, and one might say wholesale in *A Question of Power*. The novelist's preoccupations would seem to suggest a steady progression from the first novel to the third into ever murkier depths of alienation from the currents of South African, and African, matters of politics and power – indeed in *A Question of Power* we are taken nightmarishly into the central character's process of mental breakdown, through lurid cascades of hallucination and a pathological blurring of the frontiers between insanity and any kind of normalcy. It is precisely this journeying into the various characters' most secret interior recesses of mind and (we must not fight shy of the word) of soul, that gives the three novels a quite remarkable cohesion and makes them a sort of trilogy. It would not be too far-fetched to liken their cohesion to that which has earned for Wilson Harris's first four novels the collective title of 'The Guiana Quartet'. It seems to me that with Bessie Head, as with Harris, each novel both strikes out anew, and also re-shoulders the same burden. It is as if one were observing a process that involves simultaneously progression, introgression, and circumgression; but also (and here I believe lies her particular creative power) organic growth in both her art and her central concerns. For all our being lured as readers into the labyrinth of Elizabeth's tortured mind in *A Question of Power*, and then, as it were, left there to face with her the phantasmagoric riot of nightmare and horror, one nevertheless senses throughout that the imagination which unleashes this fevered torrent resides in a creative mind that is exceedingly tough. It is not just that the fictional character emerges worn down yet regenerated and incredibly alive still after her long ordeal, but that her experience at the narrative level is also a figuring of the creative imagination in our time – that that process is both part of the multi-layered theme *and* the method of its communication. And that process as an embodiment of the novelist's art is a tough, demanding labour.

I should have begun at the beginning, and I shall now go back to the first novel, but I have paused first over the shaping of *A Question of Power* because I do see these three novels as very closely related to one another, and the third in many ways helps to explicate the first and second.

There are two major clues to the overall homogeneity of Bessie Head's novels. It is impossible to avoid noticing how frequently the words 'control' and 'prison' (and phrases and images of equivalent value) occur in all three novels, in many different ways certainly, and probably not as an altogether conscious patterning. 'Control' occurs in contexts tending towards the idea of control over appetites felt as detonators that set off the explosions in individual lives, no less than in the affairs of mankind, which leave those broken trails of blasted humanity that are a peculiar mark of our times. 'Prison' occurs in more varied uses, but most often related to a voluntary shutting of oneself away from what goes on around one. Sometimes it may be straight escapism or alienation, but more often it suggests a willed control over a naturally outgoing personality, an imprisonment not for stagnation but for recollection and renewal – a severely practical self-imposed isolation which is part of natural growth. Like the silk-worm's cocoon, it is made for shelter, while strengths are gathered for outbreak and a fresh continuance.

*When Rain Clouds Gather* opens with a dramatic departure from South Africa. Makhaya has served his term in a political prison, he is on the run, and we see him climbing the barbed wire fence into Botswana between the half-hourly police-van patrols with their sirens wailing across the veld. Yet the exhilaration of escape from a whole country that is a prison has been qualified before the escape is even described; in the very first paragraph of the novel there is an ominous note in the reference to Makhaya's intended sprint '. . . to the Botswana border fence and then on to whatever *illusion of freedom* lay ahead'. And only a few lines later we learn that '. . . the inner part of him was a jumble of chaotic discord' (p. 7). It is Makhaya's inner discord and bitterness that have driven him from home, and, although that discord has obviously been touched off by his black man's experience of apartheid, his climbing the fence into Botswana owes more to his need to come to terms with his personal inner chaos than to an overt political motive. He has no scheme of political action in mind, no concrete plan for the future, just a strongly felt need to get away from it all and find himself anew, somehow, somewhere. He is very much an urban South African and scornful of the rural, conservative tribal customs and beliefs he finds in Botswana, yet the landscape and the elemental, simple ways of life of the Batswana are balm to his jangled black sensibilities.

A chance encounter soon brings him to the village of Golema Mmidi, not a normal tribal village but an atypical community which includes remarkable individualists from other parts of Botswana: Dinorego with his homespun wisdom; Mma Millipede who has adapted the religion of the white missionaries 'to adorn and enrich her own originality of thought and expand the natural kindness of her heart' (p. 69); and Paulina Sebeso, the lonely, intensely passionate young widow. They have endured great griefs and bitternesses and are trying to make new, ordered lives for themselves in Golema Mmidi. New life is possible chiefly because Gilbert, the English agricultural expert, is helping the community to make a self-sufficient agricultural economy for itself. Himself in flight from a ghastly, comfortable but emotionally arid English middle-class background, Gilbert flings himself into the mundane problems of crops, irrigation, and building; identifies himself completely with the people, and marries Dinorego's daughter. Not on any theoretical principle, but simply because the offer is made to him, Makhaya becomes Gilbert's assistant. There are long conversations between them about curing-sheds and co-operatives, millet and tobacco crops, witchweed and cattle. Yet the novelist invests these banal activities with a strange intensity of interest. To the characters, Golema Mmidi may be a kind of pastoral retreat after their earlier rough encounters with life, but the haven is a place of tough, demanding labour, of recurrent crises, of improvisation and ingenuity, of the constant threat of disruption from a power-hungry, resentful local chief. Their co-operative efforts constitute an image of creativity in which sweat and imagination, harsh reality and an ultimate dream to be fulfilled are mixed in just about equal proportions. Out of this creative, co-operative enterprise of constructive energy Bessie Head generates a powerful sense of potential fulfilment for characters who have jealously guarded, enclosed, shut up tightly their private individualities. Against a political background of self-indulgent, serf-owning traditional chiefs and self-seeking, new politicians more interested in power than people, the village of Golema Mmidi is offered as a difficult alternative: not so much a rural utopia for the Africa of the future to aim at, as a means of personal and economic independence and interdependence, where the qualities that count are benign austerity, reverence for the lives of ordinary people (whether university-educated experts or illiterate villagers), and, above all, the ability to break out of the prison of selfhood without destroying individual privacy and integrity.

Makhaya's quest for personal freedom was a flight not only from South Africa's police-van sirens and the burden of oppression, but also from the personal demands upon him of his immediate relations. The last thing he is looking for when he enters Botswana is a new network of intimate relationships or a new struggle against a different oppression. And of course he finds both. That is why the 'peaceful haven' idea in the book is really very deceptive. Golema Mmidi is no Garden of Eden, even if its potentialities are indeed richer than the South African life Makhaya left behind could offer him. This potential is registered in a number of lyrical passages that describe the bush, the trees, the landscape, the sunrise, and the sunset in Botswana. Here is one of them:

> There, directly in the path of the setting sun, Makhaya was in the habit of coming to watch the sunset. Just as at dawn, the sun crept along the ground in gold shafts; so at sundown it retreated quietly as though it were folding into itself the long brilliant fingers of light. As he watched it all in fascination, the pitch black shadows of night seemed to sweep across the land like an engulfing wave. One minute the sun was there, and the next minute it had dropped down behind the horizon, plunging everything into darkness. On intensely cold nights, it threw up a translucent yellow afterglow, full of sparkling crystals, but otherwise it puffed itself out into a thin strip of red light on the horizon. As his eyes became more and more accustomed to the peculiar beauty of Botswana sunsets, he also noticed that the dull green thornbush and the dull brown earth were transformed into autumn shades of warm brown, red, and yellow hues by the setting sun. (pp. 78–9)

At one level *When Rain Clouds Gather* is a tale of innocence and experience. What differentiates Makhaya from the other characters is his greater knowledge of evil. Dinorego comes to understand this difference between himself and Makhaya:

> There were things in Makhaya he would never understand because his own environment was one full of innocence. The terrors of rape, murder, and bloodshed in a city slum, which was Makhaya's background, were quite unknown to Dinorego, but he felt in Makhaya's attitude and utterances a horror of life, and it was as though he was trying to flee this horror and replace it with innocence, trust, and respect. (p. 98)

Makhaya does find innocence, trust, and respect, though not as unqualified absolutes. He has to give of himself both in physical labour and in the opening of the cell door to his private sanctum. His marriage to Paulina Sebeso near the end of the novel is, of course, also a finding of himself, with the ghosts of his former 'gray graveyard' life no longer visible, now, in the merciful darkness of Paulina's hut (p. 158). It is a different kind of freedom, coloured by new responsibilities, as indicated in the wry comment that he would be so entangled 'with marriage and babies and children that he would always have to think, not twice but several hundred times, before he came to knocking anyone down' (p. 187).

The precise relationship between individual freedom and political independence, and between a guarded core of privacy and an unbudding towards others, may seem rather elusive, perhaps even mystical, in my reading of the novel, and I see it as one of the weaknesses of *When Rain*

*Clouds Gather*. It is a straightforward narrative with no unexpected tricks of technique and very down-to-earth in the minutiae of an agricultural hard grind of a way of life. Most of this aspect of the novel I have deliberately ignored, because I find that below this level of the novel's existence, there is another kind of novel speaking to the reader, a shadow-novel that works in the dimensions of allusiveness and embryo symbolism. There are moments of melodrama and excessive romanticism, but the real life of the novel is of creativity, resilience, reconstruction, fulfilment. Of the six major characters, four are themselves Batswana but all are in one sense or another handicapped exiles, learning how to mend their lives in the exacting but ultimately viable sands of Golema Mmidi. It is the vision behind their effortful embracing of exile that gives Bessie Head's first novel an unusual maturity.

*Maru*, published in 1971,[3] three years after *When Rain Clouds Gather*, immediately proclaims itself as technically a very different sort of book. The first six pages present the outcome of the events narrated in the rest of the novel, and, though they are essential for our adequate grasp of how those events unfold, they don't make sense at first, not until one has read to the end. The opening is thus both a species of sealed orders for the reader and an epilogue. And are we sure, at the end, that the two chief male characters, Maru and Moleka, who are close, intimate friends until they become bitter antagonists, are indeed two separate fictional characters, or that they are symbolic extensions of contending character-traits within the same man? Again, the story is solidly rooted in a particular, concretely evoked way of life, a busy administrative village in Botswana. Maru and Moleka work at desks in offices, Maru is hereditary Paramount Chief elect, waiting to be installed after his predecessor's death, and in the meanwhile getting on with the business of government. There are civil servants and teachers and classrooms with children being taught in them. But in *Maru* these workaday affairs form the framework for the real novel, which is a drama about inner conflict and peace of mind and soul. In *When Rain Clouds Gather*, Dinorego believes in a God who is everywhere and Mma Millipede has her own version of the Christian God, but in *Maru*, the character Maru carries his gods within him. We are told: 'He never doubted the voices of the gods in his heart' (p. 8). Those gods lead him into making an implacable enemy of his closest friend, they lead him to marry a woman of Bushman origin (an untouchable in the eyes of his Batswana fellow-tribesmen), and they lead him to renounce his chieftainship, even though he is better suited to govern justly and wisely than the brother who will take his place. With three trusted companions and his bride, he travels a thousand miles away to start a new austere life of subsistence farming. A more transparent imaging of the renouncement of political responsibility and power could hardly be devised. But with Bessie Head things are never so simple. Maru is not merely indulging a personal predilection for a carefree, untrammelled life. We are told:

> It was different if his motivation was entirely selfish, self-centred, but the motivation came from the gods who spoke to him in his heart. They had said: Take that road. Then they had said: Take that companion. He believed his heart and the things in it. They were his only criteria for goodness. In the end, nothing was personal to him. In the end, subjection of his whole life to his inner gods was an intellectual process. Very little feeling was involved. His methods were cold, calculating and ruthless. (p. 73)

Here lies a typical Bessie Head irony. Maru's methods, 'cold, calculating and ruthless', are the normal methods of those who seek and wield power, and yet Maru's role in the novel is the very antithesis of power-wielding. He renounces the kingdom of political power in favour of the kingdom of love. But before he does so, he manipulates, engineers, 'fixes' the delicate relationships among himself, his sister Dikeledi, his friend Moleka, and Margaret the Masarwa woman, with whom both he and Moleka are in love. With the help of his three spies, Maru is able to manoeuvre Moleka against his real will to marry Dikeledi, who loves him; Maru is then able to marry Margaret, whom Moleka really loves. And Maru can exert such a persuasive influence upon Margaret that she begins to learn to love him, though it is Moleka with whom she has been secretly in love since her arrival in the village.

What makes the reader credit the wisdom and moral respectability of the gods whose voices speak in Maru's heart, is that they are not mere masks for his egotistical indulgences. Like Moleka, Maru has been profligate in his sexual adventures before Margaret comes to Dilepe as a new schoolmistress. At the end of his affairs Moleka was always unhurt, triumphant, but whenever one of Maru's affairs ended, Maru would have to take to his bed with some indefinable ailment. We are told:

> Maru always fell in love with his women. He'd choose them with great care and patience. There was always some outstanding quality; a special tenderness in the smile, a beautiful voice or something in the eyes which suggested mystery and hidden dreams. He associated these things with the beauty in his own heart, only to find that a tender smile and a scheming mind went hand in hand, a beautiful voice turned into a dominating viper who confused the inner Maru, who was king of heaven, with the outer Maru and his earthly position of future paramount chief of a tribe. (p. 35)

The differences between Maru's and Moleka's conduct of sexual escapades are symptomatic of the fundamental differences between their innermost beings:

It was only Maru who saw their relationship in its true light. They were kings of opposing kingdoms. It was Moleka's kingdom that was unfathomable, as though shut behind a heavy iron door. There had been no such door for Maru. He dwelt everywhere. He'd mix the prosaic of everyday life with the sudden beauty of a shooting star. Now and then Maru would share a little of his kingdom with a Miss so-and-so he had acquired through Moleka. But it never went far because it always turned out that Miss so-and-so had no kingdom of her own. He used to complain to Moleka that people who had nothing were savagely greedy. It was like eating endlessly. Even if they ate all your food they were still starving. They never turned into the queens and goddesses Maru walked with all his days.

Throughout this time, Moleka was the only person who was his equal. They alone loved each other, but they were opposed because they were kings. The king who had insight into everything feared the king whose door was still closed. There was no knowing what was behind the closed door of Moleka's kingdom. Maru had no key to it, but he knew of its existence because if he touched Moleka's heart with some word or gesture a cloud would lift and he would see a rainbow of dazzling light. (p. 34)

What moves the concerns of this novel away from the level of mere private agony and personal fulfilment is the nature of the two men's loves for Margaret. Ultimately the differences rest upon Margaret's role as a Masarwa among the Batswana. When she first arrives in Dilepe, the headmaster and civil servants think she is a half-caste, and bear no animosity against her on that score. But the moment she openly announces that she is in fact a Masarwa, the unspeakable has befallen the official world of Dilepe. It is as if a fair-complexioned coloured teacher in a rural white South African government school had calmly announced that she was coloured and wasn't even trying 'to pass for white'. The humiliation to which Margaret is subjected (despite the full possession of knowledge and skill that the white woman whose name she bears helped her to acquire) makes of her a representative of all racial oppression everywhere. Although she is befriended by such influential members of the community as Dikeledi and Moleka and, more deviously at first, by Maru, and although her tormentors are discomfited, she has tasted again her childhood experience of being an isolated outcast, 'like the mad dog of the village, with tin cans tied to her tail' (p. 9).

Maru's almost god-like perspicacity justifies his seemingly devious methods of preventing Moleka from obtaining Margaret's love. Maru knows that because his kingdom is of love, he has the strength to marry Margaret and live by all the consequences. He knows that

> Moleka would never have lived down the ridicule and malice and would in the end have destroyed her from embarrassment. (p. 9)

I hope my account doesn't make Maru seem intolerably priggish and morally smug, for Bessie Head doesn't slip over that particular precipice. Maru is no god. He remains a man with doubts. We know from the beginning that he and Margaret have not got away to another Garden of Eden. Rich and fulfilled and symbolically healthful as their life together is, it nevertheless has shadows and questions over it. Though Maru has obeyed the voices of the gods in his heart and trusts them, the closed door in Moleka's heart still hides an uncertainty:

> Perhaps he had seriously miscalculated Moleka's power, that Moleka possessed some superior quality over which he had little control. Was it a superior kind of love? Or was it a superior kind of power? He'd trust the love but not the power because the power could parade as anything. (pp. 9–10)

This doubt and with it his willingness to give up Margaret, despite his deep love for her, if he should one day be proved wrong about Moleka, comes in those pages of introductory epilogue that I mentioned earlier, and throughout the novel influences our view of Maru and his actions.

On the one hand Maru's marriage is a deeply personal thing. He knows he 'could not marry a tribe or race' (p. 109). On the other hand the marriage also carries a considerable political symbolism. Here are the final two paragraphs of the novel:

> When the people of the Masarwa tribe heard about Maru's marriage to one of their own, a door silently opened on the small, dark airless room in which their souls had been shut for a long time. The wind of freedom, which was blowing throughout the world for all people, turned and flowed into the room. As they breathed in the fresh, clean air their humanity awakened. They examined their condition. There was the fetid air, the excreta and the horror of being an oddity of the human race, with half the head of a man and half the body of a donkey. They laughed in an embarrassed way, scratching their heads. How had they fallen into this condition when, indeed, they were as human as everyone else? They started to run out into the sunlight, then they turned and looked at the dark, small room. They said: 'We are not going back there.'
>
> People like the Batswana, who did not know that the wind of freedom had also reached people of the Masarwa tribe, were in for an unpleasant surprise because it would be no longer possible to treat Masarwa people in an inhuman way without getting killed yourself. (pp. 126–7)

Much more than *When Rain Clouds Gather*, *Maru* is a novel about interior experience, about thinking, feeling, sensing, about control over rebellious lusts of the spirit; and, ironically, ambiguously, in Bessie Head's comprehending vision, it is also a more 'political' novel than *When Rain Clouds Gather*. I am not sure that the two things are satisfyingly fused, even whether it is the sort of novel in which they *should* be so fused, but I am much impressed and moved by the power with which they are conveyed. That power resides in the vitality of the enterprise, which projects the personal and the political implications in such vivid, authentic parallels that one feels they are being closely held together, like the lengths of steel on a railway track, which fuse only in optical illusion and are indeed useless if they don't maintain their divided parallelism. It is also a novel full of creative enactments: Maru's carefully willed and painstakingly planned bringing together of himself and Margaret, and Margaret's painting of her outcast's experience in the strange, evocative paintings that move Maru, Moleka, and Dikeledi deeply. That apparently 'obvious' political message in the closing two paragraphs must also be seen as a plea for creative, benign political action seen in the light of Maru's austere life of integrity as he wrests a precarious living from the soil of a new locale.

Bessie Head's most recent novel, *A Question of Power*, is clearly more ambitious than its two predecessors, and less immediately accessible, and altogether a more risky undertaking. The movement here is even deeper (and more disturbingly so) into the vast caverns of interior personal experience. The setting is closer to that of *When Rain Clouds Gather*, a remote Botswana village with a medley of exiles and foreign-aid helpers showing the Batswana how to make semi-desert sands more fertile. There are two prime exile-figures, the visionary, dynamic white Afrikaner who has escaped the other prison of apartheid, and the central character, Elizabeth, whose mental stresses and breakdown take her into ultimate isolation and absolute exile. In addition she is a coloured South African exile in Botswana.

Bessie Head's common-sensical rootedness in the earthy level of everyday reality is still there to anchor for the reader the terrifying world of Elizabeth's hallucinations, but it is the events of that world that dominate the book. Even more than in the two earlier novels, one finds an intimate relationship between an individual character's private odyssey of the soul and public convulsions that range across the world and from one civilization to another. To see Bessie Head's handling of Elizabeth's mental instability as a clever literary device to make possible an epic confrontation between Good and Evil within the confines of a realist novel, is to underestimate the achievement. One wonders again and again whether the phantom world that comes to life whenever Elizabeth is alone in her hut could have been invented by a novelist who had not herself gone through similar experiences, so frighteningly and authentically does it all pass before one's eyes. But there is no confusion of identity between the novelist and the character, and Bessie Head makes one realize often how close is the similarity between the most fevered creations of a deranged mind and the insanities of deranged societies.

Elizabeth's nightmares are dominated by two characters, Sello and Dan, of whom the former in fact exists in the village of Motabeng, though Elizabeth doesn't know him personally. Part I of the novel, called 'Sello', presents him as a monk-like hallucination sitting in Elizabeth's room at night, who seems to be revealing spiritual truths to her imagination. Though Sello is elevated to the role of a God of Goodness, he has as an *alter ego* Medusa, of Greek mythology, who symbolizes all that is personally vicious and vile and socially destructive and obscene. By the end of Part I, Elizabeth believes that her monk-like guide has duped her and is both Evil and Good in one. I do not pretend to have mapped out for my own ordered satisfaction the full values and equivalences of the myriad figures who people Elizabeth's cinematic nightmares. What is clear by the end of Part I is her utter disillusion and hopelessness, which come from the extraordinarily comprehensive free-wheel ranging over cultures and their myths, from Osiris, Medusa, the Indian Mahamaya (who trapped men in their own passions), to the Buddha, Christ, and ordinary common people as God, from Greek and Hebrew to Jews in Nazi Germany, coloured people in South Africa, Elizabeth's own alienation as a coloured exile among the Batswana villagers. Her private sufferings re-enact the sufferings of all the despised and rejected and oppressed of human history, and Sello as God remains ambivalent, passive, at times overwhelmed by the evil that strangely seems to be a function of himself.

But Sello does have an active, clearly marked-off antagonist, and Part II is named 'Dan', after him. The Sello/Dan polarity is a development of the Maru/Moleka contrast in the earlier novel. Early in Part I we learn that 'Dan understood the mechanics of power'[4] and that Sello's injunction that 'Love is two people mutually feeding each other . . .' (p. 14) will prevail. In Part II Dan also achieves a status of divinity, yet he is at times merely an extension of the Medusa. In Part I Elizabeth's torturings at the hands of Medusa are symbolized into humanity's sufferings. In Part II Elizabeth's even greater anguish arises from Dan's ability to violate her mind with the most depraved obscenities. She witnesses his gargantuan sexual exploits with an incredible succession of sexually insatiable females with such names as Madame Loose-Bottom, Squelch Squelch, The Womb, and Miss Pelican-Beak.

I think that in part at least this sexual cess-pit that so terrifies Elizabeth is a dredging up of the deeply hidden horrors and depravities that lie un-acknowledged within every human consciousness. One must remember that Elizabeth's epic purgatory is the process of her mental illness, and it is the remorseless intensity and completion with which her confrontation of the horrors in history and the horrors within herself are presented that constitute what I referred to at the beginning as Bessie Head's toughness of mind. Because there are connections established between Buchenwald and the direction in which Elizabeth's personal moral life could turn, between the lust for power over black or yellow or white and the lust for personal sexual excitations. But the illness turns out to have been also a curative process, even though the patient is left exhausted and wrung dry.

The characteristic Bessie Head irony comes out in the fact that even as Elizabeth, the South African coloured refugee among the Batswana, finds herself screaming in her nightmares that she hates black Africans, she is none the less in what appears to her the almost dream-like world of her workaday activities in the co-operative vegetable garden, forging, steadily and genuinely, links of personal regard and affection with the Batswana villagers and with the foreign helpers. The last words of the novel are 'a gesture of belonging' (p. 20) as Elizabeth settles herself for her first un-tortured night's sleep in three years, annealed both spiritually and socially, as in imagination she places one soft hand over her land.

I do not believe that Bessie Head's novels are offering anything as facile as universal brotherhood and love for a political blueprint for either South Africa or all of Africa. In *Maru* common sense is described as the next best thing to changing the world on the basis of love of mankind.[5] What the three novels do say very clearly is that whoever exercises political power, however laudable his aims, will trample upon the faces and limbs of ordi-nary people, and will lust in that trampling. That horrible obscenity man-kind must recognize in its collective interior soul. The corollary is not liberal abstention from action, but rather modest action in very practical terms, and with individual hearts flushed and cleansed for collective pur-pose. The divinity that she acknowledges is a new, less arrogant kind of humanism, a remorseless God who demands that iron integrity in personal conduct should inform political action too. Of course the novels don't sermonize like this, but grow out of a moral basis of this kind of order. No neat solution, but, whatever our political loyalties, can we escape the validity of the problem she poses, as the TV News shows us Palestinian refugee camps, roads blocked with terrorized men, women, and children in Vietnam, the rows of children's graves in South Africa's so-called re-settlement areas, the living conditions of Commonwealth immigrants in Bradford and Wolverhampton?

In the development of the South African novel, this disturbing tough-ness of Bessie Head's creative imagination returns to us that gesture of belonging with which *A Question of Power* ends. All three novels are fraught with the loneliness and despair of exile, but the resilience of the exile characters is even more remarkable. Bessie Head refuses to look for the deceiving gleam that draws one to expect the dawn of liberation in the South, but accepts what the meagre, even parched, present offers. She isn't tempted by that vision granted to the psalmist who had endured bitter exile and could sing:

> When the Lord delivered Sion from bondage,
> It seemed like a dream.
> Then was our mouth filled with laughter,
> On our lips there were songs.[6]

Instead, we have that image of the Cape Gooseberry rooting itself sturdily in an alien clime.

### References

1. *A Question of Power* (London, Heinemann, 1974).
2. *When Rain Clouds Gather* (London, Gollancz, 1969). Other references are to the Heinemann editions noted here.
3. *Maru* (London, Heinemann, 1972).
4. *A Question of Power*, p. 13.
5. *Maru*, pp. 12–13.
6. Psalm 125, *The Psalms* (London, 1970).

# Index

▼▼▼▼▼▼▼▼▼▼▼▼▼▼▼▼▼▼▼▼▼▼▼▼▼▼▼